Praise for *Search Engine Optimization: An Hour a Day*

Search Engine Optimization: An Hour a Day *is an excellent primer for the beginner do-it-yourself search-engine marketer. It covers the basic essentials of SEO but also drills down into the challenges (both technical and business-specific) in an easy-to-read and entertaining manner. The book offers a comprehensive SEO plan with metrics for tracking your success that can be done conveniently in "an hour a day." Even if you're considering outsourcing your SEO, this book is an excellent read and a great way to understand the industry and the terminology involved.*

 —DANIEL RIVEONG, Head of SEO Services, e-Storm International

Finally, a common-sense approach to day-by-day search engine optimization. The authors offer a comprehensive yet light-hearted guide to preparing a successful SEO strategy. If you are just getting started, this book is a must read to minimize your risks and maximize your rewards. SEO: An Hour a Day is habit-forming. Readers should be prepared to get hooked on SEO.

 —P.J. FUSCO, Search Engine Marketer, Writer, and Speaker

Written with clarity and detail, the book leaves little room for confusion about what you can do to improve your Web site's rank in the search engine results pages.

 —HARVEY RAMER, Marketing Designer and Blogger, Design Delineations
  Excerpted from: http://blog.designdelineations.com/2006/08/09/search-engine-optimization-an-hour-a-day-book-review/

I'm always being asked to review the latest book on marketing. With a hectic schedule, it can be tough to get any time to read any of them, but I just made time to read Search Engine Optimization: An Hour a Day.

 You have to give credit to authors Gradiva Couzin and Jennifer Grappone for putting together an excellent book that combines practical advice sprinkled with humor—very much needed to prevent this topic from being too dry.

 I didn't pay for my copy of the book, but would have no hesitation in buying a copy for anyone new to the industry!

 —ANDY BEAL, SEM Expert
  Excerpted from: http://www.marketingpilgrim.com/2006/08/book-review-search-engine-optimization-an-hour-a-day.html

A well written SEO tutorial...by the time you have reached the end of the book you will be pretty proficient in the obscure art of SEO.
 —Pandia.com
  Excerpted from: http://www.pandia.com/sew/253-search-engine-optimization-with-a-feminine-touch.html

SEO: An Hour A Day *is a great book.*

 The authors focus consistently on your business needs. They're not trying to tell you that you need to do something for the good of the world—they're telling you that you need to do something to accomplish your specific business goal. That practical and realistic emphasis on business oriented needs makes the book a great reference.

 If you want to understand what your professional consultant is doing, or use this book as a kicking off point to learn how to promote your own sites, you'll have made a great choice.
 —JOE DOLSON, inter:digital Strategies
  Excerpted from: http://www.interdigitalstrategies.com/blog/reviews/search-engine-optimization-an-hour-a-day-book-review/

If you've ever put off doing search engine optimization (SEO) because you know it's so time consuming, here's the book for you.
 —Web Marketing Today
  Excerpted from: http://www.wilsonweb.com/seo/seo-daily.htm

New to the sometimes confusing and seemingly arcane world of making search engine friendly web sites? A new book offers a systematic, common-sense approach to the art and science of SEO.
 —CHRIS SHERMAN, SearchEngineWatch.com
  Excerpted from: http://searchenginewatch.com/showPage.html?page=3618296

The book will give you the knowledge that you need and will then supply you with a plan so that you can carry out SEO in an orderly fashion. Much more than this, the book cleverly helps you to identify the results that you want from your web site. The experience that the authors have working with all sizes and shapes of organisations is used to good effect and you will find that there is added value in helping you to get different departments to work together.
 —J.F. HIGGINS, bancassurance.co.uk
  Excerpted from: http://www.amazon.com/Search-Engine-Optimization-Hour-Day/dp/0471787531/ref=cm_pdp_review_teaser_product/103-5445543-6918200

Search Engine Optimization

An Hour a Day

Jennifer Grappone

Gradiva Couzin

Wiley Publishing, Inc.

Acquisitions Editor: WILLEM KNIBBE
Development Editor: HEATHER O'CONNOR
Technical Editor: MICAH BALDWIN
Production Editors: DARIA MEOLI, SARAH GROFF-PALERMO
Copy Editor: JUDY FLYNN
Production Manager: TIM TATE
Vice President and Executive Group Publisher: RICHARD SWADLEY
Vice President and Executive Publisher: JOSEPH B. WIKERT
Vice President and Publisher: DAN BRODNITZ
Book Designer: FRANZ BAUMHACKL
Compositor: MAUREEN FORYS, HAPPENSTANCE TYPE-O-RAMA
Proofreader: IAN GOLDER
Indexer: TED LAUX
Cover Designer: RYAN SNEED
Cover Image: GETTY IMAGES

With love to Todd, a superb tech consultant, ace dad,
and all-around supportive guy. —JG

To Lowell, my anchor & my answer. —GC

 # Acknowledgments

The authors wish to gratefully acknowledge our editors at Wiley: Willem Knibbe (whose savvy and wit make him an excellent person to bump into at a party, not to mention a great guy to have on your side while writing a book!); Heather O'Connor, a wellspring of cheerful redirection and helpful insight; our technical editor, Micah Baldwin; our talented copy editor, Judy Flynn; our production editors and schedule-keepers, Daria Meoli and Sarah Groff-Palermo; our compositors at Happenstance Type-O-Rama; and the other hard-working members of the production team.

We are grateful that some of the best and brightest in the field of search marketing were also the kindest. Thanks to Danny Sullivan, Jill Whalen, Kevin Lee, P. J. Fusco, and Aaron Wall for contributing their time and respected opinions to this project.

Thanks to the many good-natured members of the business community who shared their stories, successes, and challenges with us: Anna and Dexter Chow, Christine Moore, Jill Roberts, Paul Heller, Gina Boros, Susan McKenna, Sage Vivant, Mark Armstrong, and Ann Meyer. We wish them all many targeted visitors and mad conversions! We owe special thanks to Eric Fixler and Anthony Severo for providing invaluable technical reviews, and to Kelly Ryer and Sarah Hubbard for generous helpings of advice and wisdom. Thanks also to Swork in Los Angeles and Nervous Dog Coffee in San Francisco for the caffeine injections and free wireless!

We also thank our cherished friends and former Fine Brand Media colleagues, especially Jan Schmidt, Willo O'Brien, and Elizabeth Waller, for their contributions to this project. We would be remiss if we did not also thank David Brennan, who has been a very good-natured SEO guinea pig through the years. And thank you to Richard Bennion, who forced Gradiva into this line of work in the first place.

As luck would have it, our families are full of people with amazing talents for things linguistic and technical. Thank you to Barbara Gold, Laura Gold, Margaret Morris, and Alex Robinson for ideas, enthusiasm, and other warmhearted intangibles and especially to our beloved husbands, Todd Grappone and Lowell Robinson, for their love and support. And to our most beautiful and wonderful children, thank you for making this book a part of your daily lives too. Yes, Bennett, there are pictures in this book. Yes, Enzo, we made it with our 'puters. Yes, Jonah, you can press some buttons too. Yes, Zehara, Mommy's coming back. We love you all.

About the Authors

Jennifer Grappone is a Los Angeles–based search marketing consultant whose work has resulted in many targeted hits and happy clients in various industries including media, entertainment, software, and non-profit. Starting out as a writer/producer/director of industrial and corporate videos, Jennifer followed the dot-com boom and became a project manager for large-scale web development projects before working exclusively in SEO in 2000. Jennifer advocates a holistic approach to SEO, one that combines elements of good writing, usability, search-friendly site design, and link building. You can often find Jennifer hunched over a laptop in any number of wireless cafes in Northeast LA. Stop by and say hello!

Gradiva Couzin has been working in search marketing since its early days in 1998. Since then, she has improved the search presence of organizations ranging from small businesses working on a shoestring to Fortune 500 companies. Her SEO strategy creates win-win solutions by improving the match between searchers and websites. With a history as a civil engineer and experience in website and database development, Gradiva enjoys the technical side of SEO and loves to facilitate communication between techie and non-techie types. She is also an accomplished artist, painting oil portraits on commission. Gradiva lives and works in San Francisco's Bernal Heights with her husband and two small children.

Contents

Introduction

How is your website doing on the search engines? Need a little help? Well, you're holding the right book in your hands. This book will walk you through the steps to achieve a targeted, compelling presence on the major search engines. There are no secrets or tricks here, just down-to-earth, real-world advice and a clear program to get you where you want to be. And, with luck, you'll even have a little fun along the way!

If you could think of the person that you would most want visiting your website, who would that person be? Traditional advertisers (TV, magazines, newspaper, direct mail) might describe this person in terms of their demographics: 18 to 24 years old? Male or female? Wealthy or not so wealthy? But in the world of search, our focus is very different. This is how we think:

 Pearl of Wisdom: The person you *most* want to find your website is the person who is searching for you!

Who could be a more perfect target audience than someone who is already looking for your company, your product or service, or just the sort of information you've got on your website? The trick, of course, is to figure out who those people are, develop an extremely targeted message for them, and put it where they will notice it.

Search Engine Optimization (SEO) encompasses a wide variety of tasks that improve a website's presence on search engines. Maybe you've heard a few SEO catch-phrases—*meta tags*, *keyword density*, or *PageRank*—but you don't know exactly how to tie them all together into a meaningful package. That's where this book comes in!

Why SEO?

There are many good reasons to pursue SEO for your website. If you're a numbers person, you may find these stats compelling:

- A 2004 survey found that in business-to-business (B2B) purchasing decisions, 63.9 percent of respondents stated that a search engine would be the first place they would go to research a product or service. (Source: Enquiro/MarketingSherpa)

- Research conducted in 2005 by search engine consulting firm OneUpWeb.com showed that top 10 placement in Google increased site traffic to five times its previous levels in the first month.

- A 2005 survey by search marketing firm iCrossing found that search engines are the most popular tool for researching products and services before making an online purchase, and of these searchers 74 percent use search engines to research products and 54 percent use search engines to find the website from which to buy.

But if you do SEO for no other reason, do it so you won't be handing website visitors over to your competitors on a silver platter! Here are a few embarrassing situations that SEO can help you avoid:

- A potential customer is trying to find your phone number so they can call in an order. Searching for your product name, they come across your competitor and call them instead.

- The good news is that your website is #1 on Google! The bad news is that your #1 rank is wasted on a tedious technical PDF that you didn't even know was on your site!

- Congratulations: You've accrued 157 high-quality links to your home page over the years! But since your last website redesign, you've spent the last six months with 157 links to your "File not found" error page!

The best thing about SEO is that when it's done correctly (follow the advice in this book and you'll always be on the up-and-up), it benefits both you and your site visitors! The reason:

Pearl of Wisdom: Good SEO helps searchers get where they want to go.

How? By providing a clear path from need to fulfillment. By making sure your message is simple, accurate, up-to-date, and most important, put in front of the right people.

Why an Hour a Day?

Like water filling an ice-cube tray, SEO can fill up all the hours in the day you are willing to give it. So let's get this painful truth out of the way right now: Good SEO takes work—*lots* of work.

Now you're probably wondering, "How *little* time can I spend on SEO and get away with it?"

SEO is an amorphous, open-ended task. It includes a wide variety of activities, ranging from HTML edits to reading news blogs. It would be overwhelming to try to learn every aspect of SEO at once, but jumping in without a game plan is not the most effective strategy either. You're busy, and SEO is not your only job. So for you, the best way to learn SEO is to roll up your sleeves and *do* something, an hour at a time. Complete one SEO task a day and you'll see substantial results.

One of the benefits of breaking your SEO campaign into bite-size one-hour morsels is that you'll have time to digest and learn. You can take care of your day's assignment in an hour and have plenty of time for thinking and reflecting the rest of the day.

How Long Until I See Results?

The SEO process includes a lot of waiting: waiting for search engines to visit your site, waiting for other site owners to respond to your link requests, and oftentimes waiting for others within your organization to complete your requested HTML edits. Nobody likes to wait, and nobody really believes us when we tell them this:

 Pearl of Wisdom: Believe it. SEO requires patience.

This book sets you up for a long-haul SEO process. We take you through a one-month prep period in which you'll bring together all of the components you'll need to begin a successful SEO campaign—one that's just right for your unique situation. Then you'll launch into Your SEO Plan, a customizable hour-a-day routine designed to increase quality traffic and improve your site's presence in the search engines. Your SEO Plan is three months long, but you may start to see improvement in just days.

After three months of following the Plan, your website will have a solid foundation of results-minded optimization. Your SEO campaign will be moving along and becoming more and more specific to your needs and strategies. You will have smart analysis in place to determine which strategies are working and which aren't—and you'll drop the duds and focus your efforts in directions that are working for you.

Most importantly, after three months of following the Plan, you will be a fully fledged search engine marketer. You won't need day-by-day assignments anymore because you will be forging your own path. You will have great habits and tools for keeping your campaign buffed, and you'll be well on your way to teaching *us* a thing or two.

Who Can Use This Book

Truth be told, SEO is not hard. It's not rocket science, and it certainly doesn't require a degree in marketing, design, or anything else for that matter. While SEO is not hard, it can be tedious. It requires diligence and organization.

Our plan will work for just about anyone who is willing to make the hour-a-day commitment. We offer specific advice for

- small organizations
- large organizations
- one-person operations
- business to business (B2B)
- business to consumer (B2C)
- nonprofits
- bloggers
- adult sites

You certainly don't need to be selling anything to need SEO! All you need is a website that would benefit from an increase in targeted traffic.

Even if you're considering outsourcing some or all of your SEO tasks, it's a good idea to become familiar with the SEO process before you pay someone to take it over. Obviously, we've got nothing against companies who hire SEO specialists—they're our bread and butter!—but nobody knows your own business like you do. You are, therefore, uniquely prepared for this task.

We don't like jargon and we've tried to avoid it here (except, of course, when we teach it to you so you can impress others!). You'll learn concepts on a need-to-know basis and never waste your time on dead-end tasks. We don't bog you down with SEO history lessons, but we don't skimp on the important background knowledge either. Between the "Eternal Truths" and the "Right Now" of SEO that we've included in this book, we've got you covered. We know you're busy, and this book is written accordingly.

What's Inside

The heart of this book is Your SEO Plan, a three-month day-by-day program for improving your website's presence and increasing targeted traffic. We've divvied up the days into tasks that we estimate will take about an hour each. Depending on your circumstances, your familiarity with the subject matter, and the logistics of your website, it may take you more or less time to complete certain tasks.

The Plan is preceded by the preliminary planning and information you'll need to carry it out. That means you should read this book from the beginning and work through Your SEO Plan in order from start to finish.

Here's what you'll find inside.

Part I: Foundation

Chapter 1, "Clarify Your Goals," helps you frame your thinking about your website and your goals in an SEO-friendly way.

Chapter 2, "Customize Your Approach," provides guidance for adjusting your Plan to suit the special advantages and challenges faced by different types of organizations.

Chapter 3, "Eternal Truths of SEO," gives an overview of the longstanding, or "eternal," factors in effective search engine optimization. Learn these truths to bring longevity to your SEO success.

Chapter 4, "How the Search Engines Work Right Now," presents a current snapshot of the world of search.

Part II: Strategy

Chapter 5, "Get Your Team on Board," offers been-there-done-that advice for eliminating intra-organizational hang-ups that are common in SEO.

Chapter 6, "Your One-Month Prep: Baseline and Keywords," is all about preparation: researching, organizing, and setting the direction for Your SEO Plan. Several worksheets and templates will help you along the way.

Part III: Your SEO Plan

Chapter 7, "Month One: Kick It into Gear," launches Your SEO Plan with basic website optimization, a link-building method, and a starter pay-per-click campaign.

Chapter 8, "Month Two: Establish the Habit," shows you how to use your site's structure to your SEO advantage, teaches you the best habits for keeping current with SEO trends, and helps you choose an all-important method of tracking and measuring your SEO success.

Chapter 9, "Month Three: It's a Way of Life," takes your SEO campaign further with content building, improving your return on investment, and in-depth troubleshooting.

Chapter 10, "Extra Credit and Guilt-Free Slacking," gives you practical tips on reducing your SEO workload if your schedule is less than perfect and helps you dig deeper in specific areas if you are especially enthusiastic.

This Book's Companion Website

In addition to the chapters you hold in your hand, you can find extra information and resources on our companion website, www.yourseoplan.com.

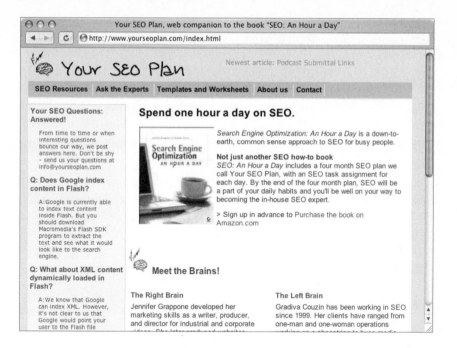

There, you can download all the worksheets and templates you need for the Plan and find plenty of useful SEO links and tips as well. When we're not saving the world one website at a time, we'll be uploading articles and answering your "Ask the Experts" questions on the website. We hope it will become one of your most useful bookmarks!

Conventions Used in This Book

 We've been working together in close quarters for so many years now that sometimes it seems our brains are fused. Gradiva tends toward the "left brain" side of our collective SEO brain, with enough logic, math proficiency, and analytical thinking for both of us. On the other hand, Jennifer is more of a "right brain" thinker, with a flair for writing and a preference for the creative aspects of SEO. One thing we agree on: Good SEO requires a little left brain *and* a little right brain! Throughout this book, you'll see the "left brain/right brain" icon wherever we think you need the view from both sides.

 We love to learn from others' mistakes and successes, and you can too! Look for the shovel icon accompanying stories from the real world: case studies, expert opinions, and even some tragic tales from the trenches. We've changed most of the names to protect the privacy—and reputations—of the parties involved.

 This pearl represents a special tip or tidbit of wisdom that you may find especially helpful.

The "Now" icon indicates an SEO task that's assigned to you. When you come across one of these, it's time to set the book down and get to work!

We wrote this book with the busy professional in mind, so all you need to commit to is the hour-a-day plan. But sometimes, you might be inclined to take your campaign a little further. For you go-getters, we've provided the extra credit icon.

And for those of you who spend most of your time wishing you had more time, here's the icon for you. Next to the slacker icon, you'll find options for trimming down your tasks without compromising results.

If you're dying to roll up your sleeves and do something *right now*, your enthusiasm is noted and appreciated. Fire up your computer and we'll be waiting for you on page 1!

Foundation

So, you want to differentiate your website from the millions of others out there on the Internet? Great! Let's get started! Whether you're starting from scratch or just looking for a new approach, the hardest part of embarking on a Search Engine Optimization (SEO) *campaign is knowing where to begin. In Part I, we walk you through a little self-reflection and search engine basics to lay the groundwork for Your SEO Plan:*

1

Clarify Your Goals

A good Search Engine Optimization (SEO) *campaign needs to be laser-focused on your business goals, so it has to start with a healthy dose of thought and reflection. In this chapter, we'll walk you through the key questions you'll want to consider before you get started.*

What Is SEO?

OK, let's see a show of hands: How many of you are reading this book because you want a #1 rank in Google? Yeah, we thought so. As SEO consultants, we know how good it feels when your website makes it to the top of the heap. Listen, we sincerely hope you get your #1 Google rank, but it won't help you if it's bringing in the wrong audience or pointing them to a dead-end website. So don't think of SEO as just a way to improve your site's ranking.

The term Search Engine Optimization describes a diverse set of activities that you can perform to increase the amount of targeted traffic that comes to your website from search engines (you may also have heard these activities called *Search Engine Marketing* or *Search Marketing*). This includes things you do to your site itself, such as making changes to your text and HTML code. It also includes communicating directly with the search engines, or pursuing other sources of traffic by making requests for listings or links. Tracking, research, and competitive review are also part of the SEO package.

SEO is not advertising, although it may include an advertising component. It is not public relations, although it includes communication tasks similar to PR. As a continually evolving area of online marketing, SEO may sound complicated, but it is very simple in its fundamental goal: gaining targeted visitors.

Do I Need to Perform SEO for My Website?

It may seem like a no-brainer, but actually, the answer is not necessarily Yes. If any of the following examples apply to you, you may not be in need of an SEO campaign right now:

- You have a website that you really don't want strangers to find, such as a training tool for your employees or a classroom tool for your students.

- Your site is already ranking well, you're satisfied with your sales, and you don't want to rock the boat.

- You're in a big hurry—say, you'll go out of business without a major upswing in revenue in the next couple of months. This is not to say that SEO can't help you, but good SEO takes time. You may need to focus your energies elsewhere right now.

- Your site is going to be completely rebuilt or redesigned in the next couple of months. If that's the case, read Shari Thurow's book *Search Engine Visibility* (New Riders, 2002) about how to build a search-friendly site from the ground up. If this is you, you'll want to keep our book on hand, though, for use as soon as your new site is launched.

If this list doesn't apply to you, we think you're ready to begin your SEO adventure!

It is a rare site indeed that couldn't use a little improvement in the SEO department. And, with the importance of SEO on the rise, if you don't need it today, it's a good bet you'll need to brush up your SEO smarts for tomorrow. So even if you don't think you need SEO right now, we recommend that you take the time to work through the questions in this chapter and make sure that your goals aren't begging for a little help.

What Are the Overall Goals of My Business?

Most likely, the fundamental goal of your business, when you get down to the bottom of it, is to make money by selling a product or service. However, there may be nuances to even such a straightforward goal as this. And there are a whole host of other possible goals and subgoals that your business is likely to have.

Perhaps yours is a large company with branding as an important long-term goal. Maybe your company wants to make money with certain products but is willing to take a loss in other areas. Maybe you are starting up with investor backing and do not need to turn a profit for years. Perhaps you are a nonprofit, with a goal to improve the world and inspire others to do the same. Whatever way you're leaning, your business goals will affect your SEO campaign strategy.

For instance, consider the fictional situation of Jason, a founding partner at Babyfuzzkin, a company selling unique, high-end baby clothes. This business makes its money directly through online sales. It's a small operation, so there is a limit to how many orders the business can handle. The Babyfuzzkin fantasy would be a steady flow of, say, 100 orders per month. But there is more to the story: Eventually, the partners would love to get out of the direct fulfillment of orders and instead secure some contracts with big-name brick-and-mortar vendors.

In the case of Elizabeth, a marketing director at ElderPets, we have a different situation. ElderPets is a nonprofit organization that provides meals, walks, and veterinary care assistance to animals belonging to elderly and infirm owners. The company relies on financial contributions and volunteers to fulfill its mission. At ElderPets their fantasy is to decrease the time and effort spent on fundraising activities such as silent auctions and community dog washes and begin attracting more contributions online, which would in turn allow them to help more pets in need. In addition, they are constantly looking for more volunteers.

Though Jason and Elizabeth have different goals in regard to their respective websites, we have an exercise they can both perform to get the most out of their planned SEO. We've created a Goals Worksheet to guide clients like Jason and Elizabeth, and you can use it as you consider the questions in this chapter. You can download the Goals Worksheet at our companion website, www.yourseoplan.com. At key points throughout this chapter, we'll ask you to stop, reflect on your own business, and write down your own vital statistics. Once you've worked through the questions, you'll have a strong vision of the "why" of your SEO campaign—and you'll be ready to move on to the "what" and "how" in Parts II and III.

 Now: Download the Goals Worksheet from www.yourseoplan.com.

Now take a moment and look at "Business Goals" on your Goals Worksheet. Tables 1.1 and 1.2 show how Jason of Babyfuzzkin and Elizabeth at ElderPets might fill out theirs, respectively.

▶ **Table 1.1** Summary of Business Goals for Babyfuzzkin

Primary Goal	Sell clothes directly to consumers online
Additional Goal	Sign brick-and-mortar contracts

▶ **Table 1.2** Summary of Business Goals for ElderPets

Primary Goal	Help more animals in need
Additional Goal	Attract more donations
Additional Goal	Attract more volunteers

 Now: Take a few minutes to write down your overall business goals in "Business Goals" on your Goals Worksheet. Don't be afraid to indulge in fantasy!

What Function Does My Website Serve?

It's not uncommon to hear that the reason a company built a website is "to have a website." While we all love a little bit of circular logic before breakfast, if you're going to put a lot of time and money into promoting your website, it's important to have a good idea of what it's doing for you.

Most websites are built out of a combination of basic building blocks. Whether your site is a web-based store seeking online sales; a personal blog seeking community connections; a political or religious outlet seeking to persuade, uplift, or inspire; a corporate "brochure" displaying branding identity and company information; or just about any other type of website you can imagine, it will likely include some or all of the following features or elements:

- ✔ Corporate history, news, and press releases
- ✔ Executive biographies
- ✔ Product and service information
- ✔ Online purchasing/donation
- ✔ Support for existing customers/clients/students
- ✔ News and current events
- ✔ Articles, white papers
- ✔ Religious, philosophical, or political content
- ✔ Online request for information (RFI) forms
- ✔ Login for restricted information
- ✔ Instructions for making contact offline or via e-mail
- ✔ Directions, hours of operation, etc. for brick-and-mortar location
- ✔ Links to other resources

- ✔ Fun, games, or entertainment
- ✔ A strong brand identityt
- ✔ Art or craft portfolio
- ✔ Educational materials
- ✔ Information specifically for geographically local visitors
- ✔ Software or documents available for download
- ✔ Media (pictures, audio, video) available for viewing/downloading
- ✔ Site map
- ✔ Archived content
- ✔ Site search function
- ✔ Live help/live contact function
- ✔ Ways for members of the community to connect with each other on the site (forums, bulletin boards, etc.)

Now, spend some time clicking around your website. You should be able to tell which of the features in the preceding list are included. How well is each component doing its job? For now, think in terms of presentation and functionality. (Is your product information up-to-date? Is your online store full of technical glitches? Are your forms asking the right questions?) Give each feature that you find a ranking of Excellent, Good, Fair, or Poor. Obviously this isn't going to be a scientific process—just make your best estimate.

 Now: On your Goals Worksheet, check off the boxes in "Website Features" that apply to your current site, making sure to note any features you hope to add in the future. Add your assessment in the rating column.

Jason and Elizabeth's checklists might look something like Tables 1.3 and 1.4:

▶ **Table 1.3** Ratings for Babyfuzzkin Features

Online purchasing/donation	Excellent
Product and service information	Good
A strong brand identity	Good
Instructions for making contact offline or via e-mail	Good

▶ **Table 1.4** Ratings for ElderPets Features

Corporate history, news, and press releases	Excellent
Executive biographies	Excellent
Online purchasing/donation	Future Goal
Educational materials	Good
Online request for information (RFI) forms	Good

How Is My Website Connecting with the Goals of My Business?

Take a look at what you've written on your Goals Worksheet. Is there a disconnect between your business goals and your current website? Is your website focused on corporate info or, worse yet, executive bios instead of your business goals? Or does the website provide only content geared toward supporting existing clients when the primary business goal is to gain new clients?

 Now: Take a moment to write down any disconnects you've identified in "Connecting Goals" on your Goals Worksheet.

Jason at Babyfuzzkin is in good shape: The business goals and website goals are in alignment, with an Excellent rating on the top business priority. Since the business goal includes not only sales but also a strong push toward future deals, the SEO campaign will need to support both.

On the other hand, Elizabeth at ElderPets may be in trouble. One of its primary goals is to get donations, but its website is currently focused on describing its mission and founders, and it doesn't even have online donation capability yet. This could pose a challenge throughout the SEO campaign.

Remember the big picture here:

Pearl of Wisdom: Your SEO campaign must support the overall business goals, not just your website.

The SEO You Have, Not the One You Want

In an ideal world, you could take your Goals Worksheet to your boss and say, "Hey! We've got a disconnect here. Let's fix it!" But let's just suppose that *ideal* is not the word you would use to describe your organization. The fact is, your SEO campaign may need to work with certain handicaps.

Over the years, we've worked with a lot of folks who have had to support their business goals with a less-than-perfect website. Here are the most common reasons we've seen for this:

- There is political opposition to change.
- There are scheduling bottlenecks: everybody else's project comes before our own site.
- The current marketing team inherited an outdated or lousy website.
- The site is floating along and isn't really anybody's responsibility.

Some Interim Solutions

It's your job as the in-house SEO expert to lobby for a website that will deliver for your company. But you may be wondering, "If my site is far less than perfect and—for whatever reason—I can't fix it right now, should I even bother with SEO?" Probably. Here are some ideas for approaching SEO while you're waiting for your site to come up to speed with your company's goals:

- Work on getting traffic, but lower your expectations for sales (or whatever action you want your visitors to perform) for the time being. When you perform your monthly rank checks during your SEO campaign, you may notice an upswing in traffic, which you can use to motivate your people to make some positive changes to the site.
- Ask for "ownership" of just one page, or just one section, and try to bring it up to snuff. Can't get a whole page? We've had customers who were given just one chunk of the home page to do with as they wished. Surprisingly, site maps

actually represent good SEO opportunities, and it may be easier to convince your boss to give you ownership of yours!

- Use your powers of competitive analysis. As you go through your Prep Month in Chapter 6, "Your One-Month Prep: Baseline and Keywords," take special care to note if your competitors' sites are doing things well in the areas in which your site is lacking. This may motivate those in power to give your recommended changes a higher priority.

- Focus on *off-page* SEO activities. While you're waiting to get your site spiffed up, you can always work on removing outdated listings and cleaning up old links to your site.

- As a last resort, if your current site is so hopeless that it's actually doing your business more harm than good, you might decide to take drastic measures and disinvite the search engines. We'll show you how in Part III, "Your SEO Plan."

SEO Infighting at UpperCut and Jab, Inc.

Here's a true story involving UpperCut and Jab, Inc. (company name and some identifying details have been changed to prevent embarrassment), which provides IT consulting and solutions for large businesses. One of the company's primary goals is new client acquisition.

In this corner: A Sales Force with Very Practical Needs They like to have lots of corporate information, white papers, and case studies online. They use these as sales tools while they are on the phone or on the road in a meeting with potential clients. Sounds like a great use of a website, and one that doesn't require any SEO or any sort of call to action. With their hands already full, the sales team does not want to waste their time responding to unqualified leads.

In this corner: A Marketing Team with a Vision The marketing team, on the other hand, would like to see the website gathering leads. They want a functioning request for information (RFI) form and a generously budgeted SEO campaign to drive traffic to it.

The plan of attack Both departments have good points, but the burden is on the marketing team to fine-tune the SEO campaign so that incoming leads are high quality and not a waste of anybody's time or money.

So who wins? Unfortunately, nobody. The marketing team was successful in driving a great deal of traffic to the RFI form! But, uh-oh, a vast majority of forms were filled out by unqualified leads. ("Does so-and-so still work there?" "Can you help me with a broken printer?") Looks like they forgot about defining their target audience. The RFI form—a potentially great lead generation tool—was eventually dropped.

The moral of the story Bringing traffic to your site is not necessarily the same as meeting your company's goals!

Who Do I Want to Visit My Website?

In the introduction we pointed out the fact that the person who you *most* want to find your website is the person who is searching for your website! And of course this is true. But now let's dig a little deeper and describe your ideal audience so that you can help them make their way to you.

Who is the target audience for your website? Surely it will include potential clients/customers. But don't forget that it may also include members of the press, employees at your own company, current and past customers seeking support, even potential investors nosing about for the inside scoop!

Using your Goals Worksheet, describe your target audience with as much detail as possible: professional status, technical vs. nontechnical (this will affect how they search or even which engines they use), age, workplace vs. home users, geographic locality.

Knowing your target audience(s) will help you make important decisions—such as *keyword* choices, directory site submittals, and budget for *paid listings*—when you start your SEO campaign.

Jason at Babyfuzzkin says, "Our target audience is parents of infants and small children, with a great sense of style and plenty of surplus income. They are probably fairly technically savvy, maybe a little short on time because of the kids—that's why they're shopping online. Also, a lot of our customers are grandparents, buying the clothes as gifts. Some parents don't want to spend as much on clothes they know are just going to get covered in oatmeal and grass stains! And the grandparents, they are a lot less savvy with the Internet. They use it from home, maybe with a slow connection, and they're located nationwide."

Elizabeth at ElderPets describes her target audience as "Caregivers or relatives of the elderly or infirm—they're usually the ones who contact us about our services. Our volunteers range from high school students hoping to beef up their college applications to retirees who don't have much money but want to do something worthwhile with their time. And then there's our donors, who can be all over the map in terms of age and income and their status as individual, family, or business. The one thing that ties them together is that they love animals."

Jason's and Elizabeth's goals and corresponding target audiences are shown in Tables 1.5 and 1.6.

▶ **Table 1.5** Babyfuzzkin Goals and Corresponding Target Audiences

Goals		Target Audience	
Primary goal	Sell clothes directly to consumers online	Primary Audience: Secondary Audience:	Parents of small children Grandparents and friends
Additional goal	Brick-and-mortar contracts	Primary Audience:	Buyers working for retailers

► **Table 1.6** ElderPets Goals and Corresponding Target Audiences

Goals		Target Audience	
Primary goal	Help more animals in need	Primary Audience:	Caregivers of the elderly or infirm
Additional goal	Attract more donations	Primary Audience:	Pet lovers with surplus income
Additional goal	Attract more volunteers	Primary Audience:	High school students, retirees

Now: Go to the "Conversions" table on your Goals Worksheet and fill out your target audiences under the appropriate column. Be as specific as you can!

What Do I Want Visitors to Do on My Website?

In SEO, the term *conversion* has come to mean your website user doing whatever it is you want them to do. So when we say "conversion," think of it as shorthand for "Score one for you—you're accomplishing your goals!"

We really enjoyed reading the results in Google when we searched for a definition of the word *conversion*. They included "an event that results in a transformation" and "a change of religion; 'his conversion to the Catholic faith.'" Wow! That's a lot to expect from your website. But one of the really fun facts about SEO is this:

Pearl of Wisdom: For your site, you can define a "conversion" however you want.

It's *your* party—you decide what you want your guests to do. Now that you have all of your goals written down in black and white, defining a conversion should be easy. Here are a few likely examples: users "convert" when they:

✔ purchase a product

✔ fill out an RFI form

✔ view a certain page on the site

✔ subscribe to a mailing list

✔ comment on a blog

✔ phone your 1-800 sales number

- ✔ drive to your retail store
- ✔ contribute to your political campaign
- ✔ change their opinion about something
- ✔ find the information they were looking for
- ✔ read a classified ad

Now look at the "Conversions" table on your Goals Worksheet. You will need to have a conversion defined next to each goal. Some of the conversion definitions will be straightforward; others may seem vague or touchy-feely. There's no harm in writing them all—we'll help you sort them out later in your SEO campaign when you're measuring results.

Jason's and Elizabeth's worksheets are shown in Tables 1.7 and 1.8.

▶ **Table 1.7** Babyfuzzkin Goals and Corresponding Conversions

Goals		Target Audience		Conversion
Primary goal	Sell clothes directly to consumers online	Primary Audience: Secondary Audience:	Parents of small children Grandparents and friends	Purchase via online store
Additional goal	Brick-and-mortar contracts	Primary Audience:	Buyers working for retailers	Make inquiry via online form or offline contact

▶ **Table 1.8** ElderPets Goals and Corresponding Conversions

Goals		Target Audience		Conversion
Primary goal	Help more animals in need	Primary Audience:	Caregivers of the elderly or infirm	View our mission statement
Additional goal	Attract more donations	Primary Audience:	Pet lovers with surplus income	Donate via online form or call our toll-free number
Additional goal	Attract more volunteers	Primary Audience:	High school students, retirees	Make inquiry via online form or offline contact

With your goals, audiences, and conversions spelled out, it's easy to connect the dots from goal to audience to desired conversion:

To achieve my **goal,** I need my **target audience** to **convert** on **this page.**

For example, Babyfuzzkin would say this:

- To achieve more **clothing sales**, I need **parents of infants** to **buy my products** on the **Clothes for Under $20 page**.

- To achieve more **clothing sales**, I need **grandparents and friends of parents** to **buy my products** on the **Gift Sets page**.

- To achieve **brick-and-mortar contracts**, I need **buyers working for retailers** to **make an inquiry** using the **Contact Us page**.

  And ElderPets might say this:

- To achieve **more online donations**, I need **pet lovers with surplus income** to **make a donation** on the **Donate Now page**.

- To achieve **a higher number of volunteers**, I need **homemakers and retirees** to **contact us** using the **Become a Volunteer page**.

- To achieve a **higher number of volunteers**, I need **high school students** to **contact us** using the **Students Volunteer Program** page.

- To achieve **being found by those in need**, I need **caretakers of elderly and infirm pet owners** to **visit** the **Our Mission page**.

 Now: Go back to the "Conversions" table on your Goals Worksheet and fill out your conversions under the appropriate column.

Which Pages Do I Most Want My Website Visitors to See?

Now it's time to start thinking about the top-priority pages for your SEO campaign. These are the pages you'll optimize when you get to your daily tasks in Part III. These are the pages that you most want people to get to from the search engines, and for best results, they should contain the most compelling content and the most useful information. Since your visitors "land" on these pages from the search engines, we call them *landing* pages (you might also hear them called *entry* pages). The main functions of your landing pages are that they speak to your desired audience and contain a call to action for your desired conversion. Figure 1.1 illustrates possible paths through your website from entry to conversion.

Often, your landing page and your conversion page will be the same, as is the case with Babyfuzzkin's Gift Sets page. This is a great situation because your site visitor doesn't have to navigate within your site to complete a conversion. Other times your conversion page will not be an appropriate entry page because your visitor will need to review other information first and then make the decision to continue. After all, the Web is a highly nonlinear space, and your visitors are free to ramble around your site in all sorts of ways.

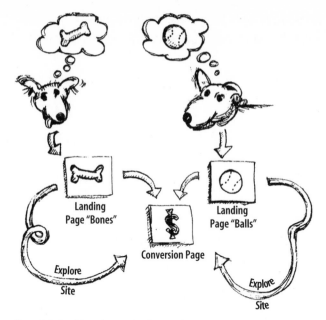

Figure 1.1 Possible paths to conversion

For the purposes of your SEO campaign, you need to ensure that for each type of conversion, there is at least one clear path between the search engine and the conversion outcome. We find it helpful to think backward: first consider where you want your visitor to end up, and then work backward to find a great page for them to enter your site.

For example, consider the ElderPets conversion:

To achieve **more online donations**, I need **pet lovers with surplus income** to **make a donation** on the **Donate Now page**.

Next, Elizabeth might work backward starting from the Donate Now page and clicking through the website to find a possible landing page:

Donate Now page → How Can I Help page → Dogs in Need page

In this scenario, the Dogs in Need page is the chosen landing page. Why? Because it's a very convincing, compelling page for this specific audience.

What makes a good landing page? One with just the right information that your target audience is looking for. Vague enough for you? Don't worry; in Part III, we'll walk you through the specifics of how to choose your landing pages and how to make sure the "right" information is on those pages. For now, we want you to begin thinking about what pages might work. If you don't have any pages that fit the bill, don't despair! Get some landing pages built if you can, or think about ways you can add compelling content to existing pages to turn them into excellent landing pages. And just a heads-up: once you start your SEO campaign, all of your top-priority pages will probably need to be revised at least a little bit as part of the optimization process.

Notice that the landing page ElderPets chose for this conversion is *not* the home page. Many site owners don't think in terms of deeper pages and think that they just want their home page to be found on the search engines. But in truth, your home page is probably only good for achieving the most general of your goals. Your deeper pages are more likely to contain a wealth of *specific* information and *specific* calls to action that you'd be thrilled for a *specific audience* to find one click away from a search engine!

 Now: Go back to the "Conversions" table on your Goals Worksheet and enter your conversion pages in the appropriate column.

How Will I Measure the Success of This SEO Campaign?

In our experience, measuring the success of your SEO campaign is the winner of the "Most Likely to Be Overlooked" award at just about every company. (Twenty-six percent of web marketers admit that they are "flying blind" in a 2005 report by Web-Trends.) Why is this? We think the cause is a combination of factors:

Lack of definition When goals or conversions are never defined, there's no way to measure your accomplishments.

Lack of communication Different departments or individuals with different goals may not be sharing information.

Technical difficulty Some types of conversions are difficult, if not impossible, to track.

Hitch up your high waters and get ready for another painful truth:

 Pearl of Wisdom: You *must* track the accomplishments of your SEO campaign.

There are a few good reasons why. Let's discuss them here.

Tracking Lets You Drop the Duds

Have you ever heard this military strategy riddle? You are waging battles on two fronts. One front is winning decisively. The other is being severely trounced. You have 10 thousand additional troops ready to deploy. Where do you send them? The answer is, you send them to the winning front as reinforcements. Strange as it sounds, it makes more sense to reinforce a winning battle than to throw efforts into a losing one.

This strategy is also reflected in the maxim "Don't throw good money after bad." You need to know which of your efforts are bringing you good results so you can send in the reinforcements, and you need to know which efforts are not working so you can bail out on them. And the only way to know this is to *track results*.

Tracking Will Help You Keep Your Job

If you work for yourself, you're the president of your own company, or you're reading this book for a hobby site or your blog, feel free to skip this section. For just about everyone else, we suspect that someone, somewhere is *paying* you to do this work. Eventually, that someone is going to wonder whether they have been spending their money wisely. Even if your boss ignores you every time you walk in the office with a tracking report, even if your department head refuses to back you up when you try to get IT support for *conversion tracking*, even if Sales tells you there's absolutely no way you can track sales back to the website, trust us; someday someone is going to want this information—preferably in a bar chart, with pretty colors, and summarized in five words or less. If you don't have the information, the measure of your accomplishments is going to default to this:

Are we #1 on Google?

And, if you're not, get ready for some repercussions!

Tracking Helps You Stay Up-to-Date

"Do it right the first time." It's a great motto and a great goal, but it's not a realistic plan for your SEO campaign. For one thing, you will need to continually re-prioritize your efforts as described in "Drop the Duds." But there's also another, unavoidable reason that your SEO campaign will need to constantly evolve: the search engines are changing too! Don't worry, this book sets you up with best practices that should have a nice long life span (in "Internet years" that is!). But you will inevitably need to be prepared for some changes. What works best today will not be exactly the same as what works best three years down the road. And the only way to know what has changed is to track your campaign.

Now that you are convinced that tracking is important, take a look at your list of conversions. Some of them will be easy to track; some may be difficult or close to impossible. Later, we'll take some time to think through possible ways to track your successes (and failures). Here are the methods that Jason and Elizabeth are considering for measuring their SEO campaign results:

Jason at Babyfuzzkin says, "Our primary goal is online sales. Probably the simplest way to track to our SEO campaign is to compare online sales numbers before and after the campaign. Our secondary goal is attracting attention from vendors. We'll track these leads back to the SEO campaign by asking any vendors that contact us how they heard about us."

Elizabeth at ElderPets describes her tracking plans by saying, "Our primary goal is donations, so we'll be watching for an increase in the number of individual donations after we start our SEO campaign. As for volunteers, we'll add a 'How did you find us?' question to our volunteer applications. As for just being found by people who need us: Our website also has a visitors counter. I've never paid much attention to it, but as a start I'll see if I can figure out if we're getting more traffic than we used to."

Clearly Jason and Elizabeth are on the right path. They've examined their goals and their websites. They've identified their targeted audiences and target pages, and they're even thinking ahead to tracking. If you're really stuck on any of these answers for your own company, take some time now to put your head together with others in your organization and hash it out. Understanding your own goals is a basic element of your upstart SEO campaign, and you'll do best if you have a firm grasp on them before you move on.

How Much Tracking Do I Need to Do?

Tracking can seem like a daunting task if you've never given any thought to it. Site owners like Jason and Elizabeth are wondering: *Should* tracking be approached with "baby steps" like the rest of SEO?

The Left Brain says Whoa there, Jason and Elizabeth: You're going to be collecting flawed data! Jason, how can you be sure that your increase in sales is just tied to your SEO efforts and not something else, like the start of the holiday season? And Elizabeth, that hit counter is not going to cut it! You need to gather data about where these people are coming from and how many of them are unique visitors. Don't you know that your counter can increase every time someone's cat steps on the "refresh" button?

The Right Brain says I admire your left-brained hunger for irrefutable facts. However, most people are too busy to make numbers-watching on that level their highest priority. I say, we encourage *any* effort at all to track conversions, as long as it's based on some logic and is done consistently. Even a little bit of tracking can bring up some interesting findings. And these findings often get people interested in learning more, which may in turn motivate people to do more detailed tracking. Believe it or not, tracking can be a creative process!

Wow! You've done a lot of thinking in this chapter. You now know that you probably need SEO for your website. You have a great grasp on your overall business goals. You know what your website is doing and whether these things are good or bad for your company. You know your target audience and your desired conversions. And, we trust, you are convinced that tracking is a necessity. Now, meet us in Chapter 2, "Customize Your Approach," for some light reading about your favorite subject: *You!*

Customize Your Approach

Let's say you want a great car wash, one that gets up close and personal with your car's curves and addresses its individual problem areas. You wouldn't trust a gas station car wash—you'd do it yourself! Likewise, the SEO plan in this book presents a method that can be applied to a wide range of SEO efforts, but you have to customize it for your particular business and website. This chapter gives you a great head start.

Chapter Contents:

It's *Your* SEO Plan
B2B
B2C
Large Organization
Small Organization
Brick-and-Mortar
Blogger
Nonprofit

It's *Your* SEO Plan

When you heard about this book, you may have had one of two reactions. Maybe you thought, "Great! A quick and easy SEO plan that I can follow!" Or maybe you thought, "Uh-oh! An oversimplified approach to something complex." Both of these reactions are perfectly reasonable. A simple approach is important, but you should be wary of anything that promises a one-size-fits-all SEO solution.

So let's make one thing clear: there's nothing cookie cutter about *your* SEO plan. And since nobody knows your organization and website like you do, guess who's in charge of the fine-tuning? You!

Small and large companies, brick-and-mortars, nonprofits, and bloggers—each type has its own set of needs, advantages, and challenges. Your assignment: Identify which categories your company is in, read our tips and guidelines for those categories, and think about how you can apply the customization to your own SEO efforts.

This is a "check all that apply" chapter—your company may fall into multiple categories. For example, let's say you run an independent toy store in Des Moines, Iowa. You would want to read at least three of the categories in this chapter: brick-and-mortar, B2C, and small organization. If you're the world leader in granulators for the plastics industry, you'd want to read B2B and large organization. Read what applies to you, but also consider reading what may not seem to. After all, part of being an SEO expert is knowing the breadth of what the Web offers. You never know where you might find something interesting and useful for your own site!

B2B

B2B sites run the gamut from the little guys selling restaurant-grade deli slicers to the huge corporation selling enterprise-level software and services. Large and small B2Bs have a lot in common when it comes to the advantages and challenges of SEO.

Advantage: Niche Target Audience Because your business depends on it, you probably already know your customer well. Your customer fits into a particular niche: restaurant owner, plant manager, candlestick maker, and so on. While your customers may not all hang out at the same bar after work, it's a good bet that they're frequenting some of the same websites. And if you don't know what these sites are, it only takes a little bit of time and creative thought to find them. If you already know what magazines your customers subscribe to, what trade shows they attend, and what organizations they belong to, you're well on your way to finding analogous sites on the Web that speak to them.

Challenge: Difficulty Gaining Links You may have heard that getting relevant, high-quality links to your website is an important SEO endeavor, because it can improve your ranks and traffic. This is going to be a challenge for you. You're not a big entertainment site or a fun *blog* with a cult following, and unless you're a giant in your industry, your activities are not automatically newsworthy. While you may have the respect of your customers, building a self-sustaining "buzz" is not the kind of thing that comes easily to a B2B website. After all, your site probably isn't built for buzz; chances are you're offering straight-up product information, corporate bios, and white papers. You'll need to move forward with a view toward increasing your site's *linkability* with noncommercial content.

Advantage: High-Value Conversions SEO is very appealing to B2Bs, for a good reason. Because each new customer or lead is very valuable to your business, your SEO campaign can make a quick and measurable difference to your bottom line by bringing in just a few conversions. Don't skimp on tracking—you'll want your SEO campaign to get credit for these high-value conversions.

Challenge: A Slow SEO Life Cycle You know why scientists love that little fruit fly called drosophila? The reason is that the drosophila has such a short life span that many generations of them can be studied in a relatively short amount of time. In a similar way, an SEO campaign can be studied and improved in a relatively short amount of time if you have lots and lots of visitors coming through and either converting or not. For a B2B, however, this is probably not the case. You will have a smaller, more targeted audience and will likely have a longer conversion life cycle. That means less information, and a slower evolution, for your ongoing SEO campaign.

Advantage: Text-Heavy Content Got FAQs? How about product specifications and mission statements? As a B2B, you probably have lots of text on your site, which the search engines love. While some site owners will be scratching their heads looking for ways to fit text into their design, you will probably have tons of text on which to focus your optimization efforts. And if not, you may have marketing materials such as white papers and PDFs ready for quick and easy appropriation onto your site. Of course, all of the text-heavy items mentioned here have the potential to be about as exciting as a glass of warm milk, so make sure you're putting out text that people actually want to read!

B2C

B2C is such a huge category that we almost hesitate to lump you all together. B2C ranges from big flower vendors making a killing on Mother's Day to one-person operations selling homemade soaps. You may have a local, national, or international customer base, and you may have anything from a phone number or a Yahoo! store to a complex, media-rich e-commerce experience. However, there are some key elements that you have in common when you perform SEO. (Don't worry about seeing so many challenges here. You can look for advantages in the other category or categories that apply to you.)

Challenge: Less-Web-Savvy Audience The people who are searching for your product or service may not be as knowledgeable about the Web as you are, and certainly not as knowledgeable as you hope they are. So, even though the Web is chock full of niche shopping sites that are worth looking into, it makes sense to give your attention first to how your site looks in the search engine mainstays: Google, AOL, Yahoo!, MSN, and Ask (formerly Ask Jeeves).

And, while you may have the benefit of marketing research and brand differentiation, your potential audience may be frustratingly unaware of your preferred labels for your own product or service. Are you selling "the finest micro-techno-fiber all-weather apparel"? That's great, but your general user base is probably searching for "blue rain-coats." In addition, they may be misspelling your product or—*the horror*—your brand name. Careful keyword research can help you tremendously.

Challenge: Unexpected Search Competition As your audience is potentially very large and diverse, so too is your competition. We mean your *search* competition, of course. You may know exactly who your top five competitors are in the "real world," but when you get down to identifying your top-priority keywords in your SEO plan, you're likely to be amazed by the sites that are clogging up the top ranks. They might be competitors you've never heard of, or they might be individual consumers talking about how much they hate your products. Or, as we often see, they may not be related to your industry at all. Did you know there's a band called "The Blue Raincoats"? Well, there is, and last we checked, it had the top nine spots in Google for the term "blue raincoats."

Challenge: Page View Conversions If, like many B2C websites, your measure of conversion is a page view—for example, if you're using traffic data to sell ad space on your site, or if your main goal is brand awareness—get ready for an exciting ride. Simply going by the traffic numbers can have you shouting from the top of the parking garage one day and weeping into your latte the next. This next bit of advice may be hard for a slick up-and-comer like you to swallow, but we're telling you because we like you: Accept that you have less control than you think you do. The Google gods are fickle. An algorithm change, or a search engine marriage or divorce, may be all it takes to sink your traffic.

Large Organization

If you're about to embark on SEO for your large organization, brace yourself, this is going to sting a little:

 Pearl of Wisdom: You do *not* have dibs on the number one spot in the rankings just because you're big.

In fact, your SEO campaign is likely to be challenged by your bulk, both in terms of your website and your organizational structure.

Challenge: Internal Bureaucracy From an organizational perspective, your SEO challenges are often a result of "too much." Too much in that your site is likely to be run by committee: designers, IT department, copywriters, and coders not to mention the executives who, with a single comment, can have you all scrambling in different directions. We know how pressed you are for time, how many different people in your organization are all putting their dirty fingers in the pie that is your website, and we know what a struggle it can be to get any changes made on your site. Here are some very common SEO tasks; see if you can get through this list without cringing about how many individuals you'll need to complete them:

- Convert graphics to HTML text.
- Edit elements of the HTML code on every page of the site.
- Remove or reduce the use of Flash.
- Create a specialized text file called robots.txt and have it placed in the root directory of the site.
- Set up a web page redirect.
- Rewrite page text to reflect more commonly searched terms.

The takeaway here is that you'll be putting a lot of extra time into internal communication and organization. You need to know your team and get them in your corner if you want to succeed at SEO. In other words: Get your team on board. It's so important it has its own chapter in this book!

Why is this door always *so sticky*?

Challenge: Brand Maintenance Another "too much" challenge for you lies in the need to keep your brand current. You have probably already witnessed several major changes to your site, steered either by real market forces or by the perceptions of your marketing department. Maybe you have a redesign every six months, frequent new products or product updates, or new branding guidelines to implement. Structurally, you may also have multiple subdomains, more than one URL leading to your home page, and lots of fragmented bits of old versions of your site floating around out there. (Think you don't? Check again. We can honestly say we haven't met one large website that didn't have something old and out-of-date live and available on the search engines.) Maybe you have all of the above, multiple times over, because you have different teams responsible for different portions of your website. Because of all these factors, the large organization has a special need to keep its "calling cards" on the Web consistent with the current state of its site. Cleaning up old and dead links and making sure your listings talk about your current products and services should be two of your highest priorities.

Advantage: Budget and Existing Infrastructure Of course, "too much" works to your advantage too. You may have a larger budget, which means that you can probably afford to buy some of the many helpful tracking and keyword tools that we will suggest in this book. And your company probably has existing marketing data about your customers, their behaviors and habits, and their budgets, which your SEO campaign can tap into.

Advantage: Lots of Landing Pages Large sites often have a wealth of opportunities for landing pages. Go deep, or more appropriately, go *shallow-wide*: think beyond your home page and main section pages when determining which pages to optimize. This shallow-wide approach—driving site visitors to a large number of unique pages on your site—can help you compensate for some of the other challenges we've discussed.

Challenge: Pay-per-Click Pitfalls *Pay-per-click (PPC)* campaigns can help you accomplish your shallow-wide goals, and your average PPC campaign is much cheaper on a per-visit basis than any form of offline marketing. But PPC campaigns for large organizations have the potential to be large and unwieldy. Even with the built-in management tools that make your PPC campaign a fairly user-friendly experience, the sheer magnitude of a hundred-plus or thousand-plus keyword campaign can be very time-consuming. PPC campaigns are an unlikely mix of the creative (word choice, campaign strategy) and the tedious (daily budget caps, maximum click price). The danger for the large company is that it's very easy to shift your attention away from the important details such as clarity of message and appropriateness of keyword choice and get distracted by the data.

Advantage: PPC Assistance Luckily, your larger budget may qualify you for helpful hand-holding services directly from the PPC engines—services where actual humans talk to you and manage the more tedious aspects of your accounts. These services are worth looking into, but always remember: nobody knows your company and brand like you do! Whether you manage the campaign yourself or hire someone else to do it, make sure someone with marketing sense and excellent writing skills is keeping an eye on it. There's nothing we hate more than seeing ads like the one below. Seriously, is this what they want people to see?

Advantage: Making News Last but not least, being large might mean that just about everything you do is automatically newsworthy—which translates into incoming links on the Web. That's great news for your SEO potential!

Small Organization

Small businesses, we salute you as the most vibrant sector of today's Web! You are the equivalent of the corner store—the "mom and pop" sites—personalizing the Web and providing an antidote to the MegaCorp, Inc. mentality and design. Whatever you're selling, you're probably doing it on a very careful budget, and you're probably doing everything with minimal manpower.

Did you read the section about the large organizations and find yourself feeling a bit envious of all that money and manpower? Don't be. SEO can be the field-leveler you need to compete with larger companies, whereas competition in offline advertising venues would be much too expensive for you. And, being smaller, your team, your site—and your SEO campaign—can benefit from a more centralized approach.

Advantage: Less Bureaucracy A busy small organization is often too tapped for resources to work on bettering its own marketing message or position—everybody else's project seems to come first. Your company doesn't have room for large teams of marketing writers and strategists. So you may be the one person who is the gate-keeper for all of these activities. Sure, it's more work for you, but on the positive side, it means you won't have to go through a huge bureaucracy every time you need to change your website. *You* have the power to make a real difference.

Challenge: Lack of Time If your business is doing well, your biggest SEO challenge is going to be a shortage of time. You might even be sweating out the notion of finding your hour a day for SEO tasks. The great news is, SEO gives back what you put into it.

slacker

Do what you can, and read Chapter 10, "Extra Credit and Guilt-Free Slacking," for ideas on how to devote your precious SEO moments to the tasks that are going to give you the best time-to-results ratios.

Advantage: A Friendlier Reception For any site, asking other sites for links is one of those lower-return tasks: very time-consuming, unpredictable results. But being small can give you a real advantage in the area of "personal touch." Do you have a really cool new product? Are you offering a discount for a particular group? Tell a blogger who might be interested in telling the world. Or you may want to reach out to satisfied customers who have websites. Even though link building might not be on the hot burner, if you chip away at this activity, you can probably increase your *inbound links* in a meaningful way.

Challenge: Small Budget Your time is tight, and your budget is modest. Probably the smartest investment you can make, in our opinion, is a pay-per-click campaign. Surprised? It actually makes a lot of sense. If you manage it closely, your PPC campaign gives you almost-instant feedback. Is your message compelling enough? Are you targeting viable keywords? Is your conversion page doing its job? With PPC, you can tweak to your heart's content for pennies on the dollar compared to other advertising methods.

Advantage: Tools to Level the Playing Field Of course you know your product or service inside and out, and your customers may seem like close, personal friends. But you might not be very well versed in your customers' Web habits and searching behavior. You may have little or no actual experience in marketing. Luckily, you don't need to be a pro—or a big business—to excel in SEO.

A recent study by The Kelsey Group found that small business advertisers in the United States currently allocate an average of 23 percent of their total advertising budget to PPC activities, and this number is expected to rise. You are big business for the search engines, and therefore, keyword research tools, directory listings, traffic analysis software, and the like are all often within the price range of the small business.

Even with a small budget, you can pick up an advantage by studying your competitors. Get ideas and insight from their websites and PPC campaigns, and use *their* resources to *your* best advantage! You may get as much out of your do-it-yourself competitive analysis as you would get from an expensive marketing study. If you've got the time and some natural curiosity, it doesn't cost you anything to look at the companies ranking in the top 10 for your desired keywords and figure out what they're doing right.

Advantage: Starting from Zero It may be that you have given no thought to SEO. Don't let that discourage you! Confession time:

Pearl of Wisdom: SEO consultants love working for companies starting out at rock bottom because you have nowhere to go but up.

But, think carefully about your plan of attack. With a small staff, it is possible to go from famine to feast more quickly than you may be comfortable with. So, if each conversion on your site creates work for you, you may want to take it slowly.

Challenge: Seductive Quick-and-Dirty SEO Schemes Don't be tempted, as some smaller businesses are, to put your money or energy into quickie link schemes or questionable practices such as *cloaking* (showing the search engines one page while showing your users another) or creating *doorway pages* (pages that have no real content and just exist to link to another page), which are likely to backfire. (We'll talk more about practices to avoid in Chapter 3, "Eternal Truths of SEO.") And please, remember that the message on your site is what will bring you conversions. If your pages are stuffed with keywords and filled with awkward text aimed at getting rankings, your business is likely to suffer in the long run. Keep your SEO campaign squeaky clean!

Little Flower Candy Co.: Know When to Hold 'Em!

Christine Moore is a former pastry chef who knows a great deal about making delectable handmade desserts using high-quality ingredients. Now she's in business for herself. Working in her own kitchen, using her own hands, she has developed a formidable reputation for making some of the tastiest candies in Los Angeles. But she admits she knows almost nothing about marketing.

Continues

Little Flower Candy Co.: Know When to Hold 'Em! *(Continued)*

And she's never had to. Thanks to great connections in L.A.'s visible foodie scene, word of mouth, and some very complimentary press coverage, her business is doing extremely well. When we spoke with her in the fall of 2005, she was looking toward the holiday season with excitement—and a good deal of trepidation. Acknowledging that the appeal of her product relies on the small-batch, handmade approach, she says, "I could ruin my reputation in one fell swoop by being greedy."

We have no doubt that an SEO campaign could bring Christine lots of new customers. But if things heat up too quickly, she may have more work than she can handle. At her current pace, she has time to get on the phone and call a Web customer to work out an ordering glitch and to be there for her family. Of course, she's open to SEO for her site, but, as Christine says, "It's hard to know whether to put the cart before the horse or the horse before the cart." Like any marketing strategy, SEO requires that careful consideration be given to the balance between a business's long-term goals and current capabilities.

Christine is in control of her company, and she is in a position to have control over its web presence. She has a good kind of problem. Her "real-world" buzz will be easy to translate into a web buzz, when the time is right!

Her site was built in a hurry, under pressure to get a store online in time for an article about her company that was about to go to press. The publication made it clear: no online store, no article. A friend quickly built her site, and Christine wrote the text just hours before it went live. Since the site was built for a ready-made audience of readers who had the URL in print, almost no thought was given to the search engines.

As SEO experts, here's what we noticed about her site: There were only two links pointing to it, and neither of them came from the large publications that have printed articles about her company. With such a rabid following and easy word-of-mouth marketing happening in the real world, she could easily get more links. Also, her site features the word *handmade* because she's not fond of the term *gourmet*. But what are her potential customers searching for? A little research would go a long way in determining if she's losing out on traffic by using the wrong terminology.

Brick-and-Mortar

If you had the chance to put one thing in front of your customers, you'd probably give them your street address, not your web address, and that's the way it should be. Your site plays second fiddle to your day-to-day business. After all, the best way to turn browsers into customers is to get them to walk through your door. You may not even be sure why you have a website, except that everyone else is doing it. So let's talk about how to make your site do its job of playing the supporting role.

Advantage: An Achievable Goal If you're not selling your product online, then the best use of your site is probably to help people find your physical location. Your SEO campaign begins with a simple goal: you want to be found when your company name is entered in the search engines. You'll focus your SEO campaign on variations of your business name and location. You're likely to get the results you are hoping for because you won't run up against too much competition for such tightly targeted keywords.

Advantage: Local Search And speaking of location, welcome to one of the hottest areas of SEO today: local search. It picks up where the local Yellow Pages left off in the last century. See Figure 2.1 for an example.

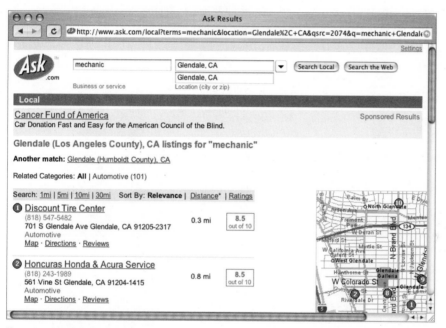

Figure 2.1 A local search on Ask

We love local search. Who wants to waste time slogging through nationwide search results when you're looking for the sandwich shop around the corner? If you're a mechanic in Glendale, California, you can put yourself directly in front of someone searching for "mechanic Glendale CA." Talk about a targeted audience! But there are a couple of things to keep in mind: First, people using local search are probably more search savvy than your average Web user. That's because local search is still relatively new, and it takes a while for the rank and file to adopt new search technology. Second, local search is changing fast, so you'll need to stay on top of it. When you implement your monthly SEO reporting, (we'll show you how in Part III) you may want to use some of it to keep track of shape-shifting results and to check the search-related blogs for developments in local search.

Maplecroft Bed and Breakfast in Barre, Vermont: The Power of Knowing Your Niche

Take a look at the Maplecroft Bed and Breakfast home page. Here's a little inn in small-town Vermont that offers a discount if you are a "librarian, quilter, or magician." You might describe the site as homey, low-budget, and low-tech, and that would all be true. But this sweet little site is deceptively well connected in the world of search.

Built by co-owner Paul Heller and designed by a family member in exchange for a vintage banjo, the site certainly does its job: it shows off the accommodations and provides a link to make a reservation. But Maplecroft is doing better than its competitors because Paul knows his niche. Here's what he says:

"My local competitors are not aware of the power of search-engine advertising (Adwords, in particular) and many are unwilling to make an investment in travel-specific search engines (BedandBreakfast.com). Our experience has shown both of these investments pay off in dramatically increased traffic.

Continues

Blogger

In recent years, *weblogs* have grown from a band of sharp-tongued outlaws to the darlings of online marketing. From Stonyfield Farm Yogurt to the Republican National Committee, it seems that everyone has a blog, or two, these days. Whether you are an individual out to bring in an income through running ads on your site or a large business with a blog on the site as a way to create relationships with potential clients, you are today's Big Thing on the Internet. Naturally, the major search engines should be catering to your every need. But you make it plenty hard for them! Your site lives and dies by content that changes every day, so it's difficult for search engines—which are also trying to index the entire rest of the Web too—to keep up. But little by little they are catching up.

Challenge: Keeping Up with New Search Options Blog-specific search works differently from standard search. Instead of going out and wandering through the zillions of web pages on the Internet every day, blog search engines sit back and watch for changes that come in through the "wires." This means that you'll need to do things a little differently to get your site included in these engines. In Part III, we'll walk you through the "need to feed" that will get your blog or podcast listed.

Until the summer of 2005, everybody was asking, "Who is going to be the Google of blogs?" Now it looks like it's quite possible that *Google* will be the Google of blogs, with its long-awaited blog search. Other major search engines were not far behind, and as of this writing, Yahoo! and AOL are chomping at the bit with blog search engines.

Despite the flood of "mainstream" search engines getting in on the blog search action, bloggers still need to be very aware of smaller, blog-specific search sites. You can find links to current biggies and up-and-comers on the companion website at www.yourseoplan.com.

Advantage: A Link-Friendly Culture Showing up on the blog-specific search engines isn't going to get you very far on its own. Blogs are part of a very special subculture on the Internet, usually called the *Blogosphere*, and you need to tap into that subculture to gain visibility. Blogs need incoming and outgoing links—lots and lots of them—to succeed. But, lucky for you, no other sector of today's Web is as link-happy as the Blogosphere.

The Blogosphere is a very social place. Even if you usually cross to the other side of the street to avoid chatting with a neighbor in the "real world," you need to force yourself to be a much more gregarious animal online. Time-consuming as it may be, reading other blogs is one of the best ways to connect yourself to a community, and ultimately build links and visibility for your own blog. But be careful: one thing you must *never* do when visiting other blogs is leave a *spam comment*, saying nothing more than "Visit my blog!" Bloggers are merciless in their punishment of etiquette-breaking behavior such as this.

Challenge: Optimizing Every Post Since your site probably doesn't have a traditional site map, with sections, subsections, and conversion pages, you won't have traditional landing pages to focus your SEO attentions on. Instead, you will have to put your time into making *every post* a better place for searchers to land. All of the SEO rules we lay out in this book for landing pages—rules like including keywords throughout text, writing great titles, and using search engine-readable HTML text—should become part of your every post.

Does it go without saying that you are going to need to update your blog very, very frequently? We sure hope so. Since your whole existence as a blogger is about writing excellent content, you're already well on your way to search-friendly site optimization.

Are You Selling Out If You Optimize Your Blog?

The Right Brain says, "Wait a minute. I'm uncomfortable telling bloggers to optimize their postings with search-targeted keywords! Shouldn't a blog be a bastion of personal expression and entertaining writing? Shouldn't the blogosphere be free of the marketing mentality that pervades the rest of the Web? We've seen it time and again: Good writing can really take a beating when a marketing agenda is attached to it."

The Left Brain says, "Right, and bloggers are all out there working on their own personal time, with no need for the luxuries in life like food and shelter. Heck, no! Blogs are well beyond the days of being just for fun; they are truly a business now. And as such, they have a legitimate need for SEO, just like any other business website. I would never counsel a blogger to dilute their message or change the blog's subject matter based on conversions—just as I don't give that sort of advice to any other website owner. But creating highly readable headlines that are compelling and clear—that's just common sense. And isn't "search-targeted keywords" just another way of saying, 'Use the text that makes the most sense to your audience?' After all, what good is a message if nobody gets it?"

Challenge: Domain Considerations One of the reasons blogging is so popular is the availability of free blog hosting services. But while free hosting is a great idea for personal sites like "The Knibbe Family Thanksgiving Web Page," it could work against your blog's SEO potential. Not only will a URL like knibbefamily.blog-mega-service.com reduce your linkability, it may also leave you subject to the advertising choices of the provider. Other bloggers will be more likely to take you seriously—and link to your blog—if you aren't using one of the free blog services that forces you to work within one of their domain names.

Advantage: A Venue for Personal Touch Any salesperson will tell you that making a sale is about trust. If you are trying to sell something through your blog, you have a great opportunity to give your audience a chance to get to know and trust you. Aaron Wall of www.seobook.com is both a blogger and expert search marketer. His blog is one way that potential customers find and purchase his e-book. But it's also a comprehensive, information-rich site that both helps others and bolsters his reputation in the industry. His advice to bloggers getting started and looking for SEO strategies: "Learn your community well, find and use your real voice, and link out early and often."

Adult Sites: Time to Get Passionate about SEO

If your website is of the adult variety, prepare yourself for a very difficult SEO experience. Besides dealing with mind-boggling levels of competition for keywords, you are also faced with several other disadvantages: a website that is, shall we say, more "visually" oriented than text oriented; a plethora of *black-hat* (questionable or unethical) SEO competitors; an entry page to boot out the under-21 crowd; and search engines that do not allow X-rated sites to advertise.

Sage Vivant, president and webmaster of CustomEroticaSource.com, has had her share of trials and tribulations working to promote her custom erotic literature website. Her many frustrations range from not being able to list her ads on Google Adwords for terms such as *gifts* and *anniversary* to being denied participation in the Better Business Bureau. "I'm extremely frustrated by having to constantly work around arbitrary moral rules relating to what is and is not 'adult.'"

So, what does work for adult websites?

- Use descriptive text. It's a real turn-on to the search engines! Find ways to add some very specific keywords, not just graphics, to your site.

- Your PPC campaign has the potential to be very pricey, so track it carefully, with a focus on cost per conversion.

- Be patient, and perseverant, with advertising rules and limitations.

- Although you're in a very competitive spot, never use unethical SEO techniques, which could get you permanently *banned* (removed from the search engine listings).

- Think beyond the search engines. Sage says, "Several years ago, I started an e-mail list and I think that was the single most successful thing I ever did. I had been afraid that people wouldn't want to hear from my business but I was wrong—response to any promotion or announcement I send out through that list is always good to excellent."

Nonprofit

Those of you in nonprofit organizations are working with a different sort of bottom line for your websites. Rather than following the corporate mantra of "money, money, and more money," you fine people are out there trying to change the world, educate, and improve society! And as a thank-you from the world of web search, you have some huge advantages in SEO.

Advantage: Linkability The culture of the Web generally adores noncommercial content—something that your website should be chock full of. And, let's face, it, giving you a link doesn't cost a thing. Any webmaster or blogger who supports your cause—or at least has no major problem with it—will see adding a link as a cheap and easy way to help out. You will want to adjust your SEO plan accordingly, giving extra effort to link-building.

And what is even better than inbound links from other sites? How about some fabulous "site of the day" awards from major web presences like Yahoo! and USAToday.com? "Site of the day" editors are always on the lookout for worthy sites, and nonprofits are in a perfect position to tap into this source of visibility and traffic. It's helpful—but not necessary—if you have something new on your site to show off. Be sure to include some time in your SEO Plan for building that "site of the day" potential. Sure, it's a little like winning the lottery of SEO, but for you, it's worth a try. Your odds are a lot better than for-profit sites' odds.

Advantage: Simple Website Structure And there's more good news: some of the characteristics that might, at first glance, seem like disadvantages for nonprofits are actually not so bad. Oftentimes nonprofits are short on cash but have plenty of untrained manpower available. Using your hour a day as management and training time for a small team of sharp-witted college students might just be the SEO strategy that brings you to the top. Another "problem" that might not be as bad as you think: an old website. That's right, your cruddy old 1999 website was probably built using no Flash, little JavaScript, and an absence of dynamic bells and whistles. Well, guess what? Those are just the things that can send *search engine spiders* packing anyway! A "classic" all-text site can be just the ticket for getting noticed by the search engines. Before you make any changes, make sure you aren't in an "if it ain't broke, don't fix it" situation.

Advantage: Less PPC Competition Many nonprofits think that there's no way that they can survive in the competitive world of paid listings. However, there are a few ways that you can, as a nonprofit, get your foot in the door. For one, it's very possible that the keywords that matter most to you are not the same words that commercial organizations are vying for. After all, nobody's out there selling "AIDS in China." Even better, both Google and Yahoo! offer free advertising programs for nonprofits. Be sure to check their websites for current programs and availability.

Challenge: Internal Issues Internal disorganization, an overworked and underpaid workforce, lack of funding, and lack of a clear bottom line could throw hurdles in the way of Your SEO Plan. If you are a small operation, you may not even have a marketing department to manage the website. And without a clearly measurable bottom line, it may be very hard for you to prove the value of your efforts. You will need to do some creative thinking to figure out a way to get that ROI measured. Is there a specific event that you can promote? A campaign or drive that can be earmarked as an SEO testing ground? With any luck, your SEO campaign will be funding itself after a few months of effort. You may be surprised to find that it becomes one of the most important outreach venues your organization will use.

Mon Yough Community Services: SEO on a Shoestring

Mon Yough Community Services is a nonprofit organization near Pittsburgh, Pennsylvania. It embodies some of the common challenges of nonprofits: lack of funding, lack of resources, and an organization that embraces "low tech." MYCS' website, developed and hosted by a company offering pro bono services to nonprofits, hasn't had a major update in seven years. If you ask Gina Boros, MIS manager, what kind of effort they put into SEO, she'll just laugh.

At first blush, it seems there's no reason to market MYCS on the Web. This is an organization whose target population is the homeless and mentally ill. Its most successful marketing efforts are in the form of bus stop advertisements, not the Internet. Pittsburgh's nonprofit service agencies are a tight-knit group, and the referrals that come are almost always word of mouth.

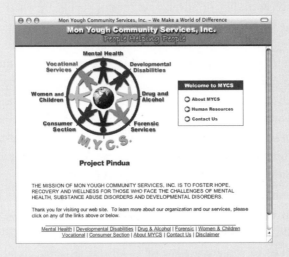

But, when you delve a bit deeper, it becomes clear that marketing its site on the Web would be far from pointless. MYCS constantly seeks new volunteers and interns to keep its therapy programs running smoothly, and website owners love linking to these kinds of opportunities. MYCS throws fundraising events: the more people attending, the more funds raised. If they're using flyers and newspaper ads to promote these, why not the website? And it turns out that there are some case managers in the region who haven't heard of MYCS. The search engines might give a little boost.

Perhaps the hardest part of Gina's job is that she knows how much she *could* do—she has a master's degree in multimedia development—if her organization just had the funding and resources. Her hosting service has a stats program, and she could check it if she had time, but who has time? She's one of three people maintaining 400 machines. She knows its branding could be more cohesive, but MYCS doesn't have a marketing department. As it is, Gina says, "I can give you maybe four examples of people who actually found us through our website".

Gina's got a plan: She's going to find some grad students, maybe from her old multimedia program, and get a new website built with labor from free internships. After that, she'll have a website worth promoting and a team on board to get moving with SEO. Good luck, Gina!

One final word of encouragement: We asked SEO luminary Jill Whalen (one of the most renowned names in the SEO industry) whether she thought do-it-yourselfers could do as good a job as professionals in SEO. Her response? "Absolutely!" You know your business—and all its nooks and crannies—better than anybody. After reading this chapter, you should have a long-view understanding of how you'll need to approach SEO so that you can make the most of your advantages and minimize your challenges. In the next chapter, we'll start talking details about the search engines. Get ready to be imbued with some Eternal Truths of SEO.

Eternal Truths of SEO

You've probably heard that SEO and the search engines change constantly, and it's true. But there are some things about SEO that haven't changed much, and probably won't for a long time to come. These Eternal Truths include basic information that you will use starting in Part III and for the duration of your SEO campaign. You don't want to chisel this stuff in stone, but it calls for something a little more permanent than a dry erase marker.

3

Chapter Contents

Robots Deliver

Search Results Are Blended

Algorithms Change

Humans Are Smart—Computers Aren't

Text Matters

It's Not Just about Rank

Search Engines Don't Like Tricks

SEO Is Not Brain Surgery

Robots Deliver

We're going to start with the basics of how the search engines work, and a major component of this is a *robot,* or *spider*, which is software that slurps up your site's text and brings it back to be analyzed by a powerful central "engine." This activity is referred to as *crawling* or *spidering*. There are lots of different metaphors for how robots work, but we think ants make the best one. Think of a search engine robot as an explorer ant, leaving the colony with one thought on its mind: *Find food*. In this case, the "food" is HTML text, preferably lots of it, and to find it, the ant needs to travel along easy, obstacle-free paths: HTML links. Following these paths, the ant (search engine robot), with insect-like single-mindedness, carries the food (text) back to its colony and stores it in its anthill (search engine database). Thousands and thousands of the little guys are exploring and gathering simultaneously all over the Internet. (See Figure 3.1 for a visual example.) If a path is absent or blocked, the ant gives up and goes somewhere else. If there's no food, the ant brings nothing back.

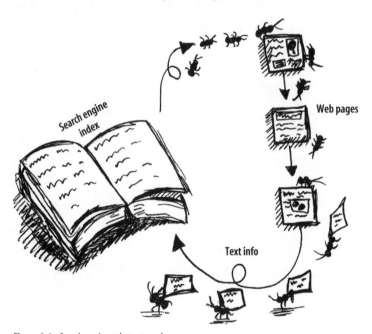

Figure 3.1 Search engine robots at work

So basically, when you think of a search engine, you really need to think of a database that holds pieces of text that have been gathered from millions of sites all over the web.

What sets that engine in motion? A search. When a web surfer enters the term "grape bubble gum" into the search engine, all of the sites that *might* be relevant for that term are brought to the forefront. The search engine sifts through its database for sites containing terms like "*grape* growers," "stock market *bubble*," and "*gum* disease." It uses a secret formula—a.k.a. search ranking *algorithm*—to sort the results, and in a fraction of a second, a list of relevant sites, many containing the exact phrase "grape bubble gum," will be returned in the results page.

There are lots of things that factor into the way robot search engines determine the rank for their main search results. But, just for a start, in order to be in the running for ranks, you need to provide HTML text to feed the search engines and HTML links as clear paths to the food. Keeping those robots well-fed and happy is going to be one of the biggest priorities in Part III, "Your SEO Plan."

A Search Engine by Any Other Name

We like to talk about search engines at parties—hey, it's how we get our clients—and when we use the term *search engines* with our pals, we really mean search *sites* like Google, Yahoo!, and MSN. But folks in the search industry can get pretty picky on terminology. Technically, a search *engine* is the software that is used to retrieve information from an indexing database, while a search *site* is a website that combines and displays all of that information, often from multiple sources. But, frankly, we don't give a hoot about the technical accuracy of the term. Everyone and his mother calls Yahoo! a *search engine*, and—with apologies to the purists out there—we do too.

Search Results Are Blended

If you've spent much time searching, you have probably noticed that the search engines are not displaying one set of homogeneous results. Most search engines take the "chef's salad" approach, displaying a mix of robot results, directory listings, and pay-per-click (PPC) ads. Your site is probably already represented by most of the types of results we're about to discuss. Knowing what each type looks like and where they come from is the first step in being able to influence your own listings in a positive way. You learned about robot results earlier; here are the other types of results that are available to searchers.

Directories

Unlike those robot search engines, directory listings are often compiled by humans. Whether these humans are editors who work for the search engines or the site owners themselves who write and submit their own listings, it is often easy to tell the difference between a directory and a robot search result. Take a look at this robot-generated listing from Google. It's called a *snippet*—text slurped directly from the web page and spat out into the search results page.

Thanksgiving **Coffee** Company - Organic **Coffee**, Fair Trade **Coffee** ...
Mirembe Kawomera **Coffee** · **Mirembe** Kawomera **Coffee** Delicious Fair Trade Certified
Ugandan **coffee** grown by Jewish, Muslim, and Christian farmers that make up ...
www.thanksgiving**coffee**.com/ - 49k - Nov 28, 2005 - Cached - Similar pages

Now take a look at this directory listing. Note the sentence-like structure, the human touch, and the category information.

Thanksgiving **Coffee** Company - Organic **Coffee**, Fair Trade **Coffee** ...
Category: Shopping > Food > Beverages > Coffee and Tea > Coffee > Organic
A selection of blends, as well as information on topics such as shade grown
coffee, organic farming and fair trade **coffee**.
www.thanksgivingcoffee.com/ - Nov 28, 2005 - Cached - Similar pages

Directories aren't likely to come out and find you the way robots will; site owners need to submit to them manually. Sometimes you can purchase a listing, sometimes they're free, and sometimes you pay for the "privilege" of having your submittal reviewed whether your site is included or not. While it's a little extra work to achieve directory listings, at least you can be relatively certain that your submittal will be reviewed by somebody and your site will have a fair chance of getting in. This is different from the robots, which do not guarantee review or inclusion.

Pay-Per-Click

No matter how blurred the line between unpaid and paid search gets in the search engine results, you, as the SEO expert, will always know the difference. That's because, while it's possible to get listed in robot search engines, *meta search engines*, and even directories without actually doing anything, you (or someone you delegate) will have to actively implement and carefully manage any pay-per-click (PPC) advertising for your own site. And, of course, there's that little matter of the checkbook too.

Here's how PPC Works: You open an account with a PPC engine. You decide which search terms you want your site to be seen for, and you write your own listing (or often, several different listings) to correspond with your chosen terms. Every time a searcher clicks on your listing, you pay the PPC engine a fee. You control the amount you want to spend for each click (your *bid*), and this is a major factor in the placement of your listing.

PPC is the SEO marketing venue over which you have the most control. It offers you a chance to micro-manage your website marketing by being able to target specific messages to specific terms, and even specific geographical locations. It gives you the opportunity to change your message on a whim, and it provides some of the most conclusive tracking around. Therefore, while PPC is by no means a requirement for good SEO, it's an Eternally Attractive Option to have available to you.

Site Feeds

Site feeds have been around for years in one form or another, but their methodology is still morphing. Available in various forms, they are Eternally Helpful for large or frequently updated sites. Just as you may use a feed to be notified of your favorite blog or news topic, the search engines use site feeds to sit back and receive information from websites without sending spiders out to constantly gather, gather, gather. Feeds work well for regularly edited websites such as blogs and news sites (feeding the content of their daily posts) and online sellers (feeding up-to-the-minute commercial information such as product descriptions and prices). You may also have heard of *trusted feed* or *paid inclusion* programs where search engines allow certain "trusted"—and, usually, paying—websites to send the engines regular updates. Generally these types of listings get thrown into the mix with robot-gathered sites and have to fend for themselves, with no special status in the ranking algorithms.

Meta Search Engines

Some people are comparison shoppers, flitting from store to store to review all the merchandise before making a decision. For people who like to compare search results, meta search engines make it easy to review listings from different search engines in one screen—no flitting from site to site necessary. Simply put, meta search engines compile and display results from several search engines and rank them according to their own algorithms. You can't use SEO to improve your presence on meta search engines directly; if a meta search engine like Mamma.com or Dogpile.com is using Google results, the way to do better on the meta search engine is to do better on Google.

Algorithms Change

Here's something that drives people crazy about SEO: You can't ever be 100 percent sure that what you're doing will be rewarded with the rank and the listing you want. This is because the search engines keep their internal ranking mechanism, even the criteria by which the ranking is determined, under wraps. Welcome to the secret formula of SEO: The Search Engine Ranking Algorithm.

The algorithm is the formula that a search engine uses to determine its ranks. It's a way of sifting through a multitude of factors, including keyword repetition and page titles, inbound links, and even the age of the site. Some elements have more weight, meaning that they are considered to be more important in determining rank, and some have less. Each search engine uses its own algorithm to determine which results to show and in which order. And each search engine changes its algorithm from time to time, often without so much as a friendly warning. So, the truth is this:

Pearl of Wisdom: You will never really know exactly how Google works

(unless you work there, in which case, give us a call sometime!).

Imagine if other forms of marketing worked this way! What if you couldn't rely on alphabetical order in the Yellow Pages anymore? What if the TV networks chose to air only the bits of your ad that *they* felt were most important? What if your billboards were periodically relocated without your consent? We're so glad you've got a good head on your shoulders because, now that you're doing SEO, you will have to find a balance between keeping up with the algorithm and keeping your sanity.

Why do the search engines guard their algorithms so closely? Because, first and foremost, they value the searcher's experience. If MSN published a guide called *Instructions for Ranking #1 on Our Search Engine*, of course you'd use it. And so would everyone else. Then all of the results on MSN would become so manipulated by site owners that relevance would disappear—investment sites could rank high for "grape bubble gum" on purpose—and searchers would drop the engine like a big useless hot potato. Even without a manual, the little bits of algorithm that people figure out themselves often get so abused that the search engines eventually devalue them.

How do you find the balance between seeking the Eternally Unknowable Algorithm and making sure your SEO efforts are effective? Matt Cutts, the popular blogger and Google employee who sometimes indulges his SEO-obsessed readers with tantalizing bits of inside information on Google's algorithm, says, "Most of the right choices in SEO come from asking, What's the best thing for the user?" Bringing targeted users to your site is, of course, the point of SEO, and that's the reason we made you clarify your audience and site goals before we started talking about how the search engines work.

We asked Danny Sullivan, probably the best known and most respected authority on search today, what he considers to be "Eternal" about SEO. His answer: "Good HTML titles, good body copy, great content, ensuring that your site doesn't have roadblocks to crawling—these have worked for nearly a decade." Notice he didn't mention anything about chasing the algorithm.

Now, you won't hear us saying, "algorithm, shmalgorithm" (though in the next chapter, we will say, "PageRank, ShmageRank"...stay tuned). One of the Eternal Truths we've learned over the years is this:

Pearl of Wisdom: Often, factors that matter most in the search engine algorithms are good for both websites and their users.

It's fine to keep an eye on the latest and greatest rumors about *exactly* how Google works, but don't go nuts or you will lose focus on what really matters: your site visitors.

Humans Are Smart—Computers Aren't

Let's face it: The search engine's job is not easy. Take a look at your filing cabinet, multiply it by about a billion, and imagine someone throwing you a couple of words and then hovering impatiently behind you, tapping a toe, expecting you to find exactly the right document in the blink of an eye. Nobody could! We humans are wonderfully intelligent creatures, but we're just a tad on the slow side when compared to computers. Unfortunately, machines are still just that: machines. They struggle with ambiguity that even a kindergarten student could handle. Not to mention misspellings, regional dialects, and punctuation. For search engines to bring back great results, they need to combine the best of both worlds: the speed of the machines and the intelligence of the human mind.

What's a search engine developer to do? Two things: First, combine results from several sources, as discussed earlier. This allows the search engines to intertwine the massiveness of the machine-driven system (robot results) with the finesse of the human touch (directory and PPC results). Second, structure the ranking algorithms to integrate "votes" from human beings. Putting the human touch into a ranking algorithm can be done in a variety of ways, and search engines continue to experiment with solutions. Counting inbound links from other websites, for example, is a way of measuring how many votes a site has from human—and presumably intelligent—webmasters. Other ideas have included measuring how many search engine users click through to your site and how long they stay. *Social bookmarking sites* and *collaborative tagging*, even comparing a person's current and past searches, are forms of artificial intelligence intended to improve the search experience.

But artificial intelligence still has as long way to go. In movies you can say to a computer, "Computer, Rotate and Enhance!" and the computer will somehow manage to turn and un-blur a grainy image from a security camera just the way you need it. In the real world, we just aren't there yet. Search engines remain very literal creatures, unable to improvise very much beyond the exact words, even the exact syntax of words, they are given. Which leads us to our next Eternal Truth.

Text Matters

You probably *can* etch this one in stone:

 Pearl of Wisdom: Text is Eternally Important in search.

The entire process of a web search is text-based, even when the item being sought isn't text at all, like a picture or video file. The search engines care about how much text you have on your site, how it's formatted, and, of course, what it says. In Parts II and III, we will walk you through the process of keyword selection and placement. To help prepare you for these tasks, you should know some Eternal Truths of text.

Keyword Selection Is Key

Careful keyword selection is the heart of the SEO campaign. Site owners who are on top of their SEO game have a list of top-priority keywords that they use on their site, with reasonable repetition, in strategic places. We never let a site go for six months without checking the keywords to make sure they're still appropriate. If a site's focus or positioning changes, new keywords are in order. If a company adds new products or services, new keywords are in order. If a new competitor comes on the scene, it's worth peeking into its site for new keyword ideas. Even if none of these changes takes place, regular keyword analysis is in order because search behavior and trends may change as well.

SEM: An Hour a Day?

When we were thinking about possible titles for this book, we had to take a little bit of our own advice: look into the minds of your users. Most of our potential readers would use the term *Search Engine Optimization* (SEO) to describe what we do, so we stuck with it for our title. But *SEO* is actually an outdated term. Industry insiders like to label our work either Search Engine Marketing (SEM) or just Search Marketing.

Continues

SEM: An Hour a Day? *(Continued)*

What's wrong with calling it SEO? The term *optimization* really only accounts for one segment of the tasks that search marketing encompasses: edits to the content of your website. Other components of search marketing, like link gathering and PPC sponsorships, don't easily fall under the banner of "optimization."

To add to the mix, many people use the terms *SEO* and *Organic SEO* interchangeably to refer to all nonpaid efforts. This would include edits to your website, as well as work involved with increasing your inbound links and usability. The complement to organic search is paid, or PPC, search. Confused yet? We'll sum it up for you:

- Search Marketing = Search Engine Marketing = the total package

- SEO = Organic Search Engine Optimization = nonpaid only

- PPC = Paid Search = pay-per-click only

Are there exceptions to the rule? Sure there are. Paying a one-time fee for a directory submittal would fall under Organic SEO. As long as your listing is going to display in search results that are not labeled "Sponsored Listing," you can probably call the work organic.

With all this potential for confusion, we're keeping it simple. In this book, it's *SEO* for everything.

Your Site Has Many Keyword Placement Opportunities

The code that makes up your web page's text falls into two categories—visible and invisible—and they are both important for optimization. The *visible text* is made up of the words that you put on your page for the world to see, including obvious things like the paragraphs of carefully crafted content aimed at your target audience but also less-obvious elements like your page title, the text inside your links, and the navigational text that tells your visitors how to use your site, such as "Click the thumbnails for a full size image." *Invisible text* refers to the words that do not display on the page but are added to your HTML code and gathered and analyzed by the search engine robots. This includes your *meta keywords tag*, *meta description tag*, and your *ALT image tags*.

Your Site's Message

We can't say it enough: Your site's text needs to be compelling, clear, focused, and directed to your users. It also needs to be formatted so that the robots can read it. This means HTML text, not *graphical text*, which the search engines can't read. If your site doesn't have any HTML text, adding some is critical to getting the search engines to give your site the visibility you desire.

Take a look at this page full of text.

Unfortunately, almost all of the text on the page is composed of GIF files, not HTML. So, to the search engines, it looks like this.

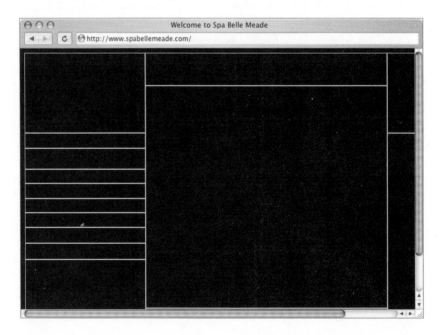

HTML Page Title

Probably the most important of the visible text elements is your HTML page title. In the code, it looks like this:

<title>Dave's Custom Bikes, Santa Cruz, California – Electric Bikes</title>

On the page, it looks like this.

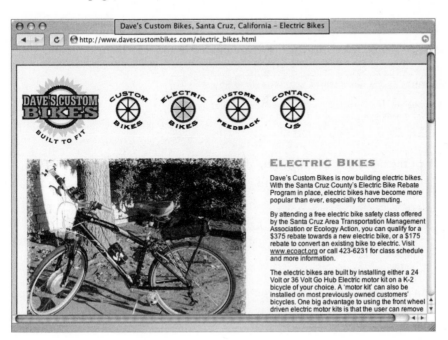

And in the search engines, it gets top billing, usually as the bolded first line of a search results page, like this.

Dave's Custom Bikes, Santa Cruz, California - Electric Bikes
... **bikes**, used **bikes** and accessories. Located in Santa Cruz, California. **Dave's Custom Bikes** is now building **electric bikes**. With the Santa Cruz County's **Electric** Bike Rebate Program ...
www.davescustombikes.com/electric_bikes.html Cached page

The page title is Eternally Important because it gets maximum exposure in the search engine results pages. If you care about getting clicks to your site, this text should be succinct and compelling, and for your best chance at conversions, it should accurately summarize the page content. We'll visit the specifics of writing great HTML page titles and meta descriptions in Part III.

Meta Description Tag

The meta description tag is an example of invisible text.

In the code, it looks like this:

<Meta name="description" content="Bobux baby shoes are the original soft soled shoes with the elastomatic ankle system that makes them easy to slip on and they stay on.">

And in the search engines, it can be displayed as the description under the page title. Notice how the searched-for keywords are bolded in the search engine results.

Bobux **Baby Shoes** Online **Baby Shoes** Soft Soled **Baby Shoes**
Leather...
Bobux **baby shoes** are the original soft soled **shoes** with the elastomatic
ankle system that makes them easy to slip on and they stay on.
🔗 | www.bobuxusa.com/ | Cached | Save

Much of the time, however, the meta description tag is passed over, and instead, a "snippet" of the page is displayed instead.

Bobux Baby Shoes Online Baby Shoes Soft Soled Baby Shoes **Leather**...
New Styles. Animals. Bows & **Mary Janes**. Flowers. Summer/Sandals.
Classics ... Bobux® baby shoes are made from **Eco-leather**, a natural
leather...
🔗 | www.bobuxusa.com/ | Cached | Save

You can't control when or where your meta description tag will display, but like your page title, it should be compelling, keyword rich, and unique for every page.

Meta Keywords Tag

The meta keywords tag, another invisible text element, is the place where site owners can list their keywords, including variations of keywords such as misspellings, that wouldn't be appropriate for the visible text elements.

In the code, it looks like this:

<meta name="keywords" content="movies, films, movie database, actors, actresses, directors, hollywood, stars, quotes">

It is rarely seen on the search engines, and that's a good thing because it's one of the few elements on your website that you can write specifically for the search engines and not your audience. This excites a lot of site owners, who think, "Finally! A way to talk to the search engine robots and tell them which terms I want to get my high ranks for!" But search engines prefer to make their own decisions on rank, and this is precisely why the meta keywords tag does not carry a lot of weight.

How Other Sites Are Linking to Yours

As we discussed earlier, search engines need human help in their Eternal Quest for that perfect ranking algorithm. They look for links to your website, not only to follow those links and find you, but also to determine more information about you. Does someone else link to your website using the words *Click Here to Find Very Fancy Foxhounds*? That's giving the search engine a clue that your website just might have something to do with foxhounds. And the search engine may go even further, looking at other words surrounding the link for more clues. If the linking page also contains the words *fleas*, *fur*, and *Finding a Breeder*, it's reinforcing the notion that your website will be a good destination for that foxhound-seeking searcher.

It's Not Just about Rank

While your ranks are the easiest aspect of SEO to grasp, don't let them be the only thing you care about. We don't mean to be dismissive of people who really, truly live and die by their Google rank. We know that there are industries that are so cutthroat and specialized that this *is* the only thing that matters. But we have found this to be true:

> **Pearl of Wisdom:** The vast majority of businesses do best when they use a holistic approach to SEO, combining elements of organic and paid search with a healthy dose of good writing and usability.

Remember, good ranks do not guarantee conversions! As you learned in Chapter 1, "Clarify Your Goals," your business goals for your website may range from online sales to political persuasion—whatever it is you want your visitors to do. Your keywords must be chosen to directly match these goals. You could easily gain some high ranks for, say, the term *hydroplaning monkey* because nobody else is optimizing for it. Of course, nobody's searching for it either. Likewise, if you make some iffy choices regarding your top-priority keywords, it's possible that you'll track top-10 ranks, month after month, and have no conversions to show for it.

Ranks Change

Let's say you are lucky enough to be getting good organic ranks for a coveted, competitive term. Congrats, but don't take these ranks for granted; any number of factors outside of your control could send your site on a nosedive:

Competitor activity Many times, SEO success is achieved not by brilliant optimization but rather as a result of the laziness of a site's competitors. If yours is the only site in your niche giving SEO any effort, you're going to come out on top. But you never know when the other guys are going to get their act together and start a successful SEO campaign.

Common SEO Misconceptions

If you're brand new to SEO, you may have a couple of incorrect notions in your head. Let's get rid of those right now:

"Our site gets a ton of traffic! We're so popular, we're a shoo-in for top ranks." Search engines don't have insider information about your overall web traffic, so they don't know exactly how popular your site is. But they can count up how many sites they find that *link* to your site, and this is one factor in how they judge your site's popularity.

"We've got to get more sites to link to us so that our ranks will improve!" If the only reason you set out to get more links is so that Google will rank you higher, you are missing the big picture. Inbound links are pathways that allow people to visit your site. They can be excellent, direct sources of targeted traffic!

"Our site is doing great! We ranked #1!" Ranked #1 for *what*? Starting now, erase "We ranked #1" from your vocabulary and replace it with "We ranked #1 **for the term** _____". Ranks are irrelevant unless they are tied to a meaningful target keyword.

"We're only going to promote our home page." SEO is not about your *site*, it's about every *page* of your site. Every single page in your site stands on its own merits and can sink or swim based on its unique combination of the factors described in this chapter. If you approach SEO as a page-by-page endeavor, you will be on a surer path to success.

"We've filled in our meta keywords tag…we're good to go!" The meta keywords tag carries very little influence with the search engines, and it's certainly not going to do much for your ranks if the rest of your site isn't shipshape. Just like any element of SEO, the keywords tag works best in the context of a holistic approach.

Your server performance The search engine robots visit your site on a reasonably frequent basis to make sure they've got the most up-to-date content to offer searchers. But what if a robot happens to visit your site while it's out of commission? If they can't find you, they probably won't rank you. You're likely to be very sad next time you check your ranks, at least until the robot comes back and rediscovers you.

Which search engine database you happen to be looking at We're talking billions of pieces of data from millions of sites. There's no way the search engines could keep it all in one database. This means that, at any given time, searchers are looking at one of a number of different search engine databases, each giving out slightly different search results. Expect that your ranks are going to hop around a bit on a daily basis. Try not to sweat these little dips or put too much stock in the little jumps.

Algorithm changes As we mentioned earlier, you never know when an existing search engine algorithm is going to morph into something different. There are so many people chasing the search engine updates, and losing sleep over the next little tweak in Google's algorithm, that a new phrase was coined to describe them: *algoholics*. We urge you not to become on of them.

A Holistic Approach Helps

All of the rank-busters we just listed underscore the need to fill out your SEO campaign to tide you over with targeted traffic should your high ranks desert you. As the investment bankers will tell you: diversify, diversify, diversify. These aspects of the SEO campaign that you'll develop in Part III will help you weather ranking fluctuations:

Buzz generation This means getting sites to link to you out of admiration (Donutopia makes great donuts! Click here!), commendation (Donutopia's Donut News wins "Bakery News Site of the Year." Click here!), or reciprocity (Please support our friend, Donutopia, who also linked to us. Click here!).

Niche directories The big search engines are not the only paths to your site. There are niche directories for aficionados of everything from animal husbandry to Zen Buddhism. A small but fervently targeted audience is not to be ignored.

A PPC campaign Pay-per-click can be a very effective way to get those targeted *eyeballs* to your site, especially if something is preventing you from breaking through the competition for organic rankings.

Good writing and usability Quality material on your site will always be there for you when the winds of algorithm fate shift again.

Remember that Your SEO Plan should focus on conversions, not just search engine ranks! If you're doing well with the SEO elements listed here, you may discover that—lo and behold!—a dip in ranking won't affect your conversions in any disastrous way.

Search Engines Don't Like Tricks

The search engines are aware of the many sneaky ways that site owners try to achieve undeserved ranks (in SEO lingo, these sneaky activities are called *spamming*). If they discover that you're trying to do this, your site may be penalized: Your rank may be downgraded, or your page—or even your whole site—could be banned. Even if your site is never caught and punished, it's very likely, we dare say inevitable, that your tricky technique will eventually stop working. Here are some practices that have been on the search engines' no-no list for so long that they can safely be labeled as "Eternally Bad for your Site":

Cloaking When a search engine robot visits your site, it expects to see the same content that any normal human visitor would see. *Cloaking* is a method of identifying robots when they visit your site and showing them special, custom-made pages that are different from what human visitors see. This thwarts the search engines in their attempt to deliver the most accurate search results to their users. In the vast universe of website technology, there are sometimes valid reasons for showing different content to different entities. Tricking the search engines to give you higher ranks than you deserve is not one of them.

Duplicate content Are you the kind of person who thinks, "If one aspirin works, why not take two?" If so, you might be thinking that if one paragraph of keyword-rich text will help your ranks, why not put it on every page in your site? Or worse, if one website brings you sales, why not make a bunch of identical websites with different names and get even more sales? The problem with this kind of thinking is that it ignores the big headache it causes for searchers. If the search engines listed identical content multiple times, it would destroy the diversity of their results, which would destroy their usefulness to the searcher. So, if the search engines catch on to duplicate content schemes, they're likely to knock you down in the ranks.

Keyword stuffing Adding a keyword list to the visible text on your page is not exactly scintillating copy. We're not talking about overly optimized text, which may come off as pointless and dry. We're talking about repeating the same word or words over and over again so that your page looks like an industry-specific grocery list. At best, sites that do this cause eyestrain for their visitors. At worst, they're risking penalties from the search engines. There's a place for your keywords list: It's called your meta keywords tag!

Invisible text When we mentioned invisible text previously in this chapter, we meant specific elements that are included within specific parameters in your site's code and recognized by the search engines to be legitimate. We did *not* mean making a ton of keywords invisible by making them the same color as the background. The search engines caught on to this one a long time ago, and they're not likely to let you get away with it.

SEO Is Not Brain Surgery

So many people feel intimidated when approaching SEO. They think its ultratechnical or it requires a huge budget. Many people think SEO requires some sort of degree or a lot of insider knowledge. But SEO doesn't take any of that.

The only thing that is really necessary for SEO is the willingness to learn. So here is our most special gift to you, an SEO mantra that you can adopt as your own:

I wonder why *that's* happening.

SEO: Art or Science?

It's an oft-repeated cliché: SEO is one part art and one part science. The Left Brain and Right Brain delve a little deeper into two Eternal Truths:

The Left Brain Says, "SEO is a Science! I originally learned SEO by using an experimental approach: trying different strategies and observing how successful they were. There's nothing fancy or difficult about science. It just means asking questions and seeking answers: *Will adding keywords to my HTML comments tag help my rankings? Which of these two landing pages will bring more conversions?*

"A PPC campaign provides the best opportunity for testing hypotheses because PPC allows you a great deal of control over your listings and your landing pages. And, most important, PPC has a quick turnaround, so you won't have to wait months for the results of your experiments. So give it a try (we'll help you do this in Part III)! Compare results for two ads with slightly different phrasing. Or build a page just for testing purposes, and see what happens when you triple the keyword density. Science is *fun*—hey, don't look so surprised!"

The Right Brain Says, "SEO is an Art! SEO can never truly be a science because you'll never be working in a vacuum. Your competition pulls a surprise move, the algorithm throws you a curveball…you can't control for these factors. Sure, your tests are fun, and they can even give you a lot of helpful insight. But anyone doing SEO needs to be comfortable working in an environment that is often more guesswork than empirical proof. Isn't it better to focus on the *art* of SEO—well-crafted text, a thoughtful, user-friendly site design, and personal connections? In its purest form, SEO is the art of persuasion!"

This is the approach that got us to where we are today; it helped us gain our SEO knowledge and it keeps the clients coming. This is how we attacked almost every SEO question or problem before SEO was a big industry with hundreds of books, e-books, and websites devoted to it. And, more often than not, this is how we still approach things. It can work for you too!

It goes something like this: You say to yourself, "I wonder why my Google listing has that weird misspelling in it." Then you spend a few minutes searching for the misspelled word on your page. If it's not there, you look for it in your meta tags. Still not finding it? Browse through the directory listings. "*Aha*," you say, "There's a misspelling in my Open Directory listing!" Now you've learned two things: one, that your Open Directory listing is feeding into your Google listing, and two, that you'd better get to work on getting that misspelling fixed.

Or, you say to yourself, "I wonder why my competitor has such good placement in that shopping directory." Then you click around until you find the "advertise with us" link on the shopping directory, figure out if that placement is a service they offer, and determine whether you want one, too.

Developing a healthy curiosity about how the search engines work, and an itch to solve interesting puzzles, is key to do-it-yourself SEO. It's a poor man's or woman's marketing study, and it's the best way to find your own path toward getting more targeted traffic.

Over the past several years, we have both drifted on and off of the SEO career path from time to time. Extended side projects and maternity leaves have caused us to focus our attention elsewhere temporarily, but we've always come back, and what's more, we've always gotten our SEO chops back and been able to offer respected, useful, and well-received consultation within a relatively short time, every time. Why? Because we have internalized the Eternal Truths of SEO and use them as our basic frame of reference. Now that you understand the longer-lasting aspects of SEO, it should be a lot easier to make sense of the "right now" qualities, which will be described in the next chapter.

How the Search Engines Work Right Now

What's the inside buzz among SEO experts? What do the search engines care about? What works? What doesn't? In this chapter, we present a current snapshot, including some of the more ephemeral facts of SEO: which search engines dominate the industry and how they work today.

4

In Pursuit of Right Now

We admit it: We were shaking in our stiletto heels just thinking about writing this chapter. The Right Now of search engines? Committed in ink, on old-fashioned paper? Give us a break. Everybody knows the Right Now of SEO changes every 5 minutes and you'd do much better finding this stuff on the Web.

Just kidding. We wear sensible shoes. Oh, and there are lots of great reasons for you to hang onto every word of this chapter.

First off, researching SEO on the Web is a difficult way to learn new concepts and get the basics down. If you set out to discover the Right Now of SEO for yourself, you're likely to run into a mishmash of organic and paid strategies, *white hat* and *black hat* techniques, and beginner and technically advanced concepts. And you are going to run into conflicting advice, naturally; you've got forums running rampant with rumors and expert and not-so-expert blogs, not to mention every Dick and Jane employed by an SEO firm who has posted an article on SEO. And here's our favorite pet peeve: SEO advice on the Web is maddeningly unlikely to be date-stamped, so you often don't know if what you're reading is current advice or yesterday's news.

So, instead of trying to jump into your own frustrating pursuit of the Right Now, read our rundown of the current search landscape. Later, in Chapter 8, "Month Two: Establish the Habit," you'll learn how to keep your knowledge up-to-date using our favorite trusted sources of information.

Now, let's get right down to the details.

Google Basics

Simply stated, Google is the standout leader in search today. It has the most *eyeballs* and the most new trends, and it's the only search engine with its own entry in the dictionary. Once a search-only entity, Google now offers a mail service, a map service, and a traffic and conversion tracking service, not to mention a diverse menu of specialty search options, including video, image, blog, and local. See Table 4.1 for handy Google facts for SEOs.

Google has been an all-out trendsetter in the evolution of the search algorithm. Link popularity? Google made it hugely important. The probable death of *paid inclusion*? Thank Google. A website's age being a factor in its ranking? Blame Google. We'll go into the details throughout the chapter, but let's face it: The world of SEO is playing Follow the Leader, and Google's at the head of the line.

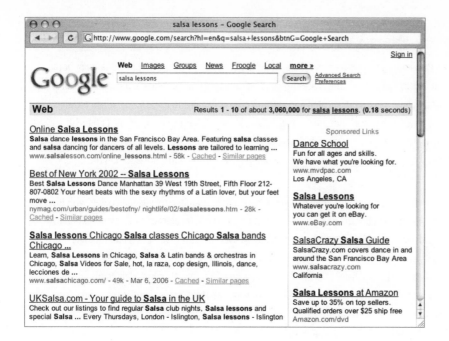

▶ **Table 4.1** Google Basics

URL	www.google.com
Percent of search traffic	39.8% (Source: comScore Media Metrix, February 2006)
Primary results	Robot crawler
Organic listings also influenced by	Open Directory
Ways to submit your site	Google Sitemaps (free, good for large or dynamic sites), submit URL form (free), or wait for the robot to find you
Pay-per-click services	Google AdWords
In five words or less	*The one to beat.*
Keep an eye on	Google Sitemaps, Google Analytics, Google Local for Mobile

The current hot topics at Google are its new SEO-friendly products. One is Google Sitemaps, a service that allows the site owner to submit a list of URLs and other factors to Google for improved indexing (but not improved ranks). And the other is Google Analytics, a robust conversion tracking service. Both products are in the beta phase of development as of this writing.

Products like these have been around for years. So why are they big news in the SEO community? Two reasons: They're free, and they come from Google.

PageRank, ShmageRank

Google's PageRank is a measurement of a page's worth based on the quantity and quality of both incoming and outgoing links. The concept behind PageRank is that each link to a page constitutes a vote, and Google has a sophisticated and automated way of tallying these votes, which includes looking at a vast universe of interlinking pages. Google awards PageRank on a scale of 0 to 10; a PageRank value of 10 is the most desirable and extremely rare. Like the Richter scale, the PageRank scale is not linear, so the difference between 4 and 5 is much greater than the difference between 3 and 4.

More often than not, pages with high PageRank have higher Google rankings than pages with low PageRank. And therein lies the link obsession. Throughout the SEO community, the scrambling for, trading, and even selling of links became such a focus over the past several years that Google modified its system and began to devalue certain kinds of links. It's widely accepted, for example, that links from content-deficient "link farm" websites do not improve a page's PageRank, and getting a link from a page with high PageRank but irrelevant content (say, a popular comic book site that links to a forklift specifications page) won't either. Google now displays updated PageRank values at infrequent intervals to discourage constant monitoring.

It's good to get links to your site, but obsessive link building to the point of excluding other areas of SEO is a waste of time. Keep a holistic head on your shoulders and remember these points:

- Google's ranking algorithm is not based entirely on inbound links.

- A high PageRank does not guarantee a high Google rank.

- A PageRank value viewed today may be up to three months old.

PageRank is still a fairly good indication of how Google regards your website's pages, and you'll learn how to gather your own measurements in Your SEO Plan. But in the Right Now of SEO, think of PageRank as a hobby, not a religion.

The Best of the Rest: Yahoo!, MSN, AOL, Ask

Taken as a group, the major non-Google search engines that we're about to discuss make up a larger percentage of the search market than Google, which means they deserve your attention. This is even more true if your organization is looking for an edge in a special area such as shopping, local, or mobile search. Non-Google search engines allow you to fill out your website's presence so that it is not overly dependent on rankings on a single site (what was that expression, something about eggs...and a basket?).

Now, we'll fill you in on what you need to know about the search engines other than Google:

- Yahoo!
- MSN
- AOL
- Ask

Yahoo!

Yahoo! (yes, the exclamation point is part of its name—a bane to copy editors everywhere) is one of the oldest and still one of the best-known search engines. Already an established presence when Google was still in diapers, Yahoo! has now settled into the number two spot. Nevertheless, with its considerable legacy and the muscle to expand its offerings through major corporate purchases (the most recent acquisition of popular social bookmarking site del.icio.us shows that Yahoo! is in tune with trendy new directions in search), Yahoo! is a force to be reckoned with. Table 4.2 shows you handy Yahoo! facts for SEOs.

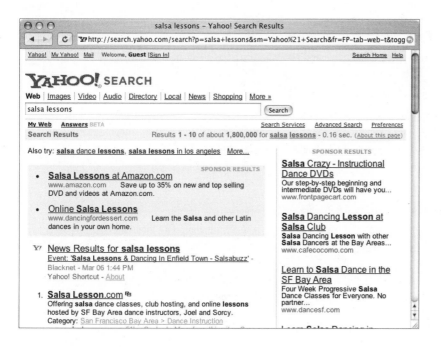

URL	www.yahoo.com
Percent of search traffic	29.5% (Source: comScore Media Metrix, February 2006)
Primary results	Robot crawler
Organic listings also influenced by	Yahoo! Directory
Ways to submit your site	Paid submittal to Yahoo! Directory, paid inclusion, or wait for the robot to spider you
Pay-per-click services	Yahoo! Search Marketing (YSM)
In five words or less	*Constant growth means survival.*
Keep an eye on	Local search, Yahoo! Mobile, Web 2.0 search

An important point to keep in mind is that Yahoo!'s market share as listed in Table 4.2 includes searches in Yahoo! properties and "channels" such as news, shopping and sports. That means Yahoo!'s percentage of "standard" organic searches might be lower than the number implies. Still, Yahoo!'s healthy share of traffic will come in mighty handy if your Google juice fails you.

Riding the Algorithm Roller Coaster

Susan McKenna is a marketing consultant who also owns an online traffic school at www.opentrafficschool.com. Her business lives and dies by its search engine traffic, which brought in close to 60 percent of its prospective students in 2005. A change in ranking algorithm can really shake things up for this type of business, as Susan learned the hard way. She says, "I was ranked #1, 2, or 3 for the terms 'traffic school,' 'online traffic school,' and 'california traffic school' on Yahoo! for half of 2004 and most of 2005. . . . And then it happened: We disappeared from Yahoo!'s results in a matter of days, dipping to 300, then 400, until we were completely off the map."

Susan jumped into action within weeks, with a sweeping site optimization campaign as well as new link-building efforts. Her ranks have been gradually climbing since then: "My traffic school is really beginning to gain traction," she says. Next, she plans to begin taking some of the content-building steps you'll read about in Chapter 9, "Month Three: It's a Way of Life."

Continues

Riding the Algorithm Roller Coaster *(Continued)*

If you're fortunate enough to have stratospheric ranks on one search engine, don't rest on your laurels. As paradoxical as it seems, doing very well on one search engine means that you should probably work on increasing traffic from other sources, just in case. It's no fun losing your ranks, but if you have a broad spectrum SEO plan already in place, it needn't run your business off the road.

MSN

In case you didn't know, MSN is a property of a quaint little organization known as "Microsoft Corp." MSN is not, shall we say, a favorite among SEO pros. In forum postings, blogs, and websites, SEOs and website owners complain bitterly about long waits for spidering, irrelevant and spammy results, and a market share number that some believe is inflated by the fact that MSN.com is the default browser home page for many computers.

Though it was very late in creating its own independent search results (as recently as 2005, MSN was still showing results from the Yahoo! database), MSN still has a chance to exceed expectations by leveraging its bulk. Check out the MSN facts in Table 4.3.

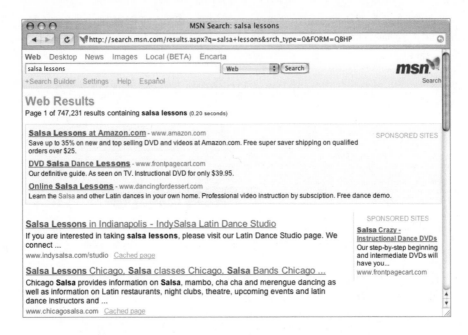

▶ Table 4.3 MSN Basics

URL	www.msn.com
Percent of search traffic	14.2% (Source: comScore Media Metrix, February 2006)
Primary results	Robot crawler
Organic listings also influenced by	Open Directory
Ways to submit your site	Submit URL form (free), or wait for the robot to find you
Pay-per-click services	Slated to replace YSM listings with its own adCenter listings in June 2006
In five words or less	*Watch out for late bloomer.*
Keep an eye on	Incentives to search (MSN Search and Win), MSN adCenter

MSN's PPC service, called MSN adCenter, is currently in beta and scheduled to be fully operational in June 2006. MSN could put up some serious competition to the current wonder twins of PPC, Google AdWords and YSM. Early reports say that the new service will offer much more targeted sponsorships, with the capability for advertisers to select specific audiences by age, gender, location, and time of day.

AOL

The most important thing to know about AOL is that it uses the Google database for search results. That means, from an SEO perspective, AOL can be safely ignored. See Table 4.4 for basic facts about AOL.

▶ **Table 4.4** AOL Basics

URL	www.aol.com
Percent of search traffic	8.7% (Source: comScore Media Metrix, February 2006)
Primary results	Google results
Organic listings also influenced by	None
Ways to submit your site	None; get indexed through Google
Pay-per-click services	Google AdWords
In five words or less	*Google is my copilot.*
Keep an eye on	Future partnership deals

AOL may continue to score a respectable share of the search market, but we don't think AOL will be generating its own independent search results anytime soon. Because of that, we won't say another word about AOL in this book. Want to do well on AOL? Do well on Google (or whoever else AOL partners with in the future). 'Nuff said.

Ask

In a move that had hundreds of SEO industry wags shouting, "It's about time!" Ask has dropped Jeeves the butler from its branding, and is redefining itself as a Google-like search engine, with a clean, search-focused interface. Most important, Ask's previous focus on "natural language" queries such as "who is the prime minister of Kazakhstan?" has given way to a focus on more standard keyword-based queries such as "prime minister kazakhstan." See Table 4.5 for basic facts about Ask.

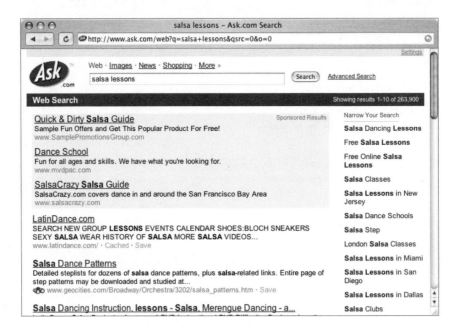

▶ **Table 4.5** Ask Basics

URL	www.ask.com
Percent of search traffic	6.5% (Source: comScore Media Metrix, February 2006)
Primary results	Robot crawler
Organic listings also influenced by	A very limited number of hand-edited "web answers"
Ways to submit your site	None
Pay-per-click services	Google AdWords, Ask Sponsored Listings
In five words or less	*Ready to catch a wave.*
Keep an eye on	Integration with Citysearch.com

With no website submittal process and little market share as of now, Ask receives little attention from the SEO industry, and rightfully so. However, we like its prospects for the future. Its business strategy seems to be floating in limbo, but the SEO world agrees that the search results are excellent, and that certainly bodes well.

Now that you've got a handle on the top search engines, we'll discuss the elements that influence their rankings.

Organic Ranking Factors

You already know that search engines use complicated secret formulas, called ranking algorithms, to determine the order of their results. You even know from Chapter 3, "Eternal Truths of SEO," that some of the most Eternally Important factors are your web page text and your HTML title tags. Now we're going to wrap what you already know into an organic optimization cheat sheet that you can peek at next time someone asks you, "What do search engines care about, anyway?"

But first, a disclaimer: The SEO profession is an upstart one, with no degrees to be earned or widely accepted canon of literature (and if there were, it'd change every five months anyway). So we're all out there trying to figure this stuff out on our own, using different test cases, chasing morphing search engines, and possessing varying levels of interest and talent in the writing and technical components of SEO. SEO experts are a diverse group, ranging from the fanatical to the rabidly fanatical, and there are radically differing opinions within the SEO community about what works and what's important. We've distilled what we believe to be the best-of-the-best advice and present it here in a simplified form.

Here's the lowdown on the most important factors:

- HTML page title
- Visible HTML text on the page
- Inbound links (quality and quantity)
- Inbound link anchor text
- Age of domain
- Lesser factors

We'll get into how to optimize all of these factors in Part III. But for now, as you read through them, think about how much attention you've given to each of them on your own site. Maybe, like a lot of site owners, you've been focusing on the bottom of the list—the least important factors—more than the biggies at the top. As you think about what matters to the search engines, keep this in mind:

Pearl of Wisdom: Each page on your website is analyzed individually by the search engines.

That means each and every page is an opportunity to optimize for the following:

HTML page title The HTML page title is today's hands-down leader, and an Eternally Important factor, in search engine ranking algorithms. As a bonus, optimizing your HTML page titles is one of those activities that will quickly affect the way your listings look in the search engines.

Visible HTML text on the page It seems obvious, but you would be surprised at how many site owners miss this simple point: In order to rank well for a particular set of keywords, your site text should contain them. True, there are examples of pages that rank well for words not actually appearing on the page (see the sidebar "Googlebombing and 'Miserable Failure'") but this is not something you want to leave to chance. You may see SEO pros insist that you need 250 or 1,000 words on a page and that 5 to 10 percent of these words must be your target keywords (SEO folks call that percentage *keyword density*).

We say this: As long as you have robot-readable text on your page (a great first step that many of your competitors, believe it or not, may have missed), you should use *as many keywords as you need to state your message clearly* and *as many opportunities to insert keywords as makes sense within the realm of quality writing*. Your marketing message is much too special to be put into a formula.

Inbound links (quality and quantity) Coming in at #3 in our list of search engine ranking factors is inbound links to your website. Why are inbound links so important in the search engine ranking algorithms? Because they can indicate a page's quality, popularity, or status on the Web and site owners have very little control over their own inbound links. (Being off-page factors, inbound links can be influenced only indirectly.) Links with the most rank-boosting power are links from a home page (as opposed to links from pages buried deep within the site) and links from *authority pages* in the *topical community*, meaning pages with their own collection of fabulous inbound links from other websites covering the same topic. The same quality factors hold true for links coming from within your site.

Inbound link anchor text We mentioned in Chapter 3 that the way other websites refer to your website is one of the ways that search engines understand your content. *Anchor text*, also called linking text, is the text that is "clickable" on the Web, and it is an important factor in search ranking algorithms. Anchor text that contains your page's targeted keywords can help boost your page's ranks. Combining this keyword-rich anchor text with relevant text surrounding the link can amplify this good effect.

Age of domain In one of the more perplexing and frustrating developments in SEO in recent years, site owners have noticed that newer domains have a much tougher time making their way up the ranks than older ones. Read more about this in the sidebar "The Google Sandbox." So far, this phenomenon has only been spotted in Google, but you know what happens when Google does something: Sooner or later the others are likely to follow suit. You have been warned.

Lesser factors There are a large number of additional, lesser factors that can influence your ranking. Google, for example, probably includes hundreds and possibly even thousands of factors in its algorithm. Things like keywords in your meta tags, image ALT tags, and page URL all have some degree of influence, as do factors that may be harder for you to control, such as the popularity of a page (as measured by the search engine's own click-through tallies) or how often it is updated. For a comprehensive list of ranking factors, including commentary from several knowledgeable SEO professionals, see this page: www.seomoz.org/articles/search-ranking-factors.php.

The Google Sandbox

The simple premise of the Google sandbox is this: Google doesn't want to list spammy sites. Some spammers, however, have been able to get sites listed quickly, get good ranks using questionable techniques, and make a buck before Google can react. Because of this, Google seems to have increased the importance of the age of a website among its ranking factors. So now, to be designated "Not Spam," one of the things a site has to do is, apparently, get older.

It's age before beauty: A brand-new site, even one with no spam qualities, may disappear into ranking oblivion for several months until it's had a chance to age its way into Google's heart.

The gossip and guessing surrounding the Google sandbox rivals that of any celebrity breakup, federal interest rate hike, or Supreme Court nomination. Questions—many, many questions—have been asked, and anecdotal answers are all we have: *Does it exist? Does it affect a whole site or just individual pages?* And we are totally serious here: *When Google's Matt Cutts smiled and nodded, did he mean anything significant about the sandbox?*

We've done some poking around under the shroud of mystery, and still, the best we can do is provide you with unconfirmed but oft-stated rumors about the sandbox:

- Commercial sites are more likely to be affected by the sandbox than .edu or .gov sites.

- Regardless of how a site finally breaks out of the sandbox, many sites are commonly released at the same time.

- Age is not the only factor involved; a sudden increase in inbound links and page overoptimization may also be penalized.

So here's what this means to you: First and foremost, don't think of Google as the only way to get traffic to your website. Nobody loves Google like we do, believe us. But the sandbox proves that Google can pretty much play whack-a-mole with sites' rankings in any way it likes. And second, wait it out. It might take months (yes, months) to get out of the sandbox. If you think your site is sandboxed, make sure it's optimized and well-linked from quality, relevant sites. Then you'll know it's ready for its debut.

Paid Placement

Every major search engine, as well as plenty of minor search engines and independent websites both large and small, displays paid listings today. Most of these listings are provided by the two major U.S. pay-per-click services, Google AdWords and Yahoo! Search Marketing (YSM).

The market is huge: According to the Search Engine Marketing Professional Organization (SEMPO), close to $5 billion was spent on paid placement advertising in the U.S. and Canada in 2005, and by all expectations this number will grow in the coming years. MSN is poised to jump into the fray with MSN adCenter.

Here are two elements of paid placement that you may encounter:

- Pay-per-click advertising
- Paid inclusion

Pay-per-Click Advertising

As you learned in Chapter 3, pay-per-click (PPC) is generally an auction-based system, with advertisers jockeying for their listings' positions based on bid price. See Figure 4.1 for an example. Until recently, the PPC auction was a fairly straightforward system in which a higher bid resulted in a higher rank. Now, Google and YSM are both gravitating toward a more complex method for determining PPC ranks. In Google AdWords, for example, the PPC algorithm is called a Quality Index, and it awards position based on several factors, including click-through rate, cost, and relevance of the ad text.

So if you were looking to PPC as a way to skirt around the Eternally Hidden Algorithm, we're sorry to say there's one to puzzle over in PPC as well. For starters, noted pay-per-click expert Kevin Lee indicated to us that PPC algorithms today are likely to favor big brands and compelling, relevant ad text because those ads would receive higher predicted click-through rates. The winds of change are blowing especially hard in the world of PPC, so do your best to stay in the know.

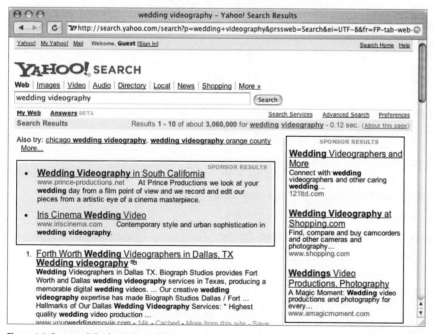

Figure 4.1 Pay-per-click advertising on Yahoo!

Both Google AdWords and YSM offer an opt-in feature that will display your listings on partner sites in addition to their own search engines. In this system, called *contextual advertising*, your listings are algorithmically matched to the content of the page where they are displayed. See Figure 4.2 for an example. You can manage your contextual campaigns separately from your search-based PPC ads.

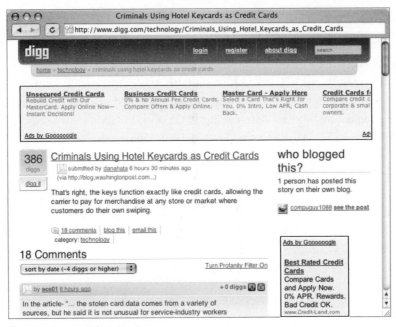

Figure 4.2 Contextual ads by Google

You can see a quick run-down of the two major PPC services in Table 4.6.

▶ **Table 4.6** Pay-per-Click Basics

	Yahoo! Search Marketing	Google AdWords
URL	http://searchmarketing.yahoo.com	http://adwords.google.com
Name of pay-per-click product	Sponsored Search	AdWords
Name of contextual placement product	Content Match	AdSense
Major partnerships (sites where ads are shown)	Yahoo!, CNN.com	Google, AOL.com, Ask.com, Shopping.com, thousands of small sites
Industry chatter	Easier for the newbie to set up but doesn't offer quite as many features as Google AdWords.	With the per-click bid becoming a lesser factor in ad positioning, some advertisers may become frustrated by lack of control.

Competition between PPC services has resulted in some significant advances in campaign tracking, click fraud prevention, and geographic targeting, and these improvements are expected to continue. The bad news is that there are so many products out there—even within the same PPC service—that the potential for confusion is very high. With more and more site owners adopting PPC, the online help systems are rather robust. But there are lots of people who choose to outsource PPC management because it can be a real headache. It *can* be done in-house, though, and it doesn't have to be that difficult if you start small and focus on the basics.

PPC is really unmatched in the power it gives you over your listing: what it says, who sees it, and when. We also love PPC as a tool for studying the response to your keyword choices. So in Chapter 8, with our guidance, you're going to set up a starter campaign and get to know the basics while you get yourself some tasty targeted clicks.

Paid Inclusion

As you learned in Chapter 3, robots aren't perfect, and there are plenty of reasons that a robot may not be able or willing to index every page on your site. Paid inclusion is a service offered by some search engines that provides a workaround for these imperfections by allowing you to submit a list of URLs that you want them to index and recrawl on a frequent basis. Usually these services also allow you to submit your own dolled-up description of each page and to view basic statistics of the traffic that flows from the search engine to your paid URLs. Paid inclusion does not guarantee a boost in ranks, but it often does guarantee more frequent spidering and, in some cases, the very attractive possibility of having your own description used in the listing instead of a text snippet.

Paid inclusion in this form is currently offered only by Yahoo! (MSN and Ask dropped their programs in 2004). Google, which never offered a paid inclusion service, now offers a *free* version of paid inclusion, called Google Sitemaps. You can learn more about how to set up Google Sitemaps in Chapter 10, "Extra Credit and Guilt-Free Slacking."

Whenever the subject comes up, the general consensus of the SEO community is that the death of paid inclusion is imminent. One reason is that the search engines' ability to index pages has improved steadily over the years. Combine that improvement with the pressure of Google's free Sitemaps service and who knows? Maybe paid inclusion will be nothing more than a memory soon.

SEO Trendspotting

SEO trends move fast, so it's OK to jump in where you are! Use this primer to get clued in to some of the current jargon and trends in SEO.

Personalized Search Coming soon to a search engine near you: *personalized search*, meaning search results that vary based on the searcher's profile and past behavior. Personalized search may be applied to organic or PPC results and could be used to target users who, for example, have made certain previous searches or have made online purchases within the last 48 hours. In organic SEO, personalized search would throw a wrench in the works by making rank tracking nearly impossible and adding further complication to already mysterious ranking algorithms. But in PPC, it has excellent potential as a targeting tool.

Social Search *Social search* is any system that uses community-sourced information to determine search results. Although social search is still only a small percentage of overall search traffic, it's a trend to watch. There have been many attempts in the past to incorporate the wisdom of the masses into search results, but social search really hit the big time when Yahoo! bought up several companies that use this type of system (flickr and del.icio.us are the most well known) in 2005 and 2006.

Mobile Search Mobile search is like one of those up-and-coming neighborhoods that never quite ups and comes. Web developers are still working out the kinks of building websites in formats that can be viewed on mobile phones and handheld devices. Meanwhile, search engines, most notably Google and Yahoo!, are working hard to place themselves in the middle of this growing search sector, especially by combining local and mobile search. The SEO community remains on the sidelines, watching and waiting to see if mobile search will ever really take off.

Persona/Scenario Not a new marketing concept, but one that is making its way into mainstream SEO. This is simply a more creative and in-depth way of defining a site's target user than with simple demographics. So, for example, instead of targeting "women in their 40s who drive minivans," you might think instead about a persona, *Barbara, who is 42*, and her scenario: *She has two daughters, both A students in private school. Barbara enjoys infrequent but expensive outings with her husband in her affluent suburban town.* Personas and scenarios can be helpful in determining your targeted keywords or identifying your landing pages.

SEO Slang

Just like any other topic with a big online following, SEO has its own colorful vocabulary. There are far too many terms to include here, but here's a sampling of what you might come across in your own SEO endeavors:

SERP An acronym that stands for "Search Engine Results Page," that is, the listings you see when you use a search engine. It is our opinion (as it is with other right-minded folks) that this acronym has an ugly ring to it, so we've decided to ban it from the book!

White hat/black hat Stereotypically speaking, *white hat* refers to "squeaky clean" optimization activities, ones that stay squarely within the search engines' guidelines. *Black hat* refers to under-the-radar (and often below-the-belt) activities, such as quickly launching a site with poor-quality, *scraped*, or no content; making some quick cash; and then dumping the domain and starting over with another site. There are also SEOs who proclaim to be gray hat, who do their work somewhere in the middle.

Tripping a filter Since search engine algorithms are almost entirely automated, infractions and slipups are often caught and penalized via automatic analysis. When a page has set off an algorithmic red flag, SEOs say it has tripped a filter. This is especially common talk in forums, where you may see someone speculate, "My page is gone from the index. I think I tripped a duplicate content filter."

Everflux A term used by Matt Cutts of Google to refer to the constant addition of newly crawled and recrawled sites into Google's index, resulting in minor ranking shifts that occur on a daily or even hourly basis.

Now that you've had your fill of background knowledge, join us in Part II where you'll create an SEO strategy that will set you on the right track for Your SEO Plan.

Strategy

Before you can implement Your SEO Plan, you need to develop a workable strategy. In this part, you'll begin by getting your internal team on board and identifying the various disciplines that are necessary for effective SEO. Next you'll spend a month performing the brainstorming, research, and assessment to point you in the right direction for your ongoing campaign:

II

Get Your Team on Board

5

Search engine optimization is truly a team effort. A great SEO campaign encompasses skills that nearly always surpass those of any individual: writing, marketing, research, programming, and, yes, even a little bit of math. In this chapter, we guide you through the all-important task of getting your team on board, from techies coding your HTML edits to salespeople tracking conversions.

Chapter Contents

The Challenge of SEO Team Building
Marketing, Sales, and Public Relations
IT, Webmasters, and Programmers
Graphic Designers and Style Developers
Writers and Editors
Executives and Product Managers

The Challenge of SEO Team Building

You're busy, and SEO isn't your only job, so we're pretty sure you won't be thrilled to hear this:

Your SEO campaign will incorporate a wide variety of tasks: writing and editing, web page design, programming, ad copy creation, research, server log analysis, conversion tracking, and interpersonal communication for link building. If you're doing this all yourself, bravo! You're just the sort of multitasking do-it-yourselfer that thrives in SEO. If your entire company can't ride to lunch on the same motorcycle, we're putting you in charge of coordinating the SEO team. Either way, once you've read this book, you'll be the in-house SEO expert, so the responsibility for all of these tasks ultimately falls on you.

Before you close this book forever and run for the antacid, let's clarify a bit. We're not saying that you have to be the one to code the website or set up the server log software. We're saying you need to know enough to be able to speak intelligently to the people who do these tasks. And here's the hard part: You also need to convince them to spend some of their precious time working on Your SEO Plan.

Why is it, after all, that organizing an SEO team is so hard? We have observed three common reasons:

- SEO requires efforts from multiple departments and a variety of skills, such as marketing, sales, IT, PR, and creative/editorial.
- SEO is a new discipline and doesn't have established processes in the corporate system.
- The SEO budget will have to come from somewhere. That means somebody may have to give up some funding.

This chapter is here to guide you through the SEO crusade within your organization. There are some common patterns of resistance you might meet in each of the departments discussed here, and we'll share with you the most effective ways to counteract them.

Pearl of Wisdom: As with any team-building effort, building your SEO team will be an exercise in communication. Educate your team about SEO and you will be rewarded with their participation and enthusiasm.

But remember this: They're probably just as busy as you are, and that's why we advocate a pace-yourself approach. Don't overwhelm them with information—just the SEO rules that pertain to the task at hand. Likewise, there's a lot of knowledge to be gained from your colleagues as you work on SEO together, but don't expect to learn everything at once. SEO is a flexible and forgiving process, so take your time becoming a jack- or jill-of-all-trades.

"But I Don't Have One of Those!"

In this chapter, we discuss ways that you can approach various departments within your organization to get help on your SEO campaign. We are well aware that, due to size or focus, your organization may not include each of the separate departments described here. If this is the case with you, figure out what entity takes on these roles: Who is it that closes the deals with customers? That's your sales department. Who edits your website? That's the IT department. Look to that entity—be it a small staff, an entire department, or Erica on Every Other Tuesday—for the SEO help you need.

Even if you're planning to go it alone with your trusty hour-a-day book and a cup of coffee by your side, this chapter should offer some insight on approaching the work with the right "hats" on.

We have worked in many situations in which team participation was less than ideal for an SEO campaign, and we know how this can reduce the campaign's effectiveness. What happens when those carefully prepared page edits aren't implemented, keywords aren't incorporated into site rewrites, or a planned-for PPC budget never comes through?

 Pearl of Wisdom: Without your team on board, SEO suffers.

Besides being very frustrating for you, it can be a huge waste of time and money. Here are thoughts for keeping the enthusiasm going within all of your departments:

Marketing, Sales, and Public Relations

Marketing, Sales, and Public Relations make up a corporate SEO trifecta. Get all three excited about your SEO campaign and you'll have built your "brain-trust" foundation for success. Here's some food for thought that might come in handy when you need to deal with these departments.

Marketing: VIPs of SEO

In most organizations, the majority of the tasks relating to SEO will be performed by people in the marketing department. We're guessing you're a member of this department yourself. It's a natural progression: the marketing department may already be handling the website as well as *offline marketing* such as print ads, television, radio, billboards and *online marketing* such as banner ads and direct e-mails.

The marketing team will likely be instrumental in the SEO tasks like keyword brainstorming and research, writing text for descriptions and page titles, writing pay-per-click (PPC) ad copy, managing PPC campaigns, and executing link-building campaigns.

The folks on the marketing team have, quite literally, the skills to pay the bills, and they probably don't need any convincing that SEO is a worthwhile effort. What they will need, however, is some organization and some focusing.

What does your marketing team know about the importance of robot-readable text, keyword placement, and PPC campaign management? Maybe a lot. Maybe nothing. Maybe they know something that was worthwhile a few years ago but is now outdated. Since you're in charge of the SEO team, it will help you to know what the general knowledge level is and then think of yourself as the on-site SEO educator.

We have found that marketing staffers are almost always open to a little education about how the search engines work, as long as the information is provided on a need-to-know basis. For example, whenever we brainstorm for keywords with a marketing manager, inevitably their list contains terms that are extremely vague ("quality") or so specific that nobody is searching for them ("geometric specifications of duckpin bowling balls"). When we trim down that list, we always explain the basic concept of *search popularity* vs. relevance. But when it comes to educating the team, a little bit of information at a time is key; you don't want to drown your colleagues in too many details.

But what if you're not working in such a receptive environment? Maybe you are the only one convinced of the positive powers of SEO. Perhaps, for reasons of budget or time, you don't have the buy-in you need to move forward. Perhaps other marketing programs are taking precedence or the department can't seem to make the leap from offline to online marketing. If that's the case, it's time to convince the marketing manager of the importance of your SEO project!

Here's one way to approach it: Focus on the needs of the marketing department. Yes, it's time for you to go into therapist mode and do a whole lot of listening. Is there something that they've been dying to get done? A new tagline, perhaps? Maybe some changes to the corporate website? Are they feeling overworked? Do they secretly want to drop one segment—say, billboard advertising—out of the marketing mix? Are they having trouble getting help from the IT department? Tell them SEO can help.

SEO can provide the trackability that they've been waiting for. It may provide justification for dropping less-successful advertising venues. It can forge new alliances between Marketing and IT. On the "warm and fuzzy" side, it may provide an outlet for a creative soul who feels trapped in marketingspeak and wants to do more creative writing. And SEO is an extremely telecommuting-friendly enterprise. Is there a new dad in the department who would love to spend a portion of his week working from home?

Once you've found some common ground and the enthusiasm is starting to grow, look through your conversion goals from Chapter 1, "Clarify Your Goals," and consider starting Your SEO Plan with a a pilot project that you can focus your SEO efforts on together. Pick something close to the hearts of the marketing staff: a recent or upcoming launch, a section of your site devoted to a special event, a promotion, or a product line that's down in the dumps. Cherry-pick if you can! It's important that these early experiences be positive ones.

What If You're at the Bottom of the Pecking Order?

If you're on the bottom of the food chain in your organization, you may be either ignored or micromanaged by the people you answer to. Here are some tips that might work for you no matter what department you're dealing with:

- Create monthly reports, even if nobody's looking at them. As consultants, we have often asked ourselves, "What's the point of documenting everything if nobody reads our reports?" But it always comes down to this: we need them for our own reference. After a couple of months, search engine results begin to blur together—don't expect to keep this stuff in your head.

- Keep your reporting to a monthly schedule, even if you are asked for more frequent data. There are rare exceptions to this rule, such as extremely short-lived promotions or unusually volatile PPC campaigns. But for almost everything else, it really is helpful to set expectations that SEO is about long-term trends, not daily numbers.

- Deliver meaningful information. When you e-mail your boss a spreadsheet detailing your ranks for the last six months, you're delivering necessary information. But you can turn that into *meaningful* information when you summarize it in your e-mail: "Dear Boss, This month, three of our top-priority keywords made an entry into the top 30 in Google. Five of our keywords improved in rank, but our ranks for the term 'industrial strength pencils' continued to slide."

- Likewise, if you have to deliver bad news, always deliver a plan of action for addressing it. You're the in-house SEO expert, like it or not, and your boss is looking to you for guidance. The boss doesn't want to hear, "Holy moly! Google dropped all our pages!" The boss *does* want to hear, "It looks like our pages have been dropped from Google. This is probably a temporary problem, caused by Googlebot trying to crawl our site during our server outage last week. I'll resubmit the pages using Google's free submittal form and keep a close eye on the situation."

- Don't take all the credit for your success. This is not just to be humble, it's also because you actually *aren't* responsible for every SEO success. Even if you do everything right, you can't control what your competitors are doing or the nature of the next big search engine algorithm change. If you set your boss's expectations along these lines, you won't be blamed for every little failure, either.

Selling SEO to Sales

In Chapter 1, you gave a lot of thought to the fundamental goals of your business. Your sales department will be happy to hear that your SEO campaign will be bringing in not just traffic, but targeted traffic that leads directly to sales. You will be looking for their help in the following areas of SEO: keyword brainstorming, assistance with conversion tracking, competitive analysis, and insight into the customers' Web habits.

Since Sales often has the most direct contact with customers, they will have excellent ideas to add to your keyword brainstorming sessions. And if your conversions are of the easy-to-measure variety, such as online purchases, they'll probably enjoy monitoring conversion rates on a PPC campaign and adjusting accordingly.

On the other hand, you may have a harder time getting help with conversion tracking for transactions made over the phone or in person. The sales department may not want to make the effort to figure out exactly how the person on the other end of the phone got their number, or they may feel that grilling the customers about how they found you will interfere with the sales process. You need to convince your sales team that incorporating this sort of follow-up into the sales process is not a waste of time because it's important for everyone to know whether the website is generating profits.

The key to bringing your sales team on board for these more difficult tasks is educating them on the connection between targeted search engine traffic and bottom-line sales:

Pearl of Wisdom: SEO *will* bring in sales if it's done right!

How can you make it easier for the sales team to track conversions to the website? One way is to set up a special toll-free number and display it prominently on your website—but nowhere else! In this way, you can easily tell which customers got the number there. (In Chapter 8, "Month Two: Establish the Habit" you'll learn more about this and other tracking options.) It's not a perfect solution because it doesn't tell you which search engines and keywords were used, but it does succeed in connecting the dots for the sales department: SEO → Website Traffic → More Phone Calls → More Sales → Bigger Bonus!

SEO and Public Relations Can Relate

If your company has a public relations (PR) department, you're in luck. If not, think about this: If you got a phone call tomorrow from a radio station wanting to do a story on your company, who would they speak with? That's your PR department.

PR folks are very well suited to work with you on your SEO campaign. They're careful about words, they're excellent communicators, and they probably know how to take the time to track their results. They are the "keepers" of the brand, creating and monitoring the face that your organization puts forth to the public. Look to PR for help with keyword brainstorming, optimizing press releases, link building, and keeping your search engine listings and other links in line with your branding.

A typical PR department is primarily concerned with getting your company mentioned in the media and making sure that the publicity is accurate and—ideally—positive. Many newspaper and magazine articles, not to mention blog postings, are triggered by press releases or other forms of contact from a PR department. And it's fair to say that search engines deserve a place among these media sources: just like magazines, newspapers and the like, search engines provide a free, ostensibly unbiased third-party source of publicity for your organization.

 Pearl of Wisdom: Your PR department can think of search engines as a particularly big media outlet.

Even more important from a PR point of view, search engines have become a key research tool for those very journalists, bloggers, and thought leaders PR is chatting up in the first place.

You might meet some resistance from a PR department that thinks of SEO as strictly a form of advertising. In truth, SEO often does walk a fine line. A PPC campaign is most clearly within the advertising classification, but other SEO tasks, such as including target keywords in press releases or gaining incoming links from business contacts, fall more directly into the PR bucket. Once you explain to your PR folks that you will be seeking their assistance only with organic SEO activity, they should be more open to the possibilities.

As the department that protects the company brand, PR will likely have a great deal of interest in the brand maintenance tasks that fall under the SEO umbrella: monitoring search engine listings and other online mentions for currency and accuracy. You may need to educate the PR team about how to find outdated information online, but once they know where (and how) to look, don't be surprised if they develop a passion for rooting out the "uglies."

What if your website is not trying to sell anything or gather leads, or run advertising for revenue? What if the only goal of your website is brand awareness? This is when you need your PR department most of all. The folks in PR are already skilled in handling those difficult-to-measure soft targets offline through clipping services and surveys. They may even be doing some tracking of online mentions. Now you need to tie their tracking efforts together with the SEO campaign to make sure that SEO gets credit where credit is due. We'll talk more about online brand-awareness tracking options in Part III, "Your SEO Plan." Luckily, PR people are generally very comfortable with documentation. You shouldn't have too hard a time convincing them to document their SEO successes.

"Jill-of-all-trades" at Tachyon Publications

Tachyon Publications, a small fantasy and science fiction press, is lucky to have Jill Roberts as managing editor.

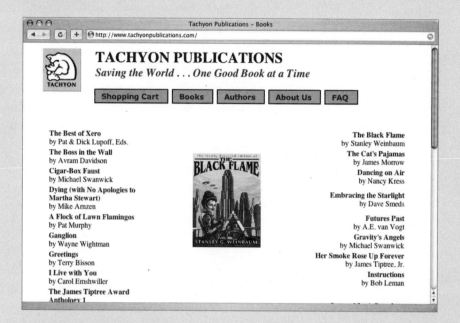

Jill is bright, hard working, and multitalented. "I do *everything*," Jill says cheerfully, "from book production to bookkeeping." Depending on the day, you may find Jill coordinating cover art for an upcoming release, representing Tachyon at a convention, or arranging the cookie tray at a local author appearance. Jill is also the keeper of Tachyon's mailing list and in-house editor of the website. She explains, "I write the text for the site, and enter it into the templates in the content management system, using some HTML tags."

By our count, Jill fits into several classifications, including marketing, sales, PR, editorial, and IT. And, by writing the website text and e-mail newsletters, Jill is doing her part to influence SEO. "The website is one of the ways that Tachyon is most visible, since we don't have a storefront," says Jill.

Like many small businesses, Tachyon is great at its core business—publishing books—but has difficulty finding the budget to build a multidisciplined SEO team. (As Jill puts it, "Small presses don't exactly rake it in.") The Tachyon web "team" is actually a handful of busy people squeezing the website work into small cracks of spare time. And for most of the company's existence, nobody was really in charge of keeping the site in line with the company's goals.

Continues

"Jill-of-all-trades" at Tachyon Publications *(Continued)*

This situation created some fairly serious hiccups along the way. Recently, Tachyon had to abandon two website redesigns because they did not meet the company's needs. "Neither version was based on a marketing plan, or by a website designer, which, I am happy to say, the third (and hopefully final) version will be," says Jill.

This struggle to redesign the site helped Tachyon recognize that it was time to make a change. The company is now building a more cohesive team to improve its Web presence. Jill says, "It took me a couple of years to convince my boss to hire a web designer," but eventually he did hire a part-timer. And Tachyon is now using an on-call marketing consultant who, according to Jill, "responds to our cries for help with amazing rapidity." Even though she's not a marketing expert—yet—Jill is on the right track, and she's got a little help when she needs it.

It's a familiar scenario: In trying to conserve money, a small company can actually waste both money and time when web presence is not given the expertise it requires. It's worth the invest-ment to identify weak spots and look for creative, but not necessarily pricey, solutions to get the right people on board.

Jill says, "I've always wanted our site to be full of great content, easy to find and navigate, and visually appealing. I think we're getting there." We say, now that you have the resources available for a well-run SEO campaign, you're bound to get there faster!

IT, Webmasters, and Programmers

Whether it's an IT department of 60 or a single programmer hiding out in the server closet, your SEO campaign is going to need a *lot* of help from your company's techni-cal experts. Not only will they be the final implementers of edits to your website, but they hold the keys to many important technical features of the site that can spell SEO success or failure.

What if you're a smaller organization and you are the one handling your own technical needs? Count yourself lucky in many ways—you won't have the workload and communication conflicts that often arise between SEO and IT . But once you start doing SEO in earnest, be ready to plug into the tech mindset a little more often than usual.

At a minimum, you will need IT to help with edits to website content, conver-sion tracking, server settings, programming standards, and the robots.txt file.

Sound overwhelming? It can be, if you don't prepare yourself. We suspect that dealing with your technical staff is going to be the most challenging part of your in-house SEO adventure. We have observed three major areas of difficulty:

- IT and Marketing speak such different languages it may be hard to get the communication rolling.

- IT is likely to be extremely cautious about taking on any additional workload.

- It may be difficult to find a way that SEO excellence benefits the IT department. There's a lot to say here, so let's discuss these three issues in more detail.

Communicating with IT

Your first task in working with IT will be finding a common language. Your IT comrades are technical thinkers. They like numbers, logic, specifications, and processes that can be repeated. They are less fond of mysterious or amorphous organic processes. They probably won't be responsive to a request unless they fully appreciate the logical reasons behind it.

Ideally, you will go into this conversation with some amount of technical skill under your belt. You may even want to take a crash course in HTML. But even if you think that HTML stands for "HoTMaiL" and a "server" has something to do with getting your eggs Benedict before they get cold, you can still develop a good rapport with your IT department if you follow this simple rule:

Pearl of Wisdom: Never fudge about your technical knowledge.

That's right, you need to be very honest about what you know and don't know. Express your needs, and let *them* do their jobs by telling you the right way to get things done. Bringing IT on board as a partner rather than a servant in SEO can make all the difference in your ongoing success.

Of course, you may not want all the information that IT is prepared to share with you. You probably don't want or need to know the details of why something can't be done. If your eyes glaze over at the first mention of "meta refresh," don't just stand there feeling miserable and trying to nod convincingly. Keep the focus on the overall goals: You need something done. Is it possible or not? If not, what alternatives are available? There is a give-and-take in play here. If you ask for a layman's explanation, and genuinely try to understand, you might learn something about the way your site is structured that will help you and Your SEO Plan. If you explain your SEO needs clearly, avoiding marketing jargon, your IT team will come to understand your SEO needs better and be more helpful to you in the long run.

A word of caution: If you are lucky enough to get your IT department extremely enthusiastic about SEO, you may find some ideas coming your way that fall into the realm of "black hat." We once had a meeting with a large multidepartmental team. We had just finished going through a point-by-point explanation of the SEO plan we had developed for their site when we saw a man in the back seem to get very excited. His hand shot up, and he said, "Wouldn't it be even better if we just used the web server to show the search engine robots one thing but the site visitors would see the regular page?" Yep, he had just "thought up" the concept of cloaking. Of course, his intentions were honorable; he was using his technical knowledge in a way that he thought would benefit the company. As SEO team leader, be prepared to communicate the things that will get your site into trouble—and find common ground with those who proclaim to be SEO know-it-alls.

Some of those techie qualities that may seem, at first, like challenges might ultimately work to the advantage of your SEO campaign. For example, IT folks are more likely than other departments to actually follow specifications. That means that if you all sit down and agree on a file-naming convention, you can probably count on IT to carry the torch. Second, your IT department is likely to be very process oriented. While you may find it frustrating to wait three months for a simple HTML change, at least you can trust that the task will be handled and documented in an orderly fashion. And third, what some may call "geekiness," others recognize as an enthusiasm for learning new things and lots of energy for the challenges that SEO will bring.

The IT Workload Conundrum

Like most departments, IT teams are feeling overworked. But even worse, their work is likely to be unrecognized and underappreciated. Unfortunately, your SEO campaign will probably require a large number of relatively small tasks from IT. And these tasks can't be done all at once because you need to assess and adjust throughout the campaign. If you are frustrated that it's taking weeks to get even simple requests handled, please realize this:

 Pearl of Wisdom: IT really hates when you call things "simple."

Here are some possible issues to consider:

- Are there a large number of different people all clamoring for simple changes? If so, it's only fair that your request is handled in order.

- Could the task be more complicated than you think? If you don't have the tech savvy to know exactly what it takes to get your task done, be very careful about throwing around the word *simple*!

- Do the folks in the IT department understand the reasoning behind the change, or do they think it's just a whim on your part? Educate on a need-to-know basis; giving them a solid background will help the process.

If you consistently find yourself bumping into roadblocks in the IT department, look for some creative solutions:

- If you have cumbersome work request procedures, can the department create an "Express Lane" for small SEO requests, bypassing the normal pathways?

- Can the department keep your work orders open for a little while, allowing you to make adjustments?

- Is there an individual in the department that can be "yours" for a certain number of hours per month? Have a sit-down with the department leadership and figure out a way to make it happen.

IT tasks needed for your SEO campaign are almost never urgent. This means that, if you agree to it, they can fit into some of the slower times in the department.

If, like a lot of smaller companies, your IT department is outsourced, you will probably find that you need more hours—at least up front—to get your site up to snuff. Although it can be frustrating to wait, stockpiling several little SEO requests and submitting them on a weekly or monthly basis may save time and money. If your IT "department" is a friend, it may be time to stop asking for favors and either figure out how to do it yourself or set up a payment situation. SEO will generate quite a few site modifications over time, and you'll fare best if you don't leave them to the ups and downs of your friend's generous nature.

How SEO Benefits IT

Can you believe it? Your SEO campaign can actually be a positive thing for the IT department. Here are a few examples:

Interdepartmental collaboration Bringing together the efforts of marketers, wordsmiths, artists, and techies is a very positive thing. Surprising new relationships, new alliances, and synergies can result.

Recognition for IT It's not often that IT tasks can directly result in sales and profits. This is one of those times. Participating in the SEO campaign can bring the IT department out of the obscurity of the computer rooms and give them some of the attention and acclaim that they deserve.

New toys Because the SEO campaign can depend on IT for so many things, such as server uptime and server log analysis, the SEO campaign may be a driving force behind getting some new hardware.

Can you think of any other ways that SEO might be positive for IT in your organization?

Graphic Designers

Graphic designers are those creative souls responsible for the look and feel of your website. In a larger organization, style developers create the style guides that all of the other web page creators have to follow. In a smaller company, you may be dealing with just a few designers or even an individual who is a combination of graphic designer and web developer. The graphics portion of the SEO team is responsible for setting up search-engine-friendly standards in the style guide, if there is one; soliciting input from the SEO team leader during site updates; and, because SEO has a way of dropping off the radar after a while, making sure that the standards are mandatory and ongoing.

If you're on your own, you won't have anyone else to persuade. But if you're assembling an SEO team that includes Graphics, you've got some convincing to do! You'll have the best chance at success with this department if you include the following steps:

- Recognize the value of the work that the Graphics department does.
- Educate about graphics-related SEO skills.
- Formalize your agreements.

Let's look at these three steps in depth.

Value Graphics

First, recognize the importance of what your designers do. Like the IT department, graphic designers often feel that their efforts are undervalued. The "look" of a site is not just an aside. In a visual medium, the look is the fundamental substance of your visitors' experience. And it's not just a cosmetic thing—your designers are responsible for *usability* factors as well. Your organization may have the benefit of user testing, or the designs may be created in a more seat-of-the-pants fashion. Either way, we can tell you this right now:

 Pearl of Wisdom: Designers want you to let *them* be the designers.

In our experience, we have found that designers' preferences are often initially at odds with optimization for search engines. A conflict between SEO and graphic designers exists because SEO is, at least in part, optimizing the website for a nonhuman visitor (a search engine robot), while designers are entirely focused on the human user experience.

As the ambassador of SEO, your job is to find common ground. Sit down with the leadership—the department head, the style guide developer, the senior designer, or whoever happens to have the website graphic files on their computer—and figure out how you can make SEO work for everybody. A website that nobody can find is worthless, but you certainly don't want a site that people immediately leave because the design doesn't speak to them. So, you must recognize and acknowledge this fact:

Pearl of Wisdom: The human audience will always be the most important.

Make a commitment to the graphics department that you will never sacrifice the human user experience for SEO.

Educate and Empower

It's important to educate your designers about the reasoning behind your SEO proposals.

Give them a quick course on the graphics-related factors that you learned about in Chapter 3 and 4. Again, it's best not to overwhelm with too many details, so you should limit your explanations to elements that you are looking to change. Is your designer attached to a JavaScript pull-down navigation? Show how most search engines won't follow those links. Stuck on big graphic headlines? In Part III, we'll tell you how to get a peek at your website the way that search engine spiders see—or, more appropriate, don't see—these elements. Show this to your designers for a shocker!

Naturally, there may be too many changes to make in one fell swoop. Go for the big-ticket items first—for example, getting rid of frames, wrapping Flash elements in robot-friendly HTML pages, replacing major graphic headlines with HTML text, and creating a lower-priority list for less significant SEO changes. In other words, do this:

Pearl of Wisdom: Start with big changes for quicker tangible results.

After you have some results to show from the first pass, you'll have great ammunition for a second pass.

Don't be drawn in by the myth that everything that benefits SEO will be detrimental to the design and that you have to choose between a good-looking site that nobody can find and an ugly site with tons of traffic. Many of your SEO improvements, such as adding IMG ALT tags to graphics, will have no ill effect on the design. And there are some, like replacing outdated font tags with *Cascading Style Sheets (CSS)*, that your designers may have been wanting to do anyway. But most important, if your designers are able to internalize SEO factors, future designs will have a way of coming out more search-engine friendly.

P.J. Fusco: "Educate-Inform-Transform"

P.J. Fusco is a search marketing expert and in-house search engine marketing manager for a top health and beauty e-commerce group. She shared her philosophy of "educate-inform-transform," explaining that building a successful campaign is all about "empowering others with the knowledge and passion to champion a project through the organization."

Here, in her own words, is how it works:

- "When you reveal keyword research to a copywriter or editor…they take greater responsibility for the words they choose.

- "When you show a Flash programmer how the search engines 'see' their work, it's a lot easier to convince them to wrap a Flash program in more search-engine-friendly code.

- "When you show a designer that search engines can't read the words embedded in an image…all of a sudden you get more words and fewer images built in to site designs.

- "When you show a Sales & Marketing VP the return on investment made in a PPC campaign that has positively impacted top-line sales and bottom-line profits, you get bigger budgets for more campaigns."

As the head of the SEO team, you become more than an SEO expert. You also become educator, project manager, cheerleader, and most of all, communicator. P.J. sums up: "Keeping different departments informed about the status of a project takes meetings, instant messages, phone calls, conference calls, and the occasional pop-in if someone missed a meeting or conference call. It takes organization, too, in order to keep up with who is doing what, when, where, how, and why."

But despite all of your best efforts, there can still be bumps in the road. P.J. has been known to take extreme measures: "If I need the telecom team to get DNS set up for a new site, I've learned to bribe them with cookies."

Make It Official

If your organization uses a web style guide, you have a great head start. Because for SEO, rules are good! It will give your SEO guidelines longevity—so that your standards are followed not just once, but every time a new page is created. And it will benefit you when, six months down the road, you're handing off SEO reviews to someone else or you've forgotten what you'd planned at the outset.

What if there's no style guide, just one or two designers putting together pages based on what feels cool at the moment? You'll need some way to formalize your agreements and give them some long-term viability. If you can't get it in writing, a handshake will do. Set up a system for your designers to run edits by you in the future. At the very least, be sure that you're informed of major site edits so that you can coordinate a site review for SEO.

Writers and Editors

Writers and editors are the wordsmiths who craft the all-important text that your site audience, and the search engines, will see. Since SEO is so focused on text, you are going to need some writers in your corner. Writers and editors can help with these important SEO tasks: keyword brainstorming, writing or rewriting content with keywords (and linkability) in mind, writing or reviewing ad content, and establishing a process for SEO review of new content.

If you're doing this yourself, be prepared to spend a good portion of your SEO time on writing, keyword research, and related tasks.

Writers are a natural choice as SEO coconspirators. Unfortunately, SEO is often perceived among writers as something that will force them to alter, or maybe even degrade, their creative content. If you've ever seen a page of text that was written primarily for the benefit of search engines (see Figure 5.1), you know that writing for robots just isn't something that your human audience will respond to.

So, just as you did with your graphic designers, start your conversation with a promise: the human audience will always be the most important. In fact, the whole point of Your SEO Plan is to bring in that audience and speak to them, clearly, in their own language. Including your writers in the keyword brainstorming process will give them important information about the terminology your target audience is using, which they can then incorporate into their text. If you educate your writers on concepts like keywords and keyword density, that means less rewriting in the SEO review process. That's less work for you and more control for your writers.

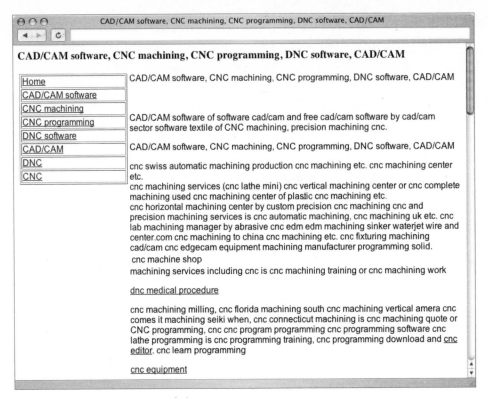

CAD/CAM software, CNC machining, CNC programming, DNC software, CAD/CAM

Figure 5.1 Some writing was never meant for human eyes.

SEO also provides an opportunity for writers to branch out and write content that isn't solely there to promote your product or service. Since linkability increases when a site offers useful or interesting noncommercial content, you can encourage your writers to add things like articles, news, and resource pages to the site. These might be projects that writers are interested in. Ask them for ideas.

Of course, one big step in making your website text more SEO friendly is to make sure the text is *actually present*:

 Pearl of Wisdom: Writers can't optimize text that isn't there.

So coordinate with the IT and graphics departments to make sure that screen real estate can be allocated for descriptive text and that graphic titles can be changed to HTML. Then you can approach your writers with specific ideas and locations for SEO-related improvements.

Executives and Product Managers

The decision makers in your organization have a lot on their minds these days: shrinking budgets, expanding competition, and out-of-control expenses could keep anyone awake at night. Why should they be open to your big ideas about SEO? Even if SEO was the boss's idea in the first place—or if you're your own boss—you still need to know, in a down-to-the-brass-tacks kind of way, what it's going to take.

Of course you want to approach your corporate decision makers with a clear vision, a plan, and a lot of cold, hard facts. But there's a catch-22 here: how can you know exactly what Your SEO Plan will cost and what it will accomplish until you have spent some time researching those very questions? Executives aren't big fans of laying out cash for an unknown outcome. So we recommend that you start the process by seeking approval for an initial, investigatory month. That's roughly 20 hours of labor at 1 hour per day, and it's all laid out for you in Chapter 6, "Your One-Month Prep: Baseline and Keywords." You'll spend your Prep Month figuring out what kind of performance your SEO campaign can expect and be able to come back to the executives with a much more complete plan on hand.

Your initial request will be introductory. Prepare it with the following information on hand:

- A general introduction to SEO: what it is and how it is being used in the marketing mix by many companies today. For starters, try the "Why SEO?" numbers from the introduction to this book.

- Your Goals Worksheet from Chapter 1.

- Some telling screen shots showing your competition outranking you, your brand looking awful onscreen, or any other SEO faux pas you can find.

- A detailed timeline for the Prep Month.

Be sure that this information is presented in the most clear, succinct manner possible. And be prepared for plenty of questions from around the table: How much will this really cost us? How long do we have to do it? Do we have the right staff in-house?

SEO is such a cost-effective marketing technique that it should be an easy sell. But change is never easy. Does budgeting your SEO campaign mean that Ellen will have to take Tim's Yellow Pages budget away? Will an hour a day of SEO mean someone is an hour late for dinner each night? No matter how persuasive your numbers and worksheets are, your plan will need to address the realities of day-to-day operations.

Once your executives are ready to move on your SEO project, be sure you get not just a green light, but a little bit of gas in the tank as well. Here's what you'll need them to do:

- Vocalize the plan to the team.
- Commit to your proposed labor and budget.
- Commit to reviewing your findings after you have completed your Prep Month.

Working in SEO can sometimes feel like wrestling a many-armed sea animal. How will you tame the beast and get some solid information to share with others in your organization? In Part III, we'll walk you through the process of choosing the who, what, and when of reporting on Your SEO Plan.

Get Your*self* on Board!

As SEO team leader, you may have to step slightly outside of your comfort zone in order to be as effective as you can be. You will have to keep yourself organized, which entails documenting results, questions, and communications as you go. And, like any team leader, you will sometimes need to repeat yourself politely until you get that requested task completed or that important concept understood. If it helps to take some of the pressure off, you as SEO project leader can comfortably adopt a friendly, easy-going approach. Since SEO isn't normally a deadline-driven process, most of the time, you'll have the opportunity to write "No rush" on your requests and mean it!

Now that you understand how to drum up the requisite levels of enthusiasm throughout your organization, you're ready to start your Prep Month. As you do the research in the next chapter, you're likely to uncover some interesting, and possibly surprising, findings about your own site that you can share with your team.

Your One-Month Prep: Baseline and Keywords

Your goals are in place, you have a good understanding of how the search engines work, your team is ready—finally it's time to get into your SEO campaign! We'll walk you through it, day by day, in tasks that we estimate will take an hour or less.

6

This month you'll handpick your most effective keywords based on a combination of gut instinct and careful research; then you'll assess your site's standing in the search engines. This is critical prep work for next month's optimization tasks.

Chapter Contents
Your SEO Idea Bank
Week 1: Keywords
Week 2: Baseline Assessment
Week 3: Competition
Week 4: Baseline Monthly Report

Your SEO Idea Bank

Maybe you're an anarchist at heart and it takes divine intervention to get your feet into two matching socks. But more likely, you're just so overworked that it's impossible to keep every sticky note and e-mail where it belongs. You need help—and we're here for you! Before you begin your hour-a-day tasks, follow these simple steps to start your new SEO lifestyle with a "headquarters" on your computer. We call it your SEO Idea Bank!

Step 1: Create a home for your SEO files. Choose a location on your computer or network where your SEO files will live. The most important thing is to make sure that there's just *one* consistent spot where your SEO files are stored.

Step 2: Download tools from yourseoplan.com. On the companion website to this book, www.yourseoplan.com, you'll find the worksheets and templates that we'll be referring to throughout this chapter. Take the time to download these now and save them in your SEO Idea Bank:

- Keywords Worksheet
- Site Assessment Worksheet
- Rank Tracking Worksheet
- Task Journal Worksheet
- Competition Worksheet

And don't forget to copy your Goals Worksheet from Chapter 1, "Clarify Your Goals," into your SEO Idea Bank as well. From time to time throughout the rest of this book, we'll send you to the website to fetch some more helpful documents for your SEO Idea Bank.

Step 3: Start an SEO task journal. Your SEO Task Journal is a place to document what you've done, what questions have cropped up, and what you need to do in the future. Your Task Journal will prevent you from duplicating your efforts and help you keep track of what you were thinking last week and the week before. It's also a convenient holding pen for ideas and random thoughts that come up while you are working on Your SEO Plan.

One of the fun things about SEO is wandering down whatever path your explorations take you. But if you only have an hour and you actually want to accomplish something, you're going to need to keep yourself on track. Rather than going off on every tangent that is thrown your way, file those thoughts away in your Task Journal for later.

If the Task Journal isn't your cup of tea, use whatever organizational method works for you. You may be happy using a simple Microsoft Word document, and changing the font to ~~strikethrough~~ when the topic is resolved. But feel free to get fancy. Consider experimenting with an online database in your own personal Yahoo! Group at groups.yahoo.com, or an online to-do list through a service such as tadalist.com.

With your SEO Idea Bank in place, you're ready for the fun stuff: choosing keywords!

Week 1: Keywords

Ask any SEO pro what the single most important part of an SEO campaign is and we bet you'll get this answer: "Keyword choice!" Here's why: The keywords you choose *this week* will be the focus of your entire optimization process. Keywords (also referred to as keyword phrases, keyphrases, keyterms, and just terms) are the short, descriptive phrases that you want to be found with on the search engines. If you put the time into choosing powerful keywords now, you are likely to be rewarded not only with higher ranks, but also with these benefits:

- A well-optimized site, because your writers and other content producers will feel more comfortable working with well-chosen keywords as they add new site text

- More click-throughs once searchers see your listing, because your keywords will be highly relevant to your site's content

- More conversions once your visitors come to your site, because the right keywords will help you attract a more targeted audience

As SEO expert Jill Whalen told us, "There is more than one way to skin the SEO cat.... There is no special formula that will work for every site all the time." And this applies to your keyword targeting strategy. We suggest that by the end of this week, you should have 10 target keyword phrases in hand. We believe that this is a reasonable level for an hour-a-day project. But you may be more comfortable with 2 or 20 keywords. We welcome you to adjust according to your individual needs.

Here are your daily assignments for this week:

Monday: Your Keyword Gut Check

Tuesday: Resources to Expand and Enhance the Keyword List

Wednesday: Keyword Data Tools

Thursday: Keyword Data Gathering

Friday: Your Short List

Your Name Here

Recently, we were chatting with our friend Mark Armstrong, an auto mechanic in San Francisco. Hearing that we were working on an SEO book, he shared a common frustration: "All I want to do," he said, "is find the official website for this supplier out in Chicago. I know the *name* of the company, but even when I enter their name in the search engines, their website is nowhere to be found. Now that is just ridiculous! There should be some system where companies always come up first for their own name."

Continues

Your Name Here *(continued)*

We couldn't agree more, and there actually once was such a system, called RealNames. Unfortunately, RealNames is no longer functioning, which is a shame because it filled a real need in search—just ask our friend Mark! And where there is such a strong need, we have to believe that the search engines will find a way to meet it. Google has introduced a version in its toolbar (later in the chapter, we'll show you how to download this handy tool) but not in its main search results. So for now, there's no guarantee that your site will come up first when someone searches for your organization's name. That's why we always recommend including it on your list of top target keywords.

Monday: Your Keyword Gut Check

Today you're going to do a brain dump of possible target keywords for your organization. You'll need two documents from your SEO Idea Bank: the Keywords Worksheet and your Goals Worksheet.

 Now: Go to your SEO Idea Bank and open up the Keywords Worksheet and your Goals Worksheet.

In the Keywords Worksheet you'll find columns with the headings Keyword, Search Popularity, Relevance, Competition, Landing Pages, and Target Audience. Today you're only worried about the first column: Keyword.

Now, take a look at the list of conversions that you came up with on your Goals Worksheet in Chapter 1. You'll use these as jumping-off points for your keyword brainstorming session.

We met Jason back in Chapter 1 when he was thinking through his target audiences and the goals of his SEO campaign. Jason's company, Babyfuzzkin, sells unique, high-end baby clothes. We're going to follow him through his keyword week.

For now, you'll jot down whatever comes to mind, and save the fine-tuning for later. Here are a few ideas to get you started:

Be the searcher. For each conversion you wrote on your Goals Worksheet, take a few minutes to put yourself in the mind of each target audience that you listed. Imagine that you are this person, sitting in front of a search engine. What do you type in the search box?

Name who you are and what you offer. No keyword list is complete without your organization's name and the products, services, or information you offer. Make sure to think about generic *and* proprietary descriptions. Jason may jot down more generic words like "baby shower gifts" and "baby clothes," but he should also include trade-marked names like "Babyfuzzkin" and a list of the brand names he's selling. Likewise, if it's equally accurate to describe the products for sale on your website with the terms "spray bottles" or "X7 MistMaker Series," add both to your list.

Name the need you fill. It's not just what you offer, it's the itch that your product or service scratches. So Jason might write down "baby shower gift ideas" or "baby clothes free shipping." If you sold home alarm systems on your site, you might want to list terms that describe your customers' needs, such as "protect my home" and "prevent burglary."

Think seasonal. Does your product or service vary from season to season? Do you offer special services for special events? Think through your whole calendar year. Jason at Babyfuzzkin may want to list words like "baby swimsuits" and "Size 2T Santa Sweaters." A spa resort may want to list things like "Mother's Day Getaway Ideas" and "Tax Time Stress Relief."

Embrace misspellings and slang. Here's something you probably know better than any SEO expert: alternate spellings and regional variations on your keywords. Jason bristles when he gets mail addressed to "Baby Fuzzkin" or "Babyfussing," but he knows his company name is easy to get wrong, so he'll add those to his list. On a regional note, a company selling soft drink vending machines had better remember to add both "soda" and "pop." You do *not* need to consider variations in capitalization because search engines are not sensitive to caps (besides, the vast majority of searches are lowercase). However, you should include singular and plural forms on your list for further evaluation.

Locate yourself. In Chapter 2, "Customize Your Approach," we suggested that brick-and-mortar organizations include variations on their company name and location in the keywords list. If your company does business only in Michigan, you really don't want to waste your SEO efforts on a searcher in Nevada. And, did we mention that search engines sometimes aren't all that smart? They do not necessarily know that "NY" and "New York" are the same thing. So be sure to include every variation you can think of.

**Self-packaged
yellow tropical
fruit snack**

Now that you've got an idea of what you're looking for, you can choose to brainstorm your list alone, or, better yet, brainstorm with members of your PR, sales, marketing, and writing teams. This can work well as an e-mail exercise, too; just shoot out a request for your colleagues to send you their own ideas for keywords.

When Homographs Attack

Homographs are words that have the same spelling but different meanings. For example, *invalid* means both "not valid" and "a person who can't get out of bed." Search engines have struggled with homographs since their inception.

As mothers to young children, we have a strong interest in making sure our homes are lead-free. So naturally, we use the search engines to learn how. Unfortunately, the word *lead*, meaning "a soft heavy toxic malleable metallic element," happens to have a homograph: *lead* meaning "travel in front of." The environmental lead testing search results are crowded out by pages with information on leadership! In order to get the information we need, we have to lengthen our search phrases: "lead abatement," "lead contamination," and "lead poisoning."

Acronyms are particularly susceptible to this problem. One site we know (we've changed the name and identifying details to prevent embarrassment), Massive Media, Inc., has spent years targeting the term "AMC," which is an acronym for one of its products. But just in the top 10 Google results, this term is represented by the following entities:

- AMC Theatres
- The AMC network movie channel
- The Appalachian Mountain Club
- Albany Medical Center
- Australian Maritime College
- American Mathematics Competitions
- Applied Microsystems Corporation

None of these has anything to do with what Massive Media was trying to promote! Clearly, in targeting this acronym, it was navigating the wrong waters. It doesn't make sense to spend your energy competing with such a broad field.

If you are unfortunate enough to be promoting a company or product with a name that shares spelling with a common word or acronym, you will need to brainstorm on what secondary terms your target audience is likely to add and combine words to find a more appropriate term to target. Possibilities are the geographical location of your company, the generic term for the product, names of well-known executives, or the term *company* or *inc*. And, as a general rule, don't target acronyms shorter than four letters long,

Once you start spitting out your list, don't over-edit yourself; you'll have time for editing later. For now, we just want you to get all of your keyword ideas in writing. By the end of tomorrow's task, you should have a big, hearty list—say, at least 50 keyword ideas for a list that will be trimmed down to about 10 by the end of this week.

Now: Go to the Keywords Worksheet and start your list under the Keyword column.

Tuesday: Resources to Expand and Enhance the List

On your Keywords Worksheet, you already have a nice long list of possible target phrases. But are there any you missed? Today, you'll troll on- and offline for additional keyword ideas. We've listed some of the places that additional keyword phrase ideas could pop up. There are more ideas here than you can use in just one hour, so pick and choose based on what's available to you and what feels most appropriate to your situation:

Your Coworkers If you didn't get your team involved in keyword brainstorming yesterday, be sure that they jump on board today. It will help your campaign in two ways: first, they'll provide valuable new perspectives and ideas for keywords, and second, they'll feel involved and empowered as participants in the plan.

Your Website Have you looked through your website to find all variations of your possible keyword phrases? Terms that are already used on your site are great choices for target keywords because they will be easier to incorporate into your content.

Industry Media If there are any magazines or websites devoted to your trade, take a look and see what terminology they are using to describe your product or service. Remember, now is not the time to edit your terms! So if the words are in use out there, be sure to include them on this list.

Your Website Statistics If you have access to a program that shows statistics on your website, review it to see what search terms are currently sending traffic your way. Terms that are already working well for you can be great choices for target keywords. We'll walk you through choosing and reviewing website stats in Chapter 8, "Month Two: Establish the Habit."

Your Customers If you (or anyone on your SEO team) have the ability to check in with customers about what phrases they use to describe your products or services, now is the time to get in touch with them and find out! Your salespeople might also take this opportunity to confess: "Oh yeah, it's called Closure Management Technology on the website, but when we talk with customers, we always just call it *zippers*."

Your Internal Search Engine If your website has a search box on it, it's time to get sneaky! You can use its usage information for your SEO campaign. Talk to your webmaster about collecting the following information about site visitors who use your internal search engine:

- What terms do they search for?
- What results are they shown?
- What pages do they choose to click on (if any)?

Keep a running list of top terms your site visitors are searching for; these are likely to be good target keywords for your SEO campaign.

There's plenty more that an internal search engine can do for you. Visit Chapter 10, "Extra-Credit and Guilt-Free Slacking," for more information.

"Related" terms on Search Engines Many search engines offer suggestions for related terms after you perform a search. For example, Ask has "Narrow Your Search" and "Expand Your Search" columns along the left-hand side of the search results that show a variety of terms related to your search (see Figure 6.1). These related terms can be good additional keyword choices.

Friends, Neighbors, and the Unexpected One major problem we have observed with keyword choice is that businesses tend to become too caught up in the insider terminology they use to describe themselves. If your target audience goes beyond industry insiders, be sure to seek out input from unexpected sources. Your friends and neighbors or even the neighbor's kid can provide surprisingly helpful ideas.

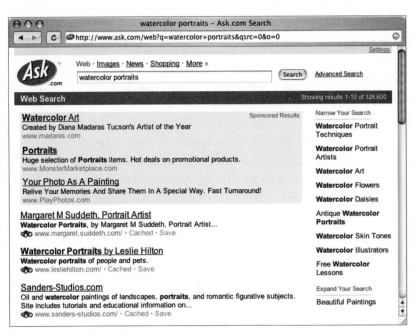

Figure 6.1 Related terms on Ask

Competitors' Websites Later this month, we'll have you digging through your competitors' websites like a hungry raccoon in a Dumpster. For the moment, try breaking up keyword writer's block by browsing your competitors' sites to see what terms they are using to describe themselves.

Now: Go to the Keywords Worksheet and add your new ideas to the list in the Keyword column.

Wednesday Keyword Data Tools

You've got a nice long list of keywords. But the list doesn't mean much to you until you find out which of these keywords are actually being used by searchers. You're also going to want a sense of how competitive the SEO field is for a keyword so you can get a handle on just how hard you might have to fight to rank well for it.

Fortunately, there are keyword analysis tools available to help you suss out this important information. And, also fortunately, there are *not so many* different high-quality options to choose from, so the decision is far from overwhelming. We'll discuss the top two here:

• Wordtracker

• Yahoo! Search Marketing Keyword Selector Tool

Today is a "study hall" day. You're going to find these tools and get your feet wet utilizing their capabilities.

Wordtracker

Wordtracker is the dominant tool for keyword research in the SEO industry. In a nutshell, it tells you how many people are searching for the terms you may want to use on your site. It does this by monitoring and recording searches on meta search engines throughout the Web. You can use it to get an estimate of how many searches will be performed for a given term, and it is also an excellent source of related terms and common misspellings (see Figure 6.2).

Wordtracker doesn't give an up-to-the-minute snapshot—its data reflects searches that took place a few months before you retrieve it. Wordtracker is available at www.wordtracker.com for a fee. We know how you hate to spend money, so now is the only time we'll tell you something like this:

Pearl of Wisdom: The Wordtracker fee is indispensable in your SEO efforts.

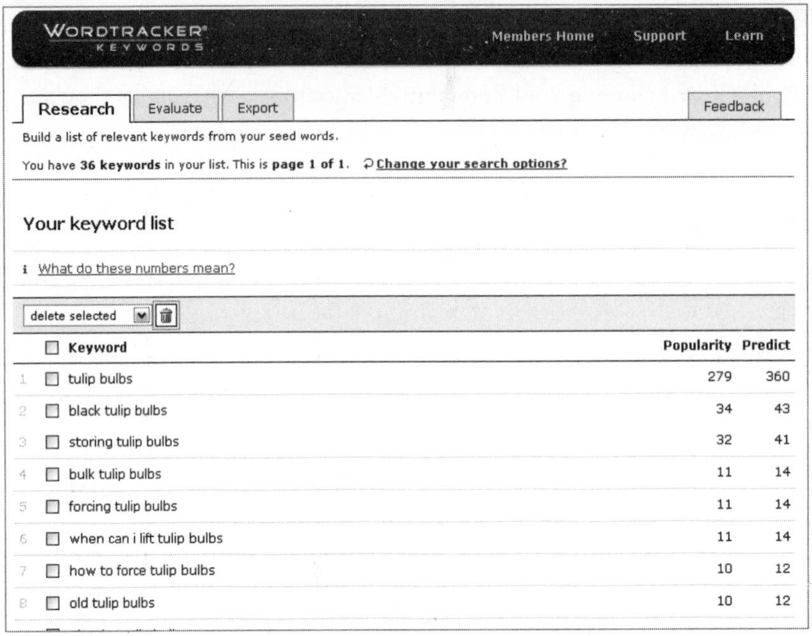

Figure 6.2 Wordtracker keywords data

We suggest that you use Wordtracker today and tomorrow as the primary tool for whittling down your long keyword list into something meaningful. If you need to be frugal, Wordtracker makes it easy for you: you can purchase low-cost subscriptions in one-day or one-week increments.

Wordtracker isn't hard to use, so we'll leave the step-by-step instructions, if you need them, to the folks who made the tool. You can download their user guide once you have logged into the system. There is also a FAQ and other resources on their website. Be sure to read up on the different databases (Comprehensive, Compressed, etc.) available within the system so you can choose the best one for your needs.

 Now: Sign up for Wordtracker and test-drive it using some of the keywords from your list.

Yahoo! Search Marketing Keyword Selector Tool

Buried in the interface of Yahoo! Search Marketing (YSM), one of the primary providers of pay-per-click (PPC) services, is its Keyword Selector Tool. This free tool taps into data on searches performed throughout the YSM search network.

It's sometimes hard to find the URL for this tool. Start from the YSM Resource Center homepage, http://searchmarketing.yahoo.com/rc/srch, and look for a link labeled Keyword Selector Tool. If you don't find it there, or if the URL has changed, you can always find the current link on our companion website at www.yourseoplan.com.

There are two nice things about the YSM tool: it's free, and it's simple. All you do to use it is enter a keyword phrase. Up will pop a list of related terms along with your original term and the number of searches that took place throughout the YSM network over the course of a month (the data is usually a couple of months old). However, YSM has many fewer features than Wordtracker, and because it uses PPC data, it combines terms that may not be combined by nonpaid engines. For example, YSM sees the words *clothes* and *clothing* as being the same—this is called *stemming*—while any organic search engine would not. It also does some funky things with alphabetization. So for example, if you search for the term "send in the clowns," YSM will return information about the term "clown in send sinatra the," with all the words in alphabetical order. See Figure 6.3 for an example.

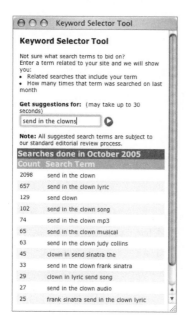

Figure 6.3 Yahoo! keyword data for "send in the clowns"

Now, you're a smart one, and it won't take long before you can see that a term like "clown in send sinatra the" is so ludicrously unlike the English language that nobody is really searching for it in that order. Stemming and alphabetization limit the usefulness of the YSM tool, but it's still a great way to spot popularity trends.

By the way, here's a tip that can save you a bunch of time: YSM data is available within the Wordtracker tool too. Last we looked, Wordtracker was still calling YSM's data the Overture database (Overture was bought by Yahoo!), so be on the lookout for changes in labels here.

Now: Switch to the Yahoo! Search Marketing (aka Overture) database within Wordtracker, or go to the Yahoo! Search Marketing site, and test-drive it with some of your favorite keywords.

No keyword research tool is perfect, and you should always double-check the data you get with your gut instincts. We use Wordtracker for most of our keyword data gathering. We use YSM primarily to find related terms, to double-check trends in popularity that we find with Wordtracker, and to plan PPC campaigns. Your finances and preferences will dictate whether you use one or both.

Thursday: Keyword Data Gathering

Congratulations—you're over the hump in your first week of SEO! You have a long list of possible keywords and tools in hand to help you analyze them. Today you will fill in those all-important columns on your Keywords Worksheet:

Search Popularity How many people are actually searching for a given term

Relevance How well a keyword connects with your site and conversion goals

Competition How many, and how well, other sites are targeting a given keyword

Finalizing your top target keywords will require a balancing act between all three of these factors. We'll look a little more closely at each of them here.

Search Popularity

Both YSM and Wordtracker provide values for keyword popularity (see Figure 6.2 and Figure 6.3). However, we recommend Wordtracker over YSM for two reasons: First, Wordtracker pulls from a larger network of searchers. Second, as we mentioned in your Wednesday task, Wordtracker is much more specific about word syntax. For example, YSM may combine "IL" with "Illinois," and you will never know which one is actually more popular with searchers. Wordtracker gives you the option of looking at the specific differences in terminology that you need to know in order to choose the "just right" keywords.

It can be time consuming pulling up the search popularity values for every term on your long list, but you can save time by copying and pasting several words at a time—or your whole list—into the search popularity tool. If you're good with Excel, you can even export the search results from Wordtracker for easy import into your Keywords Worksheet!

Jason at Babyfuzzkin used Wordtracker to determine the search popularity of his long list. We've selected a few of his results to show in Table 6.1:

▶ **Table 6.1** Search Popularity for Babyfuzzkin's Keywords

Keyword	Search Popularity
baby clothes	2125
unique baby clothes	134
infants	747
infant	376
designer baby clothing	65
designer baby clothes	438
baby gift	588
baby gifts	1629
baby shower gifts	614
unique baby shower gifts	667
cool baby clothes	236
layette	66

Don't pay too much attention to the absolute values of the numbers here. Search popularity values provided by these services do not give you the total number of searches throughout the entire Internet, so you should only use them for comparing the *relative* search popularity between two terms.

You may notice while you gather your popularity numbers that you find other tempting keywords that you hadn't previously considered. Add them to the list! You'll begin slicing and dicing this list very soon, but for now it won't hurt to add more promising ideas.

Now: Go to the Keywords Worksheet and use your keyword data tool to add search popularity values to the Search Popularity column.

With these numbers in black and white you'll have a much stronger command of which terms are going to be good performers for you.

Relevance

Relevance is in many ways a judgment call: How would a searcher feel if they searched for this term and found your site? Would your site answer their question or resolve their need? Does a good landing page for this term currently exist on your site, or could one be built? We are going to ask you to classify relevance on a scale from *Very Poor* to *Excellent*. Your relevance values should also incorporate the following perspectives:

Your writers/editors Ask yourself if the people that write content on your website will be comfortable using this term to describe your products and services. Better yet, go ask *them* the question.

Other sites that come up in the search Try entering the term into a search engine and see what other sites come up. Are the top-ranking websites from organizations that are similar to yours? Surprisingly, in SEO you often do want to be situated in the vicinity of your competitors. If a searcher enters a keyword and sees a page full of weird, seemingly unrelated results, they are likely to try again with a different search.

Value of the conversion Your relevance level should also take into account the value of the conversion for a term. For example, if the two terms "ginger syrup" and "crystallized ginger" are equally well matched to your site but you believe that people searching for "crystallized ginger" are going to be more valuable conversions (because it's a much more expensive delicacy!), then that keyword should get a boost. It's guesswork and intuition at this point, but after a few months, you'll have some tracking under your belt and a much clearer understanding of the conversion values for different terms.

Here's a detailed examination of a few of Jason's keywords. These examples should give you some guidance for thinking about your own keywords:

"infants" Relevance Rating: Poor Think about all the different things that someone might be looking for when entering the word "infants" into the search engine, ranging from gifts to medical advice. Yes, it's true that Babyfuzzkin's products do fall within this range, but so do millions of other sites. Here's a tip you can count on:

 Pearl of Wisdom: It's very rare that a one-word term is going to pass the relevance test—unless it's your business name!

Look at any one-word keywords on your list. In what other context, other than your immediate conversion goal, could searchers be using them?

Keyword: baby clothes, Relevance Rating: Good We would rate this relevance level as *Good* because it uses two rather generic words to accurately describe the product that

Babyfuzzkin sells. But it also encompasses lots of things that Babyfuzzkin doesn't sell. Searchers could use this term to look for used clothes and large chain stores in addition to boutique items like Jason is selling.

Keyword: unique baby clothes, Relevance Rating: Excellent This keyphrase uses a modifier—"unique"—to more clearly describe the product that Babyfuzzkin sells. You may be wondering, "Is a subjective word like 'unique' a good candidate for targeting?" It is, but only if you think it's accurate, and if you think people will use it to search for your product! So while "unique" may be appropriate for you to target, there's probably no point in targeting boastful terms like "best" or "finest." Sure, we know your offerings are the best, but is "best truck liners" really more relevant than something more specific on your list, like "heavy-duty truck liners"?

Keyword: cheap baby clothes, Relevance Rating: Very Poor We would rate this relevance level as *Very Poor* because Babyfuzzkin is a high-end product and does not match the description "cheap." While it may be tempting to target popular or appealing terms like "cheap," if it does not describe your product or service, it is going to be a wasted effort and a bust for conversions.

Keyword: unique baby shower gifts, Relevance Rating: Excellent This term describes Babyfuzzkin's products very specifically. As this example shows, highly relevant terms are often longer.

Keyword: Babyfuzzkin, Relevance Rating: Excellent You can't get a tighter match than the company name!

> **Now:** Go to the Keywords Worksheet and use your own judgment to add your values to the Relevance column.

Competition Level

In SEO, you've got to choose your battles. Sure, we'd all love to have great ranks for the most popular terms: "real estate," "games," "golf," or "Angelina Jolie." But the time and money spent for good ranking on these terms can be prohibitive. That's why the Competition Level column of the Keywords Worksheet exists: so you can know what you're getting into and set your expectations accordingly.

There are lots of ways to assess the competition level for a keyword; see the sidebar "Sizing Up the Competition" for some of our favorite methods. We're going to ask you to rate your keyword competition level from *Very Low* to *Very High*. What's most important is that you use the same measuring stick for all of your terms.

Sizing Up the Competition

The Left Brain and Right Brain look at different perspectives on estimating competition levels for keywords on your long list:

The Right Brain says, "You know your business, so you know what aspects of your business have more, or stronger, competitors. If you work for a bank, you don't need the numbers to tell you that the term 'low mortgage rates' is going to be very competitive. But for terms that are less obvious, you can do a competition gut check by searching for that term, and looking for the following indicators:

- "Do most of the sites in the top several pages of results appear to have the same conversion goals as you? Do you recognize some of your known competitors in there? Did you just find new competitors that you hadn't known about before? This is only one part of the competition landscape, but it's an important one."

- "Are most of the sites in the top several pages of results trying to sell something related to your term? Even SEO newbies can see that the vast majority of sites that show up for 'low mortgage rates' are trying to sell mortgages. But search for 'low literacy rates' and you can really see the difference—there's much less of a feeling that the site owners are jumping up and down, shouting, 'Over here!'"

- "How many sponsored listings do you see for the term in question? Sites that are selling something are likely to spend more time and money optimizing, so terms with a lot of commercial results are likely to be more competitive."

The Left Brain says, "Industry insight is important, but quantitative values give you more solid ground to stand on. Anyone estimating competition levels for a keyword should research these numbers:

- "How many pages on the Web are already optimized for the term? To estimate this value, you can perform a specialized search on Google and find out how many sites have that keyword in their HTML page title tag. Just type **allintitle: 'keyword'** into the search box. For example, Jason would type **allintitle: 'baby clothes'** to find out how many websites are using that term in their HTML title. (See our companion website at www.yourseoplan.com for other useful search tricks.)"

- "What are the top bid prices for the term on PPC services? In Part III, we'll explain how to set up accounts and check these values."

Here are the competition levels, and the thinking behind them, for a selection of Jason's picks:

Keyword: infants, Competition Level: Very High On a gut level, most single-word searches are going to rate as very competitive; there are just too many sites in the world that contain this term. Quantitatively speaking, the allintitle search on Google shows that there are over 2.2 million websites with the term in their HTML titles.

Keyword: baby clothes, Competition Level: Very High This term is also rather competitive. Obviously, there are numerous companies, some very large, that sell this product online and will be competing for this search traffic. You can click as far down as Yahoo!'s 10th search results page and there's no end in sight to the companies selling baby clothes. Google shows almost 200,000 pages with the term in their HTML titles.

Keyword: unique baby clothes, Competition Level: Moderate This one may not be so cut and dried. This is still a very competitive term at first glance: there's really not much difference in the "feel" of the competitor listings for this term as compared to the listings for "baby clothes." But with only roughly 300 pages showing on Google with this exact phrase in their HTML title, this term goes into the *Moderate* competition bracket.

Keyword: unique baby shower gifts, Competition Level: High There are only roughly 900 pages showing on Google with this exact phrase in their HTML titles. You might be tempted to call this one Moderate. But here's where the gut feeling comes in: *Unique* is a marketing word, making this term more commercial in nature. And take a look at the MSN search results in Figure 6.4. This is way down on page 15 of the search results, and you can still practically envision the websites trying to elbow each other out of the way to sell you their baby clothes. We would rate this term as *High* in competition.

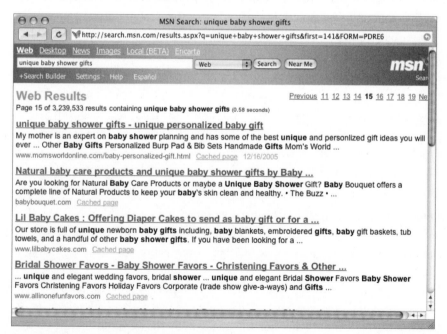

Figure 6.4 MSN search results for "unique baby shower gifts"

Keyword: babyfuzzkin, Competition Level: Very Low Actually, the competition level for this keyword is nonexistent. There are no sites ranking for it, and there don't appear to be any sites targeting it in their keywords.

 Now: Go to the Keywords Worksheet and add your values to the Competition column.

Friday: Your Short List

Your Keywords Worksheet is full of useful information. Now it's time to whittle down your list into a manageable group of 10 or so top target keywords! Here are the steps to a nicely honed list:

- The Keyword Balancing Act
- Combining Keywords
- Matching Keywords and Landing Pages
- Finalizing Your Short List

The Keyword Balancing Act

The most useful keywords will strike a balance between popularity, relevance, and competition. We're going to ask you to identify some of these more balanced keywords. Here are some examples of a good balance:

Lower Popularity/Higher Relevance A low popularity/high relevance combination means that even if there are not so many people searching for the term, the ones that do come are more likely to click on your listing, and ultimately convert on your site.

But don't go *too* low! Unless you have a reason to doubt the data, searches with zero popularity scores should probably not even be considered, except for your company name or a trademarked product name.

Higher Competitiveness/Higher Relevance If you are drawn to a competitive term, be sure that it is balanced out with a very high degree of relevance.

Higher Popularity/Lower Competition/Higher Relevance This is the ideal balance. If you can find terms that are used heavily by searchers, are closely tied to your conversion goal, and are targeted by a reasonable number of competitors, you want them on your short list!

Consider Jason's keyword list. The term "baby clothes" is popular, but it's extremely competitive and does not balance that disadvantage with a high relevance level. Not a good choice. On the other hand, "unique baby shower gifts," while on the high side in competition, balances its disadvantage with a very high relevance. See

Table 6.2; this term has great potential for Babyfuzzkin! Jason has flagged it using "highlight" formatting.

▶ **Table 6.2** Babyfuzzkin's Keywords

Keyword(s)	Search Popularity Wordtracker	Relevance	Competition Level	Landing Page URL
baby clothes	2125	good	very high	www.babyfuzzkin.com/clothes
infants	747	poor	very high	www.babyfuzzkin.com/clothes
unique baby shower gifts	667	excellent	high	www.babyfuzzkin.com/clothes

Now: Go to the Keywords Worksheet and highlight the terms that have the best balance between competition, relevance, and popularity.

Combine Keywords

Once you have your preferred terms flagged, look for terms that can be combined. For example, in Jason's case he can combine the terms "baby clothes" and "unique baby clothes" into just one term: "unique baby clothes." This is a great way to get double duty out of your SEO efforts, combining the search popularity of both terms.

If you are including geographical information with your keywords, now is the time to combine it with your other terms. For example, a manicure salon in Franklin, Missouri, may want to combine keywords to create the keyword phrases "manicure Franklin Missouri" and "salon Franklin Missouri."

Now: Go to the Keywords Worksheet and add combined terms to the list. Flag these as you go. They belong in your short list too.

Match Keywords to Landing Pages

For a keyword to perform well in the search engines, it needs to be matched to a landing page on your site that would be an excellent destination for someone searching for this term. A good landing page for a keyword will satisfy your visitors' needs, answer their questions, and direct them toward conversion if appropriate. Be sure the page contains information that is closely tied to the search term. And don't make the rookie mistake of only thinking about your home page:

 Pearl of Wisdom: Your home page will likely be the best landing page choice for your company name but not for many of your other keywords.

Let's say you work for a toy store. For the search term "godzilla action figures," a good landing page is the page that contains the description of the Godzilla action figures you're selling and a link to purchase them. For the more generic term "action figures," a good landing page might contain a menu of all the action figures you're selling with links to learn more about each one. By the way, the landing pages you select today do not need to currently have your keyword of choice on it; they just need to be relevant to the keyword. We'll help you add keywords later, in Your SEO Plan.

If you can't think of an existing page that is a good match for one of your keywords, you have two choices: plan to build a new landing page, or drop the keyword out of your short list.

 Now: One by one, step through your flagged keywords and assign a landing page to each one.

Finalize Your Short List

You've researched, you've analyzed, you've combined, and you've assigned. Now, it's time to drop those last few not-ready-for-prime-time terms!

We're going to ask you to trim your flagged list to your top 10 or so. You probably already have a good idea of which ones are your favorites, but in case you're still on the fence, here are some ways to frame your thought process:

Am I being inclusive? While you were assigning landing pages, did you discover that you have flagged too many terms for one audience or that you left a conversion out in the cold? You didn't fill out your Goals Worksheet in Chapter 1 for nothing. Use it now to help choose keywords that reflect all your target audiences and conversions.

Does my keyword have a good home? If you love a keyword but you can't find an existing landing page for it, now is the time to examine your reasoning for flagging it in the first place. Does it represent a legitimate opportunity or goal for your organization? Do you have the resources to build a page around this term? Do a reality check now, because it doesn't make sense to build Your SEO Plan around terms you can't optimize for.

Am I overcrowding a landing page? For best optimization, each landing page can accommodate only a small number of search terms (one to three is a good rule of thumb). If you're noticing that you entered the same landing page over and over again for many of your terms, you should ask yourself whether this is a problem with your site (i.e., whether you have too many different topics on one page), whether you can drop some of the extra terms, or if you just need to use your noodle to identify some additional landing pages.

Will my colleagues agree? It's important that others in your organization feel comfortable—or better yet, enthusiastic—about your top keywords. Enlist the help of your colleagues if you can! Send out your list for review, or arrange a meeting with members of your team who hold an interest: writers, content creators, marketing managers, executives, and so on. With all the data you've gathered and the deep thinking you've put into your keyword choices this week, you're in great shape to sell your favorites to your team.

> **Now:** Select your top 10 or so keywords, and then copy and paste them at the top of your Keywords Worksheet under Top Keywords.

Pat yourself on the back. You've just gotten through the most important, and perhaps the hardest, week in the whole book!

Week 2: Baseline Assessment

Suppose you went on a diet but you forgot to weigh yourself at the beginning of it. A week of exercise and green leafy vegetables later, you step on a scale and it reads 163 lbs. Is it great news or a great disappointment? You'll never know because you didn't establish your baseline. This week, you'll take care of the initial assessment for your SEO campaign so you'll always know whether it's time for a celebratory ice cream sundae.

Here are your daily task assignments:

Monday: Conversions

Tuesday: Ranks

Wednesday: Indexed Pages

Thursday: Inbound Links

Friday: Site Assessment

Monday: Conversions

In Chapter 1, we explained how important it is to track the success of your SEO campaign. In marketingspeak, these measurements are called *metrics*. Today we're interested in only one thing: conversion metrics. Different organizations can have vastly different metrics, ranging from the number of people buying your product to how many third graders download your science report. Whether it's online sales, brand awareness, or just eyeballs you're after, you know what your conversions are because you defined them way back in Chapter 1.

If your website has a system in place to track conversions, it's time to gather some data. The least you will want to know is this: *how many conversions has your site logged per month over the last three calendar months?* And if you can get additional information (for example, total conversion rate for *all* visitors versus conversion rate for *search engine* visitors), by all means, do. The more you document today, the more you'll know about the success or failure of your SEO campaign in the coming months.

You may know how to get this data by yourself, but if not, it's time to enlist your IT, sales, or PR team members for the information you need. If you haven't done so yet, be sure to welcome them to your SEO team, and tell them what an important task this is for the future of the organization…it may even be time to hand out some bribe cookies!

 Now: Open up a new blank document and record your three-month historical conversion numbers and any additional conversion data you can gather. Save this in your SEO Idea Bank; you'll need it again in Chapter 8.

To be sure, if you haven't been tracking conversions, you may think you have nothing to document today. We disagree. Somewhere, somehow, there must be some information about how your website is performing for you. If there's a request for information form on the site, how many people have used it? If you suspect that people are researching your company online and then ordering over the phone, see if you can get a salesperson to back you up. Or, just write down your suspicion. Even a guess is better than nothing here.

If you're pretty sure that the website hasn't given you any business, or recognition, or whatever it is you're looking for in the past three months, make a note of that, too. If you're starting from zero, congratulations! Your improvement will be very easy to measure.

Tuesday: Ranks

No matter how often we tell you not to obsess about ranks, we know you better than that. So if you're the one who spends your nights with visions of Googleplums dancing in your head, today is the day we'll let you give in to your passion!

Of course, conversions are more important than ranks, and your fundamental business goals are more important than search engine traffic. But great search engine ranks really do speak volumes, and checking your ranks can be a very enlightening experience.

Rank Assessment in a Nutshell

To start your assessment, open the Rank Tracking Worksheet that you downloaded from yourseoplan.com. On this worksheet, you'll see spaces for each of your top 10 keywords. (Adjust the number if you wish, but don't increase it much beyond 10 if you want to keep this task manageable!)

Here's how you'll do it:

- Moving one by one through your short list, search for your top keywords on Google. (To save time, you can set your search engines to display 30 results per page using the Preferences screen.)
- Scroll through the top 30 ranks. If any page on your website shows up within these results, note the rank in the Rank Tracking Worksheet. If you don't see your site in the ranks, mark "none."
- We're looking at the main Web results only! Don't record ranks in any other results sets, such as See Related, Local, or Sponsored Listings, as part of your standard rank check.
- Repeat with MSN, Yahoo!, and Ask.

Automated vs. Manual Rank Checking

There's no way around the fact that reviewing *all those* results on *all those* search engines for *all those* keywords can be a bit of a snoozer.

Some SEO professionals have dropped rank checking out of the equation altogether because it is less connected to your business goals than other metrics such as conversion tracking. Of SEOs that still perform rank checking, some use automated rank-checking software. Available programs include WebPosition, Ranking Manager, and Digital Point Solutions.

But even with all of the available tools, we still perform manual rank checking for our clients, and we insist on it for you too. Here's why:

- Manual rank checking is more accurate than automated checking. In the ever-changing search engine results landscape, it often takes a human to determine whether your listings are surrounded by directory sites, partner sites, or even sponsored listings.

- Manual rank checking keeps you in close touch with the goings-on in the search engine ranks for your target keywords. We want you to drink in the details. Keep an eagle eye out for your competition and any interesting or unusual results. Who is ranking well, and are they doing well on more than one engine? Have you spotted any possible cheaters? Did an unexpected page of your site (or a PDF or DOC file) show up? These are the kinds of things you can find if you take the time to look.

- Most search engines, including Google, frown upon automated rank-checking programs because they perform multiple queries that can create a burden on the search engine. Many of these tools actually violate the engines' terms of service (TOS).

If you absolutely *must* use an automated system (for example, your organization has a need to track a large number of keywords on a monthly basis), we recommend that you sign up with Digital Point Solutions, mentioned earlier, and get a free Google application programming interface (API) key (Digital Point provides instructions). If you do that, you will be in compliance with the Google TOS, and that means you will have our blessing too.

The Scenic Route

As we touched upon earlier, your manual rank-checking task has fringe benefits: it provides a great opportunity to watch out for "uglies": bad snippets, broken links, or any other interesting, mysterious, or undesirable results your website is showing in the search engines. Be sure to make a detailed note (or even a screen shot) of anything out of the ordinary (use the notes column in your Rank Tracking Worksheet, or enter it in your Task Journal) so that you can return to it later.

 Now: Go to your Rank Tracking Worksheet and fill in today's ranks. Write any interesting or unusual observations in your notes column or Task Journal.

Feel free to slip on your headphones as you work: rank checking is one of the more tedious SEO tasks.

Wednesday: Indexed Pages

A very basic fact of SEO is this: Before your website can rank well on the search engines, it must be *indexed*, or present, in the search engines. Is your website there to be found? Today you are going to find out by answering these questions:

- How many of my site's pages are indexed?
- Are my top landing pages indexed?
  In the next sections, we'll show how you'll do it.

Total Pages Indexed on Your Site

Follow these steps to find out the total number of pages within your domain that are present on the major search engines:

- Starting with Google, perform a search to find pages from within your domain only. Search engines have a special syntax for finding all pages in a site; for example, on Google you would type **site:*yourdomain.com*** (using your own site address in place of *yourdomain.com*) in the search box.

- Make a note of the number of pages returned. This is the total number of pages indexed from your domain. For example, in Figure 6.5 you can see that there are about 61,500 pages indexed within the domain mudcat.org.

- Repeat for MSN, Yahoo!, and Ask. This search can be tricky on some search engines. See our companion website at www.yourseoplan.com for an up-to-date list of search shortcuts and instructions.

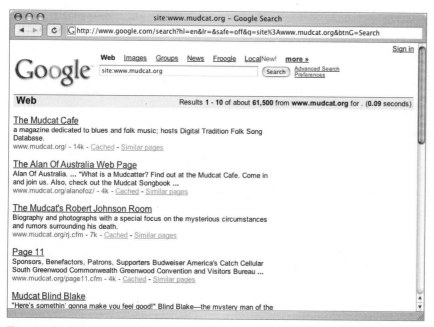

Figure 6.5 Google search results for Site:www.mudcat.org

Keep in mind that there are limitations to this value. The total number of indexed pages may include broken links and old pages on your site. Think of it as a "big picture" number for watching trends or catching big drop-offs.

 Now: Go to your Rank Tracking Worksheet and note the total number of pages indexed on each search engine.

Landing Pages Indexed

In addition to checking the total pages indexed, you'll want to determine whether each of your landing pages is indexed. After all, you wouldn't want to put a lot of time into optimizing a page that the robots can't see. Perform the following steps for each landing page:

- Enter the full URL of the landing page into Google's search box. If you get a listing for the exact page you were seeking, your page is indexed! See Figure 6.6 for an example.

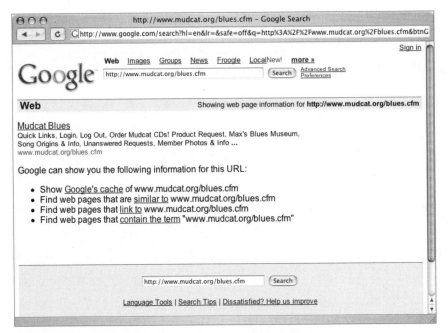

Figure 6.6 Search results for http://www.mudcat.org/blues.cfm

- If the exact page you're looking for doesn't show up for the full URL, double-check to make sure it's not indexed. Find a unique string of HTML text on your page—one that is not likely to exist on another site—and search for it in quotes. Searching for a unique term like "Robert Johnson, King of the Delta Blues. Rumors and Tales swirl with the name" isn't likely to bring up anyone's site but the one you're looking for.

- Perform the same check with Yahoo!, MSN, and Ask.

Now: Go to your Rank Tracking Worksheet and fill in Y or N for each of your landing pages in each of the four search engines.

My Site Doesn't Have Typical Landing Pages!

For most SEO campaigns, and especially for the SEO plan that an hour a day allows, it makes sense to focus your efforts on optimizing and tracking a small number of landing pages (no more than 10) on your site.

However, as we discussed in Chapter 2, there may be some of you who do not follow this system. For example, bloggers should consider every posting to be an equally important landing page. Large catalog sites may follow a shallow-wide approach, with the expectation that users can enter the website via hundreds of product pages. And for some businesses, the choice of landing pages will shift with the season.

When your situation calls for a large or changing number of landing pages, you will have to adjust accordingly: You may wish to track more pages, or just your home page, or a select group of sample pages chosen from different areas of your site. You may wish to do separate SEO campaigns in sequence, or even scale up Your SEO Plan.

Yes, this SEO plan is scalable. Give it 10 hours a day, and you can multiply your number of landing pages accordingly. Just don't forget to do the other little things in life, like bathing yourself and feeding your dog.

Thursday: Inbound Links

As you learned in Chapter 4, "How the Search Engines Work Right Now," the number of inbound links (other sites linking to your website, also known as *backlinks*) is an important part of the search ranking algorithm. Having plenty of inbound links will actually help your site in two important ways: indirectly, by improving your search engine ranking, and directly, by bringing visitors to your site through the link. In short, inbound links are valuable, and that's why Your SEO Plan will include some serious efforts in that arena.

Search engines are looking at not just the number of inbound links, but their quality too. Does the hyperlinked text say, "Click here for Computer Equipment Deals" or "Click here for Overpriced Junk"? Are the links buried deep within a domain, among millions of other outbound links? Search engine algorithms take these things into account—and so do your potential customers. You'll learn how to fully assess link quality in Part III, when you start your link-building campaign. For now, you'll stick to gathering the numbers: How many links are pointing to your landing pages?

Finding the total number of other sites that are linking to your landing pages can be quite simple: many search engines include search shortcuts that allow you to view a list of other sites that the search engine knows to be linking to specific pages within your domain. For example, on Google, MSN, and Yahoo! search for "link:http://www.*yourdomain.com/yourpage.html*" (using your own site address in place of *yourdomain.com/yourpage.html*) to find links to your page of choice. See the companion website at www.yourseoplan.com for a current list of search shortcuts and instructions.

You only need to find inbound links using one search engine, so choose the one you care most about. (Hmm…we wonder which one that will be?) And a warning: these numbers are not exact. Just use them for trend spotting.

Now: Now, using the search engine of your choice, go to your Rank Tracking Worksheet and fill in the total number of inbound links to each of your landing pages.

Friday: Site Assessment

Suppose you're a real estate investor, looking for a good money-making opportunity. You see two homes, both the same size and price. One home has been totally renovated and looks pristine. It's got a few recent add-ons and it fills up its lot nicely. The other home has some ugly carpeting over wood floors, chipped paint, and kitchen appliances that have seen better days. There's plenty of room for expansion on the lot. Clearly, you have a better chance of adding big bucks to the value of the second house after some investment of your time and money.

The same principle applies to your website. If your site is already well optimized, looking for big conversion increases from your SEO campaign may be a challenge. On the other hand, if your site is missing basic optimization, you can probably expect some good improvement in performance. This is why a site assessment is important: to identify areas in which your site is deficient, but also to set realistic expectations for results.

Take a look at the Site Assessment Worksheet you downloaded from yourseoplan .com. This worksheet provides a quick and easy way to get a handle on your site's current optimization level. Next, indicate yes or no for the following statements about each of your landing pages:

✔ This page has a unique HTML page title.

✔ The HTML page title contains my target keywords.

✔ This page contains 200 or more words of HTML text.

✔ HTML text on this page contains my exact target keywords.

✔ This page can be reached from the home page of the site by following HTML text links (not pull-downs, login screens, or pop-up windows).

✔ The HTML text links from other pages on my site to this page contain my target keywords.

We kept the worksheet short and sweet, but these quick answers provide a basic estimate of your current optimization level. And don't forget: Lower optimization just means more room to grow!

Now: Go to your Site Assessment Worksheet and fill in Y or N for each of your landing pages.

With your basic site assessment complete, you have a good picture of the current status of your website: current conversions, site ranks on the major search engines, inbound links, and your current site optimization level. This baseline assessment will serve you throughout your SEO campaign.

Week 3: Competition

Over the last couple of weeks, you've started to bulk up parts of your brain that are newly devoted to SEO. This week, we're going to use those portions of your brain to do something that you've been dying to do: snoop on your competitors. Here's how you've already gotten your feet wet in competitive analysis:

✔ You got a glimpse of your competitors' keyword preferences when you were selecting your own.

✔ You became acquainted with the top 30 players for all of your keywords during your rank check.

Now, we'll ask you to use your memory and your worksheets—and a couple of new tools and techniques—to dive all the way in:

Monday: Identify Your Top Five Competitors

Tuesday: Snooping Tools and Techniques

Wednesday: Assess On-Page Factors

Thursday: Assess Off-Page Factors

Friday: Paid Competition

Monday: Identify Your Top Five Competitors

Today you're going to choose which competitors to review in depth. To keep this week's tasks manageable, we recommend that you limit the number of top competitors you examine to five. This allows you to choose at least one from each of the three categories in the list that follows, and it leaves you with enough bandwidth to really dig in and dissect their strategies. If one of your biggest competitors doesn't have a website, then give them an honorary mention on your list. But for the purposes of this week, we want you to choose five competitors with at least some Web presence.

Your review will be the most meaningful if you select your "Big Five" from the following categories:

Business Competition Even if you know who the major players in your field are, you should check with your sales and executive team members to get the back story that you may not be aware of. For example, there may be different competitors for different products or target audiences. There may be a "new kid on the block" who's poised to enter a space that you're currently dominating. Or your company may have just lost a big job to someone in particular. Ask your colleagues to prioritize their competitors based on current issues, goals, and grudges.

Search Competition With last week's rank check fresh in your mind, you should have an excellent grasp of who's who in the top spots. Who did you see in the top ranks frequently enough to make you take notice? Whose listings were not only visible, but also well written? Whether these companies hold a candle to your organization in real life isn't relevant here. Even if they're just a blip on your business radar, if they're attracting the eyeballs that you want, you need to find out how they're doing it.

Pay-per-Click Competition Even though PPC and organic listings are different animals, they are displayed in direct competition to each other in the search engine results. So if there is a company out there who is showing up in the sponsored links for your targeted keywords, you may want to add it to your Big Five.

Search Results Competition

The left brain and right brain have different ideas about monitoring who is taking those coveted top spots in the search results.

The Right Brain says, "This is one of those SEO tasks that you can let flow over you. Search for your target keywords, browse the results and you are likely to see some patterns emerging. Maybe there is a certain site that never shows at number one but has lots of results on the second and third pages of the search results. Maybe another site is consistently in the top five for several of your top terms. You would be right to include these among your Big Five search competition."

The Left Brain says, "When I used to grade papers in graduate school, I sometimes noticed my standards getting stricter and stricter as the hours passed. Pity those kids with tests at the bottom of the pile! The same thing can happen when you use a 'hunch' approach to choosing your competition: After an hour of reviewing search results, your opinions are likely to creep. That's why I think you should choose a simple numerical evaluation method: Your potential competitor gets a point for every time their site shows up in the top 30 for your keywords—and five points for every time in the top 10. Check your searches, add up the points, and there you have it: your search competition rises to the top."

As you're going through your search and PPC competition, be on the lookout for "left field" competition. These are listings that are displayed for the same keywords that you're targeting but have no connection to your organization's focus. For example, the directors of the Green Acres Day Camp in Toronto are going head-to-head with trivia sites about the old *Green Acres* TV show. Whether you choose to review one of these sites is up to you. But if you're finding a lot more "left field" competitors than you expect, you may need to rethink your keyword choices.

Now: Use your own knowledge and your team's help to define your Big Five competitors. Add their names and home page URLs to the Competition Worksheet.

Tuesday: Snooping Tools and Techniques

Poking and peeking into other people's business is part of Web culture and one of the more entertaining aspects of an SEO campaign. When you open up a browser and look at a website, you're seeing just the content that developers intended for you to see. But there is a great deal more information available about a site, ranging from data on who owns the domain to the scripts used on the page. Here are a few tools and techniques that we have found most useful:

- The Google Toolbar
- Viewing page source
- Alexa data

The following sections include the details you need to make these methods your own.

The Google Toolbar

This is a very popular tool with searchers and SEOs alike! If you already have it, you know how useful it is. If not, get ready for a treat.

The Google Toolbar, which can be downloaded from http://toolbar.google.com/, is a free add-on to your browser (Internet Explorer or Firefox) that contains several features to enhance your web surfing experience (see Figure 6.7).

Figure 6.7 The Google Toolbar

The toolbar feature that we're most interested in utilizing for our SEO efforts is a little green bar labeled PageRank. This bar displays the Google PageRank value for the web page being viewed. As you learned in Chapter 4, the PageRank value certainly has its limitations. However, viewing it in the toolbar can give you a quick and easy estimate of how important Google thinks a certain page is. You can also use the "backwards links" feature to determine how many pages are pointing to a specific URL, but you should be aware that Google doesn't show all of the links that point to a page; some are omitted.

If you would rather not install the Google Toolbar, you can see PageRank information, and lots of other fascinating tidbits of data, at www.faganfinder.com/urlinfo/.

 Now: Go to http://toolbar.google.com and download and install the Google Toolbar.

Viewing Page Source

Anyone who's put together a website already knows how to view page source. But if you don't ever touch your site's code, this may be a new experience for you. Viewing page source is a simple way to see the inside workings of your competitors' (or anyone else's) website. *Source* is shorthand for *source code*, which is the HTML content that tells the browser what to show on the screen. In the source code, you can see all of the invisible text elements, such as meta tags and ALT tags (discussed in Chapter 3, "Eternal Truths of SEO.") You can also view the HTML title tag and other behind-the-scenes information on your competitor's page (see Figure 6.8).

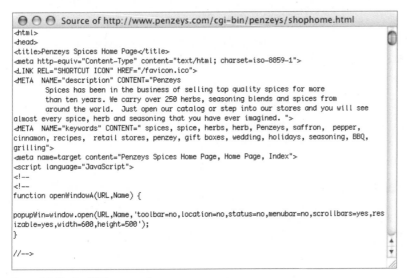

Figure 6.8 Viewing HTML source code

It's easy to view source in major browsers. Here's how:

- In Internet Explorer, select View > Source from the Explorer menu.
- In Safari, select View > View Source from the Safari menu.
- In Firefox, select View > Page Source from the Firefox menu.

On Wednesday, we're going to ask you to view source to assess your competitors. But for now, take some time to get used to viewing source code on your own site.

Now: Practice viewing page source by opening up your own website and viewing the source code on a few pages.

Alexa Data

The Alexa database, located at www.alexa.com, provides interesting tidbits of info about websites: a screen shot of the home page, traffic data, inbound links, site owner contact information, related links, and even a link to old versions of the website on the Internet Archive (aka the Wayback Machine). Most addictive of all, Alexa estimates your website's traffic rank among all sites on the Web.

Many in the SEO community have serious doubts about the accuracy of Alexa's numbers and believe that Alexa's stats are easy to manipulate, so take them with a grain of salt. But if you are looking for quick answers to general questions about a website (Is this some crazy spammer or a legit business?), Alexa might be a good place to start.

To see a website's details, search for the full URL in Alexa's search box. If you fall in love with Alexa, you can even download an Alexa toolbar to add to your browser, similar to the Google Toolbar.

 Now: Go to www.alexa.com and search for your own website URL. See what comes up!

Wednesday: Assess On-Page Factors

Today, you're going to look inside your competitors' sites to determine whether there is any evidence of SEO. You'll be researching the following elements:

- Targeted keywords
- Basic optimization
- General characteristics of the site

In the following sections, we'll go into the finer points:

Targeted Keywords

First, try to determine what, if any, keywords your Big Five competitors are targeting.

Sometimes a competitor's targeted keywords will make themselves clear if you simply review the text on their site. It's a fair bet that your competitors are targeting many of the same keywords that you are, so you can glance through their page content and look for those terms or for similar terms that you may have considered for your own site.

But are they actually targeting these terms for SEO, or did their copywriter just get lucky with word choice? The quickest way to get a read on a competitor's SEO schemes is to view the meta keywords tag. You'll need to delve into the source code to do this. Inside the tag, your competitor's keyword list might include 500 words, it might be ridiculously un-optimized (formatted as a sentence or full of words like *a*, *an*, *the*, and *quality*), or it might seem to be a tightly focused, relevant list from which you can glean a hint of a strategy. While you're in the code, look for keywords in the HTML title and meta description too.

By the way, if you've never stepped through someone else's HTML code, it can be a little disorienting. It can help to use your browser's find function (usually Ctrl+F, or Edit > Find in the browser menu) to search for the words *meta* or *title*. These should land you in the general vicinity of the tags you're looking for.

For each of your Big Five competitors, open the home page and at least one other page on their site to scan the copy and view the tags. You aren't looking to record the top 50 terms here, just the ones that seem to be in direct competition with your own conversion goals.

Now: Open your Competition Worksheet and list targeted keywords of note for your Big Five competitors.

As you're sniffing around your competitors' page content and tags, you may find a keyword here or there that you hadn't thought of. You might want to highlight these terms in your Competition Worksheet; you can save them for future research.

Basic Optimization

Now, think back to the site assessment questions that you asked about your own landing pages last week. We'll have you look at a trimmed-down version of the list, which you can use to assess the home page, and at least one interior page, of each of your Big Five competitors' websites:

✔ Does the HTML page title for this page contain their target keywords?

✔ Does the HTML text on this page contain their target keywords?

✔ Can this page be reached from the home page of the site by following HTML text links (not pull-downs, login screens, or pop-up windows)?

Answer each of these questions to the best of your ability. If they get two or more yes answers, give them a yes for basic optimization on the Competition Worksheet.

Now: Fill in Y or N in the Basic Optimization column on your Competition Worksheet.

General Characteristics of the Website

Give your competitors' websites a spin, thinking back to Chapters 3 and 4, and try to identify anything that's important about their sites' structure as it relates to SEO. Are important pages hidden behind a login or locked inside a database? Is their entire site developed with Flash, or is too much of their message presented as graphical text? (To determine whether website text is graphical or HTML, try to highlight it with your mouse. If you can highlight one letter at a time, it's HTML. If you can only highlight the entire word plus some of the background, it's graphical.) Is the site particularly text heavy? Does the site have useful, unique, or constantly changing noncommercial content that might increase its linkability?

You'll naturally be curious about lots of other, not-just-for-SEO factors as you click around your competitors' sites, like fun features that you covet for your own site. There's nothing wrong with keeping track of those elements somewhere, too (Task Journal entry, anyone?). But for our purposes, we'd just like you to jot down your general impressions in the General Site Characteristics column of the Competition Worksheet. Here are some examples of General Site Characteristics notes:

- This site has a tendency to overuse graphical text.
- Not once on this site was the long form of the acronym AMC spelled out!
- There's a ton of text, which is good for SEO, but it causes their design to suffer.

 Now: Enter your assessment of general site characteristics on your Competition Worksheet.

Thursday: Assess Off-Page Factors

Today you'll be looking at factors that are largely outside of the control of your competing site owners. Whether it's ranks, inbound links, or other algorithm-benders like Google PageRank, you want to know how the world at large is treating the sites you want to beat.

Ranks You already thought about your competitors' ranks when you named your Big Five. Maybe you singled out a competitor simply because they were ranking well, or maybe you chose one that has terrible ranks but has been stealing your "real-world" customers away. Now, summarize the overall ranking status of each of your Big Five competitors on your Competition Worksheet. This assessment doesn't need an exact value—it's enough to indicate whether they're dominant or barely there.

> **Now:** Open your Competition Worksheet and indicate the ranking status of your Big Five competitors.

Inbound Links Uncovering the number of competitors' inbound links can be a real eye-opener, especially if they seem to have good ranks without great site optimization. While you can't be sure that a large number of inbound links are directly influencing the ranks, it's a helpful piece of the puzzle.

Open the same search engine that you used to check your own inbound links in Week 2 so that you're comparing apples to apples. Using the specialized link search, determine how many links each of your Big Five competitors has pointing to their home page. Then, perform the same check for a few major interior pages of their site. The worksheet has room for three interior pages, but you can add more if you want.

> **Now:** Fill in the number of inbound links to your Big Five competitors on your Competition Worksheet.

Google PageRanks Using the Google Toolbar that you downloaded on Tuesday, determine the Google PageRank for your competitors' home page, and for the same interior page(s) you assessed for inbound links.

> **Now:** Enter the Google PageRank for your Big Five competitors on your Competition Worksheet.

While you're at it, take your Google Toolbar for a test drive through your own site today and find the Google PageRank for each of your landing pages.

> **Now:** Enter the Google PageRank for each of your landing pages on your Rank Tracking Worksheet.

Google PageRank is good to know, but it's not essential. If you're short on time, don't worry about gathering this data.

Friday: Paid Competition

Now that you know which of your competitors appear to be putting an effort into SEO, you probably have a hunch about which ones are shelling out the dough for paid campaigns. Today you'll play "spot the PPC ad" to get a sense of your competitors' activities in the PPC arena.

It can be challenging to find competitors' pay-per-click ads. Even if you go looking for a particular ad, there's no guarantee that you'll find it. Some PPC services "rotate their inventory" so that you might not be able to view a certain company's ad if you happen to be looking at the wrong time of day. Or your competitor may have an ad with such a low bid that you'd have to spend too much time trying to unearth it from 20th-page results. And, of course, your competitors can turn their ads on or off at any time, so you may never know if there's *really* a PPC campaign with your competitor's name on it.

Regardless, it's worth it to look because if you do find something, it can give you great insight into what matters most to your competitors. Here's how you'll do it:

- Moving one by one through your Big Five competitor list, perform a search for each competitor's company name on Google.

- Scroll through the top two or three pages of results. If you find an ad for your competitor, mark "yes" in the PPC column.

- If you don't find your competitor's ad, search for a specific product or service that they offer. If that turns up no ads, broaden your search to a general term related to what they offer. If you still don't find your competitor, you can feel comfortable marking "none found" in the PPC column.

- Repeat with Yahoo!, MSN, and Ask.

Remember to look at sponsored listings only, not organic search results! If you do find something that looks like a competitor's ad, click on it to make sure it actually goes to your competitor's site. There are lots of PPC ads put out by affiliate sites and resellers, and if that's the case with the ads you find, then it's not really your competitor's ad. For example, do a search for any well-known brand-name medicine, like "Claritin" (or, if you don't mind your colleagues seeing what you've got on your monitor, "Viagra" or "Rogaine"). There are lots of ads with that brand name, but only one is for the company that actually makes the product.

If you have time, you can learn a lot about your competitors by checking to see if they have directory listings. See Chapter 10 to learn how.

You've worked hard filling your worksheets—and your brain—with data and observations! Next, in Week 4, you'll compile it into meaningful information that you can share with your colleagues.

Week 4: Baseline Monthly Report

You know the famous question about a tree falling in the forest? The same applies to your SEO campaign:

Pearl of Wisdom: No matter how hard you work and what you achieve, nobody will know about it unless it's documented.

And, brains being what they are, even you *yourself* will probably forget half of what you did this month. The document you compile this week will be the basis for your future monthly reports, which will be your go-to documents for what you've accomplished, what's wrong, what's right, and where you need to go from here.

This week, you'll assemble your work from Weeks 1 through 3, add some thoughtful commentary, and present your findings in a way that provides a quick take-away for anyone who has a stake in the success of Your SEO Plan. And if you ever need to move on to new endeavors, this document and your ongoing monthly reports will be something you can easily hand over to a replacement.

We won't tell you exactly how to format your document, and we'll trust you to organize and present the information in a way that makes sense to you and your team. Some types might like splashy colors or even charts to compare the popularity of various keywords. Others might prefer a "just the facts, ma'am" approach. What's most important to us is that the information is written down for the record books:

Monday: Keywords, Landing Pages, and Competition

Tuesday: Site Visibility

Wednesday: Conversions and Red Flags

Thursday: Personalize

Friday: Quick Reference

I Hate Paperwork!

Do you hear that? Our eye-rolling detector is beeping! Someone out there is about to complain that all this documentation is useless!

In our expert opinion, the Monthly Report is a cornerstone of a well-balanced plan. Why? Because we firmly believe that data is useless unless it's interpreted in a meaningful way.

A seasoned SEO professional confesses: "One of my first SEO projects was when I worked at a web development firm, and SEO was an add-on to building a website. With SEO being a new service, we had no established system for documenting or reporting on this work. I diligently performed all the tasks for the initial discovery phase of the project: choosing keywords, assessing the site and its competitors, and making recommendations for next steps. With each of these tasks, I worked closely with our client and e-mailed him all of the related data.

"At the end of the project, my boss (who didn't know SEO but certainly knew business best practices!) suggested that I put together a final report. What did I do? I printed out my previous documents and data, stapled them all together, and slapped on a title page.

"What a disaster! The client had nothing to show his boss, nobody wanted to wade through the data, and I wasted more time re-explaining everything I had done than I would have spent writing up a summary in the first place. Worse, all of the added value from my work—the thought, research, discussion and analysis that had gone into our choices—was lost!

"Luckily, the client was forgiving. But I learned a hard lesson with that project: Document what you do and write it with a close eye on your intended audience!"

Have you guessed yet that the SEO pro quoted here is one of the authors? Lucky for you, you can learn from our mistakes! The point of week 4 is not just to document your work, but also to do the analysis and mental sifting that allows you to write about it intelligently. The way you tell your SEO *story* is what will ultimately separate you from the SEO hacks and newbies out there. Your Monthly Report is a team builder, a boss pleaser, and a mental reinforcement for your SEO learning curve, all wrapped in a sensible white-inkjet-bond-paper bow.

Monday: Keywords, Landing Pages, and Competition

You'll start your Baseline Monthly Report with a description of your activities from Weeks 1 through 3: what you did, what you discovered, and the important choices you (and your team) made. We'll start you off with a possible first sentence for each:

Your Keyword Choice

"Top priority keywords were chosen based on an analysis of popularity with searchers, relevance to our site, and competition."

Now, you've got some 'splaining to do: Explain the thought process that went into your choices. Perhaps you want to mention keywords that were considered but disqualified or the various keywords that you combined for more efficient targeting. Just a couple of sentences will do. You will want to revisit and reanalyze your keyword picks eventually, maybe as soon as six months from now, so getting this down in writing now will save you from having to reconstruct your original analysis.

Your Landing Page Choice

"Top landing pages were chosen to correspond with our conversion goals and our top-priority keywords."

Now, to make this meaningful, be sure to comment on any judgment calls you made when choosing landing pages: "I picked the 'easels' page rather than the 'artistic tools' page because I think it will be easier to edit." This is also the place to make a note of any new landing pages that need to be built and perhaps even your ideas for appropriate content on these pages. In a broad way, this section gives you a chance to have your say about anything you think is missing in your site's content.

Your Competitive Analysis

"Top five competitors were chosen based on input from the sales department and observations regarding which sites had consistent rankings in the top 30 spots on Yahoo!, Google, MSN, and Ask."

Now, feed your readers some juicy gossip: What was the most interesting and/or enlightening aspect of your competitors' search presence? Did you identify any trends that showed what you're up against? Some possible additions to this section might be "Our biggest search competitor is Nickeldyme Inc., who has a high level of optimization and consistent top-10 ranks for our target keywords" or "I could find very little evidence that any of our competitors have put any effort into SEO, which represents an opportunity for us to take the lead."

Now: Complete the "Keywords," "Landing Pages," and "Competition" portions of your Baseline Monthly Report.

Tuesday: Site Visibility

Anybody *can* look at your spreadsheets to figure out how your site is doing with regard to the hard numbers—ranks, links, and indexing—but probably less than half the people you encounter will *want to*. What's more, it's likely that the people who glaze over when they see a column of numbers will be the people you feel should know about them the most. So today you're going to boil the stats down into succinct, readable descriptions.

Indexed Pages

First, write your basic findings: "Our site's top 10 landing pages are all indexed in Google, Yahoo!, MSN, and Ask." Or "Our 'Donate Now' page is missing from Google's and MSN's indices."

What you wrote in this section has big implications for the SEO-friendliness of your site's design! Use your knowledge about robot-friendly design from Chapter 3 to explain your findings. Possible analysis would include "Having all pages indexed indicates that our site structure is amenable to robot crawling," "Our site's login requirement is probably an impediment to indexing," or "The absence of pages in the indices may be due to the fact that our site only launched last month."

We probably don't have to tell you that if your landing pages are not being indexed, something must be done about it! If you've determined that the "something" is changing your site's structure or design, you should say so in this report and make sure this report is seen by the person on your team who can make the change. This has two important benefits: One, even if you're suggesting radical changes, you're backing them up with facts. And two, if nobody does anything about the problem and it comes back to haunt you later, you have documentation proving that you made this recommendation.

Ranks

Keep the long list of website rankings out of this report unless someone on your team has a penchant for numerical details. Instead, summarize your rankings in a sentence or two. Here are some possible examples:

- "We are ranking in the top 30 for only two of our top keywords."
- "We are on the top search results page for most of our top keywords."
- "Since none of our pages are indexed in the search engines, we have no rankings in the top 30 spots."

Ranks can be influenced by many factors, and it may be premature for you to attempt to explain yours at this stage. But by the time you compile the third monthly report in Your SEO Plan, you'll have a much fuller sense of what your ranks mean. So consider adding something like this: "I will perform monthly rank checks to keep abreast of the situation." Now, here's the sentence that we *don't* want you to write: "Site optimization will be sure to bring us into the top 10 for our target keywords." Review the sidebar "A Note on Reasonable Expectations" and predict with caution.

Inbound Links

First, write the basic facts: "The total number of inbound links recorded on MSN for our top 10 landing pages is 537. This number is an estimate provided by the search engine, not a definite number."

Next, some analysis is needed. There are several approaches you can take:

- **The quality of the links:** "We have several vendor sites linking to our 'factory locations' page."

- **The quantity of links, compared to your competitors' links:** "Our home page has fewer than half the inbound links compared to Competitor X."

- **The quantity of links, compared among your pages:** "Our home page has approximately 500 inbound links, but our other landing pages have, on average, fewer than 15."

In Part III, your assignments will include the pursuit of quality inbound links. Let your readers know it: "To improve the number of inbound links, this SEO campaign will include a link-building campaign."

Now: Complete the "Site Visibility" portion of your Baseline Monthly Report.

Wednesday: Conversions and Red Flags

Here are two headlines that are going to attract the attention of the people reading your report: Conversions and Red Flags. Make sure you give them what they want to see today.

Conversions

Start with the data you were able to gather about current conversions, whether specific ("Our Sales Director logged 82 confirmed leads from our website last month") or vague ("We received $7,000 in donations last month, but it is unclear what role the website played in this").

Most likely, someone out there is not happy with your current conversion level or you wouldn't be reading this book. Be sure to include the goals and hopes of the powers that be: "Increasing sales of the new Soap Gift Baskets will be the focus of this campaign" or "We hope to improve our conversion rate (currently only 0.5 percent) by bringing in more targeted traffic." Stating this in writing shows that you're aware of what's important for your organization. If you're feeling the urge to include an estimate of how many new conversions your SEO campaign will bring in, feel free to do your best, but read our sidebar on reasonable expectations first!

This is also the place to discuss plans for future conversion tracking, if you have any. (But if you don't, don't worry! You'll get a whole week for conversion tracking in Part III).

A Note on Reasonable Expectations

Have you ever heard something like this from your auto mechanic: "Well, we can try to replace some parts, but we can't be exactly sure that it'll stop the rattling sound, and oh, by the way, it'll cost ya a bundle"?

SEO can be pretty similar. There are so many factors involved in SEO—some within your control (for example, page text and site structure) and some far, far outside of your control (for example, search engine ranking algorithms or partnerships)—that it is very hard to predict outcomes. But we know that in real life you need to have at least some inkling of what you can expect from your efforts. Mechanics offer estimates; SEO pros offer reasonable expectations. Here are some factors that can point to success for your SEO campaign: easy fixes, such as basic optimization factors that are missing from your current site; well-balanced keywords with low competition, high relevance, and high popularity; a poor current status; an enthusiastic team; a good budget for PPC; and competitors stuck in the Stone Age. How these factors combine and balance will affect your expectations. Let's look at some possible combinations and what you might conclude:

Poor Current Status/High Current Optimization/No Easy Fixes This a difficult combination. Your current optimization level is already high, which means you don't have a lot of space for improvement. You should set your expectations low, perhaps focusing on fixing red flags and your least-competitive keywords.

Fair Current Status/Poor Optimization/An Enthusiastic Team You have room to grow and a team that can make it happen. It's reasonable to expect to bump up your Fair status. But will it go to Good, Very Good, or Excellent? That depends on the other factors: competitiveness, budget, easy fixes, and so on.

High Competition/An Unenthusiastic Team/A Healthy PPC Budget With two major factors working against you, you can't expect that your organic SEO campaign will show strong results. The PPC budget just might be able to pick up the slack.

We hope we've made it clear that there is a lot you can't predict in SEO. We've done our best to give you a general idea of what you might expect, but you should be very careful not to make any promises you can't keep. Remember, reputable SEOs *never* guarantee any particular rank on search engines.

Red Flags

Through the course of your data-gathering over the last few weeks, you probably came across several red flags. These are the isolated tidbits of information that make humans so much better at doing SEO work than any kind of automated system. We hope that you remembered to note these thoughts in your Task Journal because today you'll be gathering them into your Baseline Monthly Report.

For this section, we want you to write issues that do not specifically fall under the other categories in this document, so "poor rankings" or "not enough inbound links" shouldn't go here. Red flags are issues that may be detrimental to your overall SEO health and that need to be addressed sometime in the future. Here are some examples:

- None of our files have meta description tags.

- I found several outdated listings for the following URLs available on Yahoo! and MSN....

- I found the term "X" instead of our current products in our listings.

- There are a large number of nonindustry competitors in the top ranks for our terms.

- Most of our inbound links are using the old product names and logos.

Don't get bogged down in trying to figure out exactly how to handle these red flags. As you proceed through your plan in Part III, you will be given time to address them. Just make sure to soften the blow with a statement like "I will be working to address these over the next several weeks." And you will, with our help!

Now: Complete the "Conversions" and "Red Flags" sections of your Baseline Monthly Report.

Thursday: Personalize

Use this day to tune your Baseline Monthly Report for its intended audience. You know your team and your boss, so you know whether they'll drool over a section titled "How to Bring Us to the TOP!" or a section titled "Search Marketing Best Practices." And you know if your team likes to read a lot of details or needs bullet-point summaries that they can glance through while they rush between meetings. Today, you'll spiff up your document with those bells and whistles that separate the "wha?" from the "wow!"

Finalize your document in a way that speaks to your organization's hot buttons. Possible optional sections are listed here:

- "Positive Findings" for the organization that likes to see the glass as half full
- "Highlights of Competitive Analysis" for a boss who focuses on what the other guy's doing
- Charts of relative keyword popularity, relevance, and competition for a visually oriented team
- Team planning: who will do what, for organizations with a lot of concern about staffing and labor management

 Now: Add the personalizing touches to your Baseline Monthly Report.

Friday: Quick Reference

You spent three weeks researching and analyzing data about keywords, your competition, your site performance, and optimization, not to mention your business goals and conversions from Chapter 1. But you want others to be able to "get it" in a 5-minute read (or, let's be realistic, a 2-minute skim). A Quick Reference should do the trick.

Build your Quick Reference with the following:

What is this SEO campaign trying to accomplish? You may wish to copy and paste your Conversions table, including desired conversions and target audiences, from the Goals Worksheet you completed in Chapter 1.

What are the top keywords and landing pages? List your top keywords and the landing pages that you finalized in Week 1. We recommend that you break the keywords and landing pages into two separate lists for ease of reading.

Who are our top competitors? Copy the names of your Big Five competitors from your Competition Worksheet. Use your judgment to characterize the search engine competition as a whole on a scale of Not Competitive to Very Competitive.

What is our current site visibility and performance? Rate the overall level of your site's current status on search engines and conversion performance: Poor, Fair, Good, Very Good, or Excellent. If you're finding mostly negative information in your links and status assessments, lots of red flags, and an unsatisfactory conversion rate, you're probably in the Poor slot. To get an Excellent grade, your site would need to have top page results for most or all of its target keywords, a lot of high-quality inbound links, a conversion level that you're happy with, and very few or no red flags.

What is our current site optimization level? Rate your site's current optimization level on a scale of Poor to Excellent. Review your site optimization worksheet. Do you see mostly yes answers? This means that your landing pages are in good optimization shape. A spattering of yeses and nos? Put your site in the Fair category. A whole lotta nothing? Rate your site Poor.

> **Now:** Complete the "Quick Reference" portion of your Baseline Monthly Report.

Now it's time to spread the news: Your SEO campaign is off and running! Deliver this report to anyone who has an interest or potential role in Your SEO Plan, and make yourself available to discuss it.

You've done so much for your organization and your own SEO knowledge this month! We can't wait for you to join us in Part III, when we roll up our sleeves and get into the nitty-gritty of SEO!

Your SEO Plan

You've made it through the foundation and strategy phases, and finally it's time to implement Your SEO Plan! In this part, you'll follow three months of day-by-day steps to take advantage of your site's positive attributes and address its imperfections, and you'll establish daily habits to keep targeted traffic coming to your site.

Month One:
Kick It into Gear

7

This month, you'll make a first pass at three cru-cial areas in your SEO campaign: organic opti-mization, link building, and PPC. You'll spend a week making real headway on each activity, with daily tasks that we estimate will take an hour or less. Then, this month and every month, we're leaving a week for visibility checks and reporting.

Chapter Contents

Week 1: Basic Site Optimization

Next week you're going to work hard at finding site owners and convincing them to link to you. But before you call this kind of attention to your website, you'll need to spend a full week primping, polishing, and checking for the proverbial spinach in your site's teeth.

In Chapter 3, "Eternal Truths of SEO," you learned that the text in your landing pages, tags, and titles is one of the most important and long-standing SEO factors. This week you're going to optimize them, with the goal of positively influencing how search engines view and rank your website. You'll also tackle basic site structure issues to ensure that search engine robots have easy access to your landing pages. With these improvements in place, your site will have a basic level of optimization: nothing tricky or fancy, and no time wasted on tiny technicalities, just common-sense, best-practices solutions.

You'll keep track of all your changes in one document as you go, and on Friday you'll deliver this document to the folks in charge of making edits to your website. If you're the code-slinger on the project, wait until Friday to dive into your edits! Stay in the "optimization groove" Monday through Thursday and you'll benefit from a more focused approach.

Here are your daily task assignments:

Monday: Page Titles

Tuesday: Meta Tags

Wednesday: Robot Walk-Through

Thursday: Site Text

Friday: Implementation

Full Speed Ahead

SEO is a long-term maintenance activity, comprising both productive spells and waiting periods. Your SEO Plan is designed so that your waiting time (waiting for site owners to get back to you, waiting for your team to implement your recommendations, waiting for the search engines to notice what you've done, and so on) isn't spent idly. Rather, you'll use this time to take on new activities. And even though you'll constantly move into new SEO territory as the plan progresses, you'll periodically come back to revisit and continue the work you started in earlier weeks.

The one exception is PPC management, which requires frequent quick checks. So once your PPC account gets rolling, we'll incorporate these quick checks into days that are designated for other tasks.

No fair trying to sneak in and start the Plan without getting organization-wide buy-in for your top keyword choices! If you haven't done so, do it now. It is very difficult and time consuming to change keywords after the fact. Your time is too valuable to waste on the wrong terms or to swing and miss with your conversion goals.

Monday: Page Titles

In Chapter 3, you learned that HTML page titles show up as the first line of clickable text in most search engine results. That fact, along with their considerable influence in search engine ranking algorithms, makes HTML page titles one of the most important optimization spots on your website.

Today, you're going to take a stab at writing unique and compelling page titles for each of your landing pages. We've created a document where you can keep track of these edits, called the Site Optimization Worksheet.

Now: Go to www.yourseoplan.com and download the Site Optimization Worksheet.

You'll want the Quick Reference sheet you created in Chapter 6, "Your One-Month Prep: Baseline and Keywords" handy, to keep you in tune with your goals and keywords as you write. We've compiled some Dos and Don'ts to keep you on the right track:

DO keep it short. Like a telephone answering machine that cuts you off before you finish talking, most search engines display only 40 to 60 or so characters in the listing title. So to get your message across, you should include important keywords toward the beginning of the title and make sure that the first 40 to 60 or so characters of your title form a complete thought.

DO include your keywords… Your HTML page title is important in the ranking algorithm, so it must include your target keywords! Since your space is limited, focus on the two to three keyterms that you previously matched with your landing page. Feeling a bit squeezed by the 40 to 60 character cutoff? Remember that you can combine keywords to save space.

…but DON'T overdo it! First and foremost, you want to connect with your intended audience. Excessive keyword repetition is a short-sighted strategy. Is this a marketing message or a synonym sandwich?

Baby Bedding, Crib Bedding, **Baby** Crib Bedding Sets, **Baby** Nursery ...
Baby Bedding & Nursery Crib Bedding Sets **Baby** Bedding - Huge Selection of **Baby** Nursery Bedding, Crib Bedding sets to brighten up your **baby's** nursery.
www.netkidswear.com/bedding.html - 86k - Dec 20, 2005 - Cached - Similar pages

Remember to think of the big picture! Your approach to site optimization will affect more than just ranks…it will also affect your customers' decision to part with their time and money.

DO include your name. Your organization's name will not only differentiate your listing from your competitors', it may earn you more clicks. Maybe your name carries a good reputation with it, or maybe it provides important context, making your listing more attractive or relevant. Notice how the company names in the following listings provide crucial context for the search term "bass articles."

Harmony Central®: **Bass** Resources
How to do Your Own **Bass** Setups - An **article** from The Bottom Line that leads ...
Compact **Bass** Guitar Speaker Bottom - An **article** about building light weight ...
www.harmony-central.com/Bass/ - 36k - Dec 20, 2005 - Cached - Similar pages

Smallmouth Quest Smallmouth **Bass Articles**
Smallmouth Quest is a website dedicated to **bass** fishing in North America.
Darl Black smallmouth fishing guide will provide you information on new **bass** lures ...
www.smallmouthquest.com/smallmouth_**bass**_quest.htm - 33k - Cached - Similar pages

DON'T assume your slogan does the job. Even if branding is your only objective, you need to think about whether your slogan contains your targeted keywords and, if so, whether you think it will encourage visits to your site. This listing shows a very catchy slogan.

SPLENDA® Brand Sweetener - Welcome to a World of Sweetness
Now you can purchase your favorite SPLENDA® Sweetener **Products**, including a web-exclusive SPLENDA® Holiday Kit at the touch of a button at the SPLENDA® ...
www.splenda.com/ - 21k - Cached - Similar pages

But is it really better for visibility and clicks than using targeted keywords such as "recipes," "low carb," or "diabetic health"?

DO write unique titles for each page. You've got enough competition out there. Don't add to it by pitting your landing pages against each other with identical page titles, like this site does:

Online Store - peterluger.com
Welcome to **Peter Luger**'s **Online Store** [Account] [Please Login] Search for in All Our Steaks Gift Shop Gift Certificates Steak Sauce Catalogs [Storefront] [Products] [Shopping Cart > 0 items ...
peterluger.com/cgi-bin/online/storepro.php?product=10002:Package-B   Cached page   1/4/2006

Online Store - peterluger.com
Welcome to **Peter Luger**'s **Online Store** [Account] [Please Login] Search for in All Our Steaks Gift Shop Gift Certificates Steak Sauce Catalogs [Storefront] [Products] [Shopping Cart > 0 items ...
peterluger.com/cgi-bin/online/storepro.php?product=10002:Package-A   Cached page   1/4/2006
Show more results from "peterluger.com".

Since each of your landing pages is already targeting a unique subset of your top-priority keywords, you can always find a different angle for each page title. Give each of your landing pages the chance to shine on its own merits.

DON'T duplicate site navigation in the title. Whether generated automatically or written by hand, page titles are often used as a place to mirror the navigational structure of a site. We won't say never for this because, if your site sections are named well, it can be an effective way to display keywords. For example, a furniture store might have a landing page titled "Frank's Furniture – Patio Furniture – Wicker." This works—the navigation text is very brief and includes target keywords. But most sites aren't built this way, and you don't want words like "Index," "Main Page," or "Our Products" to take up space that's best reserved for your targeted marketing message.

Now: Write optimized page titles for each of your landing pages, and add them to your Site Optimization Worksheet.

Tuesday: Meta Tags

In Chapter 3 you learned the basics of meta tags. Today you'll optimize two invisible text elements: the meta description tag, and the meta keyword tag.

Meta Description Tag

We see London, we see France. We see…your site's meta description tag? Yes, not unlike your undies, your meta description tag is something that usually stays hidden but can be displayed to the world when you least expect it. For those rare times yours is exposed, you want to be proud of what people see (and here it's probably best to drop the undies metaphor). Many sites make the mistake of leaving this tag out of their code. Today you'll make sure yours is not only present, but also written with your SEO goals in mind.

As you learned in Chapter 3, the search engines usually display snippets from your site text in their listings. Here are some possible scenarios in which your meta description tag might be displayed instead:

- When there is no HTML content on the page, such as in the case of an all-Flash or all-graphics site, or if the only content is a redirect to another page
- When someone searches for your site using your URL but no keywords
- When off-page factors make your site a relevant match for a search but no exact match is found in your site's text
- In less-sophisticated search engines that use the description tag as a workaround for their inability to display snippets

Search engines often display 150 characters or more for the listing description, so you have a lot of space—relative to the page title, anyway—to convey your message. So, if good writing comes naturally to you, you have a lot of opportunity to make this tag stand out. But if writing isn't your strong suit, this tag gives you a little more room to make mistakes. Bring in a proofreader if you need to; this is a bad spot for an embarrassing typo.

Here are some pointers for writing a great meta description tag:

Keep it informative. Think of the meta description tag as an "About Us" blurb, not a "Buy Now!" advertisement. It's your keyword-rich *elevator speech* (that's a marketing term for the description of yourself you might give in a 30-second elevator ride). It's not worth the upkeep to write this tag to promote special events or deals. And, just as it's probably not helpful to scream words like "WORLD'S BEST!" elsewhere in your marketing message, the same holds true in your meta description tag.

Pair it with the page title. While you can't be sure exactly when or how people will see your meta description tag, it's a sure bet that when it is shown, it will be right under your optimized page title. So, don't repeat your title text in your description tag.

Include your keywords… While the meta description tag may not be a huge factor in influencing rank, it may have a big influence on the searcher who is lucky enough to view it. So include your target keywords because they'll be bolded in the search results. Notice how the bolding catches your eye.

> South Metro **Jewish Congregation**
> An inviting, spiritually rich **Reform Jewish Congregation** located just outside of **Portland**, **Oregon**, for Jews by Birth, Jews by Choice, and Jews at…
> ∞ | www.smjc.info/ | Cached | Save

…but don't overdo it! Stuffing the meta description tag with a long keyword list isn't likely to help your ranks and will probably generate vast waves of indifference with searchers. Why not use this tag to give the searcher a reason to come to your site instead?

Make it Unique. Like your HTML page title, your meta description tag should be custom-written for each landing page to match its specific content.

 Now: Using your newly optimized page titles and your landing page content as a guide, write optimized meta description tags for your landing pages in your Site Optimization Worksheet.

Here's some good news if you're interested in saving time: The combination of page title and meta description tag can be used as is, or with a little trimming or spinning, for any directories that you submit your site to later. And, if you're looking for a keyword-rich tagline to add to the bottom of your page, your meta description tag can be a great starting point.

Meta Keywords Tag

As you already know, the meta keywords tag is not the most influential tag in SEO. But it won't harm you to optimize yours. Here's a quick-and-dirty method that you can use:

- Go to the Keywords Worksheet that you compiled in your Prep Month, and look through your flagged keywords.

- For each landing page, decide which of the flagged keywords you think are relevant. Insert them into Meta Keywords Tag column of the Site Optimization Worksheet.

- Add any keywords that didn't make the flagged list but that you think are appropriate and relevant.

- For each landing page, add your company name, location if applicable, and any common misspellings you can think of.
Don't overthink it. You're done.

Now: Compile optimized meta keywords tags for your landing pages and place them in your Site Optimization Worksheet.

First Impressions

Have you been wondering how people select which search results to click on—and how to make yours the one they choose? Search behavior research can help you understand and influence their click decisions:

- Research by search marketing firm Enquiro, Inc., on B2B search behavior found that 27 percent of searchers quickly scan the listings looking for words to jump out while 15 percent read titles and descriptions carefully. But 57 percent start with a quick scan and then read the listings carefully if nothing jumps out at them first. Most searchers will click on the first appropriate-looking listing they find. (Source: Enquiro.com)

- Cornell eye-tracking research shows that searchers spend 30 percent of their time reading the listing title, 43 percent of the time reading the listing description, and 21 percent of their time reading the URL. The average total time before a click choice is made is 5.7 seconds. (Source: Cornell University Computer Science & Human-Computer Interaction)

- German researchers asked users how they chose what to click on. The winning factor was clear listing text. That means you should make sure your listings contain readable text, not keyword-stuffed garble. Other important factors were relevance of the listing to the search term, a clear and easy-to-understand description of the page content, and the inclusion of the website's name. (Source: Fittkau and Maaß on behalf of eProfessional GmbH)

Wednesday: Robot Walk-Through

You're all dressed up and the hors d'oeuvres are on the table. But is there a big Do Not Enter sign on your door? You know the basics of how the robots find your site, and you know whether or not your landing pages are indexed. Today you'll knock down any barriers that exist between the robots and your landing pages. And even if all of your landing pages are already indexed, today you'll learn more about keeping robots happy so they'll always stick around for the toast.

Take a look at your Baseline Monthly Report or your Rank Tracking Worksheet to determine whether any of your landing pages are not indexed. Here are several reasons a robot might not be reaching your landing page and possible ways to fix the problem:

Robots can't follow your links. This could be as simple as a having no links from your home page or your main site navigation to one or all of your landing pages. Or maybe the links to your landing pages are created using hard-to-follow code, such as JavaScript pull-down menus or pop-up scripts. Often, this is an easy fix: just add standard HTML text links from anywhere on your home page to your landing page. (You'll probably want a site map as well. We'll cover that next month.)

No stand-alone landing pages. Maybe your site was developed in Flash, in which case it really isn't a group of individual pages but is rather one big file that's hard or impossible for the search engines to index as separate pages. Perhaps your landing pages are generated dynamically or they show up only when a form is submitted or a login ID is entered. Since robots don't fill out forms or submit login data, they won't find these pages. Or, perhaps your landing pages are built in *frames*, which means different elements of the page are broken apart into different URLs, and it's impossible to link to any one page individually.

In the long run, we'd like to see your entire site revamped as much as necessary to get robots nibbling at every little crumb, which may mean a full overhaul of your site structure. For today, our priority is getting those landing pages indexed! That means at the very least rebuilding your landing pages as completely separate, linkable URLs. If your landing pages are built in frames—Achooo! There's a lot of dust on this website! Get ready to have them rebuilt with their own URLs.

Your site asks too much from the visitor. If the queen came to visit, you wouldn't turn her away if she wasn't wearing the right hat. Treat your spiders the same way! Some websites won't display to a viewer who doesn't have JavaScript. Guess who doesn't have JavaScript? The robots! Some websites require cookies. Guess who won't accept cookies? You get the point. You'll need to eliminate these requirements on your landing pages. If you're not sure what your site requires, you'll get a better sense of it when you look at the "spider's-eye view" of your website in Chapter 8, "Month Two: Establish the Habit."

A server outage interrupted indexing. Perhaps your pages are linked and structured properly but the robot came crawling just at the moment your systems administrator spilled his Jolt Cola on the server. The robot found no site to index. There's nothing you can do in a situation like this but wait until the next indexing cycle. You may wish to consider a PPC or paid inclusion campaign to fill in the gaps while you're waiting. And if this seems to be a regular occurrence, look into a more reliable hosting situation. (By the way, for the perfect balance of caffeine and server protection, your sysadmin should switch to coffee with the little sippy lid.)

Your site is too big. Maybe your landing pages exist alongside thousands of other pages in your site. Robots don't index every page from every site, so they may simply have moved on before they got to the ones you think are most important. This is another quick fix: just be sure to add HTML links that place your landing pages no more than two clicks away from the home page.

You told the robots to stay away. That wasn't very nice of you! Next month, we'll get into the details of how you communicate with robots through a file on your site called robots.txt. Today, double-check that none of your landing pages has a tag on it that says meta name="robots" content="noindex".

Your site is being penalized. It's possible, but unlikely, that you are violating a search engine's guidelines without knowing it. If none of the other problems are striking a chord and you are absolutely sure that your pages are not present in the index, and especially if you were ever engaged in questionable SEO practices in the past, this might be your situation. It's a tough one. Probably your best strategy is to post a note in an SEO forum (you'll learn about our favorites later in the Plan) and see if the community has any suggestions.

Now: Try to identify the reasons your pages are not being indexed. Write down your findings, and determine whom you need to discuss them with in your organization.

Thursday: Site Text

Has there been something about your site's text that has been setting your teeth on edge since you started learning about SEO? Is there anything in the content that you know is working against your site's search engine visibility? Or are your keywords nowhere to be found? Now it's time to address these issues. Today is a momentous day because you're actually going to put your keyword research to good use on your site's visible text content.

Today you will comb through your landing pages for possible text improvements, documenting them as you go. You can approach documentation in a couple of ways: One way is to compile your desired changes in the "Text/Content Edits" section on the Site Optimization Worksheet. Or, depending on the layout of your site and the extent of your changes, you may just want to print out your landing pages and mark your changes on the printout.

Your goal: incorporate your two or three designated target keyterms onto each of your landing pages without going overboard and cooking up an unreadable keyword porridge. If you have any writers on your SEO team, get them on board for this session. Try these editorial strategies for making your text changes:

✔ Swap out a specific word for a top priority keyword every time it appears.

✔ Swap out a graphic containing a keyword for text.

✔ Spell out an acronym (at least in its first appearance on the page).

✔ On a case-by-case basis, swap out less-effective generic terms for keywords.

✔ Make sure your company name exists in text form once on every page.

✔ Include keywords in links wherever possible.

✔ Add keyword-rich captions to photos.

✔ Add a keyword-rich tagline at the bottom of the page.

✔ Add keywords to page headers.

 Now: Go through your landing pages and compile your list of changes on your Site Optimization Worksheet or page printouts.

Friday: Implementation

All of your desired site edits are conveniently compiled in your Site Optimization Worksheet. Today, send out these requests to your web team—or take the time to make the changes yourself.

Everyone involved in SEO implementation tasks should already have your Baseline Monthly Report in their inbox, so you should be able to deliver these requests to your team without having to explain your reasoning again! Here are some pointers for making this effort worthwhile:

Think in terms of a style guide. If your organization works from a style guide, now is the time to suggest which of your requested changes should be officially incorporated.

Many of your site text edits from Thursday are perfect candidates for inclusion in a style guide.

Know your time frame. You can move forward in Your SEO Plan for a few days without having your changes to tags and text in place. If you're not doing them yourself, these edits—and the buy-in they require—might take time. Communicate your desired time frame with your team, and get some realistic expectations from the ones who have to do the work. If you need to take a little time to get these important changes made, we won't rush you. We'll be here waiting for you when your site is ready to go!

Make yourself available. You've just handed out some serious work for your team, and they may respond with opposition or genuine curiosity. Let your team know that you're available to answer questions, and be prepared to pleasantly spoon-feed your reasoning and background information should the need arise.

Prioritize. If your team doesn't have the time to get all of these edits in place anytime soon, prioritize them in this order:

1. Fix robot barriers.
2. Edit HTML page titles.
3. Edit page text.
4. Edit meta tags.

Now that your site has its optimization spit-shine, you're ready to show it to the world. Next week, you'll get serious about building high quality inbound links.

Week 2: Link Building

You learned in Chapters 3 and 4 how important inbound links are for your website. Last month, you even dipped a toe into the ocean of link building when you used the search engines to find out how many other sites are linking to your landing pages.

Unless your site is truly wretched, there's bound to be somebody out there who is interested in linking to it. (And if you think your site is beyond linking, stay tuned! You'll get some content-building and linkability improvement lessons in Chapter 9, "Month Three: It's a Way of Life.") Put on your PR hat—or get your team's most talented communicator in the room—and get started on your SEO link-building campaign:

Monday: Your Existing Links
Tuesday: Directory Submittals
Wednesday: Surf for More Link Opportunities
Thursday: The Art of Link Letters
Friday: Send Your Letters

Surfing Is not Slacking

As SEO consultants working for a small web development firm, we were lucky to have an open-minded boss. On any given day you might have seen five other workers knee-deep in HTML edits or up to their ears in database code, but what was on our monitors? Movie fan sites, Florida vacation sites, and sports nostalgia sites. We remember the day we had to send an e-mail around saying, "Don't worry: We're not looking for new jobs. We're just researching career sites for a client!" But it was all part of the SEO job, and an important one at that.

If you're in a corporate culture where personal e-mails and web surfing is frowned upon or downright prohibited, it is essential that you get the clearance you need to access the Web in the same way that your customers and competitors do. Likewise, if there are no actual restrictions on web surfing in your company but you just feel like a slacker when you're surfing the Web, just remember what surfing does for your company:

- Surfing helps you find and assess the quality of sites linking to you and locate new sites that may want to link to you.

- It helps you find new search products and opportunities that may be useful for promoting your organization.

- It helps you to think like a searcher, using a variety of techniques to find important information.

- And it helps you get familiar with the wide range of available search engine and directory listings.

Every SEO expert has a favorite generic search term to use for testing, one that's broad and popular enough to be represented by the full gamut of paid and unpaid listings, directory listings, and text snippets, not to mention official sites, unofficial sites, and misspellings. Ours continues to be "Britney Spears." Have fun finding yours!

Monday: Your Existing Links

Today, you will assess your website's existing listings and links with an eye toward improvement. We have created a worksheet to help you in your link-building efforts.

Now: Download the Link Tracking Worksheet from www.yourseoplan.com and save it in your SEO Idea Bank.

Last month, during your baseline site assessment, you determined the total number of sites linking into your landing pages. Now you will take a magnifying glass to these sites and document them in your Link Tracking Worksheet. Here are the steps you'll take:

- Document inbound links.
- Assess existing link quality.

Document Inbound Links

On your Link Tracking Worksheet, you will see a section for existing inbound links. Today you'll identify the URLs of the first 10 or so sites that are linking to each of your landing pages. Ten should be plenty to work with for now—you will build on this list throughout your SEO Plan.

Find the URLs using one of the following three methods:

- On the search engine of your choice, perform the special search you learned in Chapter 6 for finding inbound links.
- If you have access to a website statistics program, review it for referring URLs.
- Use a backlink analysis tool, such as the Neat-O Backlink Tool built by the kind people of We Build Pages, www.webuildpages.com/tools/. This tool provides backlink URLs and also the text that the linking sites are using to link to you. Like the title says, the tool is neat-o!

Perform this step for each of your landing pages, ignoring links coming from your own site. If your site has no incoming links from other sites, you can skip the rest of today's task!

Now: Open your Link Tracking Worksheet and fill in existing linking site URLs for each of your landing pages.

Assess Existing Link Quality

As we briefly discussed in Chapter 6, search engines care about the quality as well as the quantity of inbound links. And you care, too, because a link is a direct pathway for potential customers to get to your site. Today you'll ask a few key questions about your linking sites that will help you determine if each link is going to help the right audience find the right page on your site. Later this week, we'll show you how to write to site owners to request changes to any problematic listings you discover.

The following key questions will help you assess the quality of your inbound links. It may seem like a lot to think about, but once you get a feel for it, you won't need the checklist. In fact, you'll probably be able to assess each link within 30 seconds of opening the page.

Starting with the first inbound link URL on your list, open up the page and think about the answers to these yes or no questions:

- Is this site in the same topical community as mine?
- Does the linking page content speak to my target audience?
- Are my target keywords included in the text that links to my site?
- Are my target keywords included elsewhere on the page?
- Does the link work?
- Does the link go to the best landing page choice?
- Is the link up-to-date?
- Is the link flattering, or at least noncritical?

While there are numerous factors that can contribute to the quality of an inbound link, these are the most important. The more yes answers, the higher-quality link you have. If there are any no answers, flag this URL with a note of the problem. Obviously, some problems (like a link being from an irrelevant website) can't be fixed. And if a link is coming from inside a forum post, it's good to know about, but there's no point trying to modify it. But others, especially links that don't work, are red flags that need to be addressed.

 Now: Make a note of any trouble spots in the Notes column of your Link Tracking Worksheet.

Get into the habit of asking these questions anytime you review a website and it will serve you throughout your campaign—especially later this week when you are looking for new links.

Tuesday: Submit to Directories

Ah, directories…the dinosaurs of the SEO era. Once upon a time, getting into human-edited directories was one of the most important elements of an SEO campaign. Nowadays, directory listings have fallen out of prominence. But they represent a chance to describe your site in your own well-researched, well-targeted words, and that's good for your site (and for your inner control freak!). Today, you'll learn about human-edited directories, discover the ones in your niche, and decide whether they're worth your time and energy.

Think of a directory listing as just another inbound link with a slightly different link request process (usually there's a submittal form to fill out, and specific editorial guidelines to follow, instead of a free-form e-mail correspondence). If you happen to have a nonprofit or noncommercial website, you have greatly increased potential for free links on directories.

Your directory requests will be accepted or rejected based on the judgment of human editors, and part of what they judge is whether your suggested title and description match your site's content. So if you have substantial optimization that needs to take place before this is the case, use today's task just to gather submittal information. You can perform the actual submittal when your site is ready.

We've boiled down the wide world of directories into three areas for you to review:

- The Open Directory Project
- Yahoo! Directory
- Paid or niche directories

The Open Directory Project

The Open Directory Project (ODP), at www.dmoz.org, goes by many names, including Open Directory, DMOZ, and Netscape Directory. Unfortunately, getting your site listed in the ODP can take, quite literally, forever, and its importance as a linking site has diminished greatly over time.

However, your ODP description is still used by the Google search engine as the description that displays in some search results (rather than a snippet or meta description). For this reason alone, we think that your ODP submittal is worth the time. And for sure, it's worth the price (thankfully, this submittal is free).

First, determine whether your site has a current listing in the ODP. Go to www.dmoz.org and search for your URL. (But watch out; sometimes the ODP misses URLs. If a URL search shows no results, follow up with a search for your company name.) If you find a listing for your company, assess its quality with these questions:

- Is the link functional and current?
- Is the title and description accurate?
- Do the title and description contain my target keywords?

ODP listings are so rarely updated that it's likely your listing needs some fixing. Click the "update listing" link near the top of the page and submit your edits (see Figure 7.1). The ODP provides extensive guidelines within the update submittal screens. We won't bore you by repeating the guidelines, so promise us you'll read and follow them as you go!

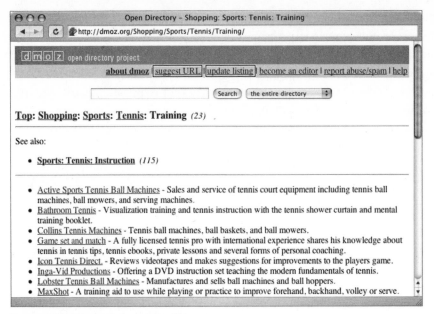

Figure 7.1 Open Directory Project submittal links

If your site doesn't have an existing listing on the ODP, you'll follow nearly the same steps to submit a new listing. However, first you must choose a good category for your site. Here are some tips to help you make the choice:

Cluster with your competition. Search the directory for your top business competitors. If they're all in the same category, you want to be there too.

Get specific. Browse the directory, starting from the biggest, top-level categories and working your way down to the one most specific to your organization. For example, if you provide tennis lessons, you don't want to be in a generic category like "Sports." You want to be in a more appropriate category like Shopping→Sports→Tennis→Training or a local category like Regional→North America→Canada→Ontario→Localities→T→ Toronto→Recreation and Sports→Tennis.

Use category tiebreakers. If you are faced with two categories that seem to fit your site equally well, choose the better-quality category page based on the link quality factors you assessed on Monday for inbound links in general. If all of the page quality factors are equal, choose the category with more editors listed at the bottom of the page. The editors are the people who review and approve your listing, but they sometimes go missing or permanently vacate their posts, so the more listed per category, the better your chances.

Once you have found your category of choice, click on the "suggest URL" link near the top of the page and follow the guidelines to proceed. Most likely, you will want to submit your home page, but it's possible that a different landing page will also work. In rare cases, if your site has landing pages with unique content, directories may include multiple listings for your site. Use the HTML page title and meta description tag you prepared in Week 1 as a launching point to write your title and description. Make sure to consider what your competition is saying (or not saying) about themselves when you fine-tune your suggested listing.

> **Now:** Submit your site to the ODP. Open your Link Tracking Worksheet and document your submittal or update request.

Now, and here's the important thing: once it's filed away in your worksheet, forget about checking up on this submittal for the next six months. It's just not worth it.

Yahoo! Directory

There's plenty of debate among SEO professionals about whether the few hundred dollars for a Yahoo! Directory listing (oh, wait, it's not the price for a *listing*, it's just the price to be reviewed…no listing is guaranteed) is worth it.

We're going to stick our necks out and give our own answer to the question: If spending a few hundred dollars (or more for adult sites) per year is going to be a significant portion of your SEO budget, don't do it. If, on the other hand, a few hundred bucks is a small drop in your online marketing budget, a listing may be worth the cost. And here's some good news for nonprofits: If your website belongs in a noncommercial category, you can submit for free.

However, keep this fact in mind: Once you have a listing in the Yahoo! Directory, the directory title and description, rather than snippets from your website, will be displayed on the Yahoo! search results pages. Is this a good thing or a bad thing? Possibly more bad than good because, even though you suggest your own listing, it's ultimately the Yahoo! editor's call and you have no control over this text. On the other hand, a complete sentence rather than a snippet might read better in your listing description, especially if for some reason you weren't able to put text on your website during your basic optimization. You will have to make the judgment based on your own website's characteristics.

If you choose to submit your site to the Yahoo! Directory, start by selecting the best category for your site, as described earlier in the section "The Open Directory Project." Click "suggest a site" near the top of the page. Follow the instructions to submit your site and payment information.

slacker   If you're pressed for time, or if this submittal is not in your budget, you can skip it. After your content is beefed up in Chapter 9, "Month Three: It's a Way of Life," you may wish to revisit the idea of a Yahoo! Directory submittal along with other directory submittals and link requests.

Now: If you choose to do so, submit your site to the Yahoo! Directory. Open your Link Tracking Worksheet and document your Yahoo! Directory submittal or update request. Be sure to include your Yahoo! confirmation code.

Paid or Niche Directories

Niche directories are small, but they can be powerhouses for targeted traffic. You know your company, and you know your niche. Now it's time for you to find directories that speak to it. Here are ways you can go about it:

What are your competitors using? Check links to your competitors the same way you did in Chapter 6, but this time take some time to read through the listings. Are there any directories listed? Click them and see if this may be a good directory for you too.

What offline opportunities do you already know about? Many publications, such as Sweets (http://sweets.construction.com) and Thomson Local (www.thomweb.co.uk) have online directory components. Check to see if your company is included in any such publication.

What comes up for your target keywords? Are there any directory pages among the top search results for your target keywords? (See Figure 7.2 for a visual.) You could benefit from their ranks by getting listed.

Last but not least, be sure to search the search engines for relevant niche directories. For example, if your organization is a day spa located in Albuquerque, New Mexico, the search terms "day spa directory" and "Albuquerque directory" will both turn up many possible niche directories. But watch out for these pitfalls as you consider niche directories:

- Many of the directories that will come up in your searches will be repurposed versions of the Open Directory. If a submittal process starts to feel a little too familiar, look to see if you've been taken to the dmoz.org domain. If you find it, you're smack dab in the middle of an Open Directory submittal.

- Don't believe the hype: If a niche directory wants a payment for your listing, you need to carefully check the link quality factors before you pull out your pocketbook.

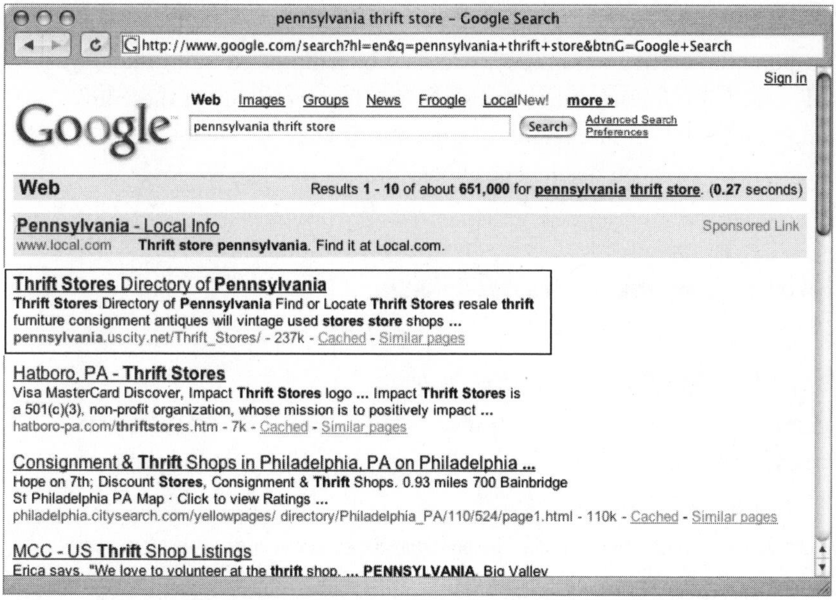

Figure 7.2 Directory in the top search results

As we mentioned earlier, your directory listings are really just like any other inbound link and should be assessed accordingly. Don't make any niche or paid directory submittals today; wait until Friday, after you've completed your other link-building activities for the week. You may decide that there are so many opportunities out there that the paid or niche directory listings aren't worth your bother.

Now: Open your Link Tracking Worksheet and document possible niche directory URLs under "New Links/Requests"—but don't do any submittals yet!

Wednesday: Surf for More Link Opportunities

Yesterday you began building the list of potential linking websites on your Link Tracking Worksheet. Today, you'll surf the Web to expand your list of sites. First, you need to know what makes a link worth chasing:

- Quality links defined
- Expanding your link requests list

Quality Links Defined

As you surf for potential linking sites today, you may be tempted to build the longest list you possibly can, with dozens or hundreds of sites. But every one of these link requests is going to take a 5-minute chunk of time out of your life—why, that's only 12 per episode of *Survivor*!—so you need to be choosy.

Quality Link or Time Sink? An Expert's Opinion

We asked blogger and search marketing expert Aaron Wall of www.seobook.com how to assess the quality of inbound links. Here were his thoughts:

"I love organic SEO, which currently is primarily driven by link building…. Many factors go into measuring link quality—to be honest, it is not entirely measurable. I like to think of a document or site as having signs of quality. Some examples:

- "Page or site is well cited from resources like educational institutions or major web companies."

- "Page links to quality related resources."

- "Page ranks well in related search results."

- "You keep running into the page even outside of search."

What about finding signs of poor quality linking pages? Here are Aaron's ideas:

- "Page will sell a link to any off-topic site."

- "Link price seems far cheaper than it should be for that kind of page…."

- "Page is hard to find in search results."

- "Site is of low quality and there is limited reason a human would want to go there or link at that site or page."

In case you didn't notice, Aaron never even mentions Google PageRank in his assessment. Google PageRank may be an at-a-glance measure of a page's significance to a search engine, but it simply doesn't give you the full picture of what a link can do for you. Thanks for the advice, Aaron!

Between Aaron Wall's factors to consider in the sidebar "Quality Link or Time Sink? An Expert's Opinion" and the link quality factors you learned on Monday, you've got a lot of tools for analysis. But there's one more angle to consider: whether the site makes it possible for you to do your link-gathering job. Make sure to take these administrative issues into account:

- Is contact information available on the site? Without it, you can't request the link.

- Does the site appear to be regularly updated? Do a quick scan for the "last edited" date or other signs of life. If nobody is manning the store, there won't be anybody to add your link.

Now that you know *what* you're looking for in an inbound linking site, here are some ideas for *where* to look.

Expand Your Link Requests List

So far, you've only scratched the surface of your potential high-quality linking sites. Here are some places you can look for additional opportunities:

Sites linking to your competitors By now, you're a seasoned pro at finding inbound links using the search engines. Do this now for your Big Five competitors. Who is linking to them? Can you get a link there too?

Any sites doing well for your top keywords Go through the top listings for your target keywords—both organic results and sponsored results—with a fine-tooth comb. These would be great places to get links.

Your clients/customers/fans Do you have a client base that is pleased with your service? Do they have websites that speak to a segment of your target audience? If so, they may be happy to provide a link to your site! Bonus points if they put your link alongside a glowing recommendation.

Your service providers/vendors Are you a major client of any organization with a Web presence that has a tie-in to your target audience? Maybe they would like to link to your site. Maybe they'd even like to list you as a "featured" client!

Your partners Corporate partners are likely to include links on their websites. Check and see if there's one for you.

Sites that already include your company name Perform a search for your company name in quotes. You may be surprised to find many websites that include your company information, maybe even a URL written in text, without making it a link! With a flick of the mouse, those could become inbound links for you.

Local and regional directories Any site that includes listings of local businesses will probably be happy to have their information updated—preferably with your organization's web listing!

Business associations and accreditations Most professional and trade associations include lists of their members. If your organization is accredited in any way, there may be a link in it for you.

Sites that are "related" to yours In Chapter 6, you learned about the Alexa database of information. One of its tastier tidbits is Related Sites, other websites that draw the same audience as yours. Take a look at your related sites for linking potential.

Sympathetic sites If your site has a religious, political, or philosophical theme, there is likely to be a large circle of similarly minded folks on the Web. These people will likely be enthusiastic about supporting one of their own. Ditto for specialized hobbies and enthusiasms.

As you surf, be open to wandering down unexpected paths—sometimes that's the best way to find new opportunities. And be sure to make a note of the site URL (location of potential link), name of site, and contact information in your Link Tracking Worksheet.

 Now: Record additional potential linking URLs under "New Links/Requests" in your Link Tracking Worksheet.

Thursday: The Art of Link Letters

If you own a website, surely you've seen them: annoying requests for links. Usually they go something like this: "Dear Webmaster. I reviewed your site and feel that it would be appropriate for a link trade. Please add the following HTML code to your home page...after your link is added, we will add your link to our links page."

Most of the time, this type of letter goes straight into the Trash folder. Follow these Dos and Don'ts to craft link letters that *do* get results and *don't* annoy their recipients:

DO include key information. At a minimum, your letter must include the following: the URL from which you would like a link, your landing page URL, your landing page title, and your landing page description. Remember to choose the best landing page on your site, which, depending on the nature of the linking page, may not be your home page.

DON'T offer a link trade. If your site is appropriate for a link, you should be able to get it without a reciprocal link agreement.

DO explain the benefits of the link... Website owners want to link to sites that their site audience will like. Specifically describe how your site relates to theirs.

...but DON'T write a novel. We're talkin' 25 words or less.

DO write from a company e-mail address. Webmasters want to know that you really come from the company that is requesting the link.

DON'T mass-mail. Figure out the name of the person you're writing to, and use it. Then, sign with your own name and title.

And finally:

 Pearl of Wisdom: DO say Thank You.

A Bulletproof Link Letter

Several years ago, we were doing some link-building efforts for a major media website that had just launched an innovative product. The product was interesting enough that we thought some of the industry thinkers with blogs might want to take a look, and maybe even write a review. So, like Little Red Riding Hood skipping into the forest, we sent out a bunch of our usual perky, polite link request letters.

Hoo boy, were we in for a surprise! Bloggers can be a little bit like sleepy dogs that wake up snapping their teeth. We received some less-than-polite responses: What were we doing pestering them? Who the heck would want this product? Why the heck did we send this e-mail?

Worse, at least one blog actually published the text of our e-mail, with our full name and e-mail address! That could have been more than a little embarrassing.

Luckily—or was it actually foresight on our part?—our letters were carefully written to avoid embarrassment to ourselves or our client. We were eminently polite and professional. We described the benefits of the product without resorting to heavy selling. And we took some time to review the blogs for relevance before sending out our e-mails. Our punishment took the form of exposure, and not worse.

Nowadays, there are blogs on every subject, from lost socks to lost souls, and surely there are some in your industry. At some point in your link-building campaign, you'll probably want to approach one. Keep these guidelines in mind when you do:

- Get to know the blog first. Read it for a while before you approach its owner.

- Remember, it's less about selling your site to the blogger and more about convincing them that your site would be interesting to the blog's readers.

- If you really want a blogger to review your product, you'll have better success if you send them a freebie. Likewise, if your product is on a page that requires a login, consider offering login information for the blogger's sole use (but don't send out login information in your first correspondence!).

And, finally, imagine your e-mail posted on the blog for the whole world to see. Would this be embarrassing in any way to you or your organization? If so, you need a rewrite.

To make your life a little easier, we've written a sample link request letter for your use. Download it from our companion website at www.yourseoplan.com.

Now: Open a new document and write your own general link request letter including your site's must-have information. Save it in your SEO Idea Bank.

Friday: Submittals and E-mails

You now have the two elements in place that you need for your link-building campaign: a list of quality sites that might be interested in linking to your site and a sample link request letter.

Today, step through the list on your Link Tracking Worksheet and, one by one, personalize and send out your link request e-mails. If you encounter a site with a "Contact Us" form, it's perfectly kosher to paste your link request e-mail into that so long as you dutifully enter your contact information into the proper fields. As you go, record the date that you requested the link, and who you e-mailed, in your worksheet. You will want this information later if you wish to send a follow-up request.

 Now: Step through your list of potential linking sites and send link requests to as many as you can.

Finally, let's take one last look at the niche directories you began reviewing on Tuesday. If any of them include a free submittal option, go ahead and do it now.

However, if a niche directory requires payment for a listing, take a step back and evaluate it further before submitting:

- As you were searching and surfing related sites this week, did the site pop up regularly?
- Are your competitors listed there?
- And, does the directory have a PPC or other advertising campaign of its own? Websites are so easy to create that there are thousands of directory sites on the Web that aren't worth the virtual paper they're printed on. Unless you can get a several-month free trial, you should be very cautious about paying for niche directory listings.

 Now: Submit your site to niche directories.

Now that you've gotten a strong start on the organic side of your SEO campaign, it's time to create a pilot pay-per-click campaign.

Week 3: Set Up Your PPC Account

Welcome to PPC with training wheels. This week you're going to develop good habits and a firm grasp of how the PPC system works, using a small-budget starter campaign. We can't tell you what "small" means, but whether you choose to invest less than $100 or more than $1,000 a month, we'll provide you with tips and pitfall-avoidance techniques that will help you spend your money wisely.

Your SEO Plan makes provisions for you to set up your PPC account and monitor it over the course of three months. This should give you enough time to judge cost-effectiveness, learn what you can expect to get for your money, and decide whether you have what it takes—both financially and administratively—to manage an ongoing PPC account.

Even if you're skeptical about PPC's place in your long-term marketing plans, we still hope to nudge you into trying PPC for the short-term:

Pearl of Wisdom: PPC can tell you a lot about your audience and your keywords in a relatively short period of time, which makes it an excellent research tool for your organic SEO efforts.

How Do I Choose My PPC Budget?

This is one of the hardest-to-pin-down factors of SEO, and one that has as many variables as a high school algebra fair. We'd love to put on our little green visors and help you arrive at the perfect number, but instead we'll have to give you some general guidelines and let you do the thinking:

Ask your boss (or whoever holds the purse strings).

Whether you like it or not, somebody may already have a number that you'll have to roll with. Let's hope your PPC campaign pulls in enough conversions to convince them to up the budget when your trial period is over!

Look to your current cost per conversion. Perhaps you already have an idea of what a conversion costs your organization based on tracking for existing online or offline marketing programs. The preliminary research you do this week may help you make an educated guess about how much you'd need to spend on PPC to meet or beat your current cost per conversion.

Consider your competition. You already know whether or not you're in a highly competitive online space. This week, with the help of the PPC engine of your choice, you're going to attach some dollar figures to your top-priority keywords. Will you need to spend $0.15 or $15.00 per click to wrestle into the top three PPC ranks for most of your keywords? The answer will inform your budget-making process.

Think about your own level of enthusiasm. Even though it's likely that your PPC campaign will run smoothly, proper campaign management takes continued interest and effort. Campaigns with larger budgets often have more keywords and more ads, taking more effort than smaller campaigns. If you don't foresee yourself having the ability or time to keep up a large campaign, scale down your budget, along with your expectations for clicks and conversions.

Because it helps you tune into your most productive keywords, a relatively small investment of funds can increase the effectiveness of your organic SEO campaign enormously.

Here are your daily tasks for this week:

Monday: Study Hall
Tuesday: Prep Your PPC Keywords
Wednesday: Write Your Ad Text
Thursday: Enter Your Data into the PPC System
Friday: Turn On Your PPC Campaign

Monday: Study Hall

Getting familiar with a new interface, not to mention specialized terminology and guidelines, is an important part of a smoothly run campaign. Today, you'll do your homework and learn about the PPC engine you want to use so that you can be a more effective advertiser in the long term.

If All Else Fails, Flip a Coin

Having a hard time choosing which PPC service is right for you? As we mentioned in Chapter 4, "How the Search Engines Work Right Now," there are bigger players and there are smaller ones in the PPC arena. The current big guns in the U.S. market are Yahoo! Search Marketing and Google AdWords. We won't tell you whether to use Google AdWords or YSM. We *can* say that unless you have a compelling reason to do otherwise, you should stick with one of the top two services for your starter PPC campaign.

If you are the kind of person who needs to scrutinize the techie details before making a choice, put on your eyestrain glasses and check out the user documentation provided by the PPC services themselves. Yourseoplan.com has links to these and other resources that will help you compare PPC services. Use these resources to learn about YSM and Google AdWords—and any other PPC provider that interests you—and decide which is the best match to your needs. The key elements that you'll want to research are outlined in this section.

 Now: Finalize your choice of a PPC engine and sign up for an account.

Spend the rest of your time today familiarizing yourself with the inner workings of your PPC service of choice. The following are the most important elements for you to understand as you attack your PPC learning curve.

Editorial Guidelines Any respectable PPC service has a list of rules with which your ads must comply. Things like limiting obnoxious SHOUTING CAPITALIZATION or limiting the use of certain terms. (For example, we recently observed that the word *Enterprise* was forbidden to any but a subgroup of Google AdWords advertisers.) Limitations on adult content and affiliate sites are also common. You should also know their editorial procedures: Do they publish your ad right away and review it later? Is there a waiting period before new ads can go online? Do they warn you before they take your advertisement offline, or do they just yank it for violating the guidelines?

Spending Requirements This probably won't be a major issue if you are planning to use YSM or Google AdWords; they both offer very low minimum spending levels. If you are considering another PPC service, be sure that you are willing to cover their minimum spending or activation fee requirements.

Keyword Matching Options If you love to micromanage, this section is for you. PPC engines, including Google and YSM, offer a variety of keyword matching controls:

- *Broad matching* causes your ad to display if searchers combine your keywords with other terms (for example, your ad for "wedding bands" will show when the term "platinum wedding bands" is searched). This may include plural forms of the term, misspellings, and synonyms.

- *Keyword exclusion* allows you to exclude searchers who use certain words from viewing your ad (for example, if you're targeting "wedding bands," you can exclude people searching for "wedding jazz bands").

- *Keyword grouping* may allow you to show one ad for several different keywords, rotate multiple ads, or manage keywords as a group.

Ad Display Options It's important to understand exactly where and when your ads will be displayed. If you're interested in a PPC service other than the two Biggies, make sure they're up front about who they partner with for ad displays. You don't want to discover your ads unexpectedly displaying in annoying pop-up windows that may be detrimental to your branding. Many PPC services also offer these types of display controls:

- *Contextual* vs. *search engine display.* Contextual advertising displays your sponsored ads on a wide variety of websites, not just search engines. Your service should give you the choice of whether you want to include contextual displays.

- *Geotargeting* allows you to display your results to searchers in a particular location.

- *Dynamic Keyword Insertion* places the searcher's keywords directly into your ad. You'll learn more about this later, when you write your ads.

Bid and Position Management Options Some bid and position management features vary among PPC services. Learn the answers to the following questions about yours:

- **Adjusting bid prices:** How do you change bid prices for individual keywords? What about for groups of keywords? Can you set parameters so that your bid automatically increases or decreases based on what your competition is bidding?

- **Budget caps:** Can you set daily or monthly budget caps? Can you set limits so that certain bidding or cost parameters are not exceeded?

- **Controlling position:** What kind of control do you have over your listing position? As you'll recall from Chapter 4, bid prices may not be the only factors at play in determining the position of your PPC listings.

Tracking and Reporting Options You will probably be pleased with the detail and flexibility of reports you can generate with whichever PPC engine you choose. Your role in PPC reporting will be less about compiling data and more about finessing the report parameters to get at the information you really want. Here are some things to look for: How recent is the data that is included in reports? Is conversion tracking an option? Is there at-a-glance information in your campaign management interface so you won't have to run a report to see how your PPC day is going?

You'll be creating monthly reports with the following information at a minimum: top performing terms, total campaign cost, average cost per click, click-through rate, and total click-throughs. Be sure you know how to find this information from your PPC service's reporting screen.

Account Services Some PPC services will help you get up and running. YSM and Google both offer setup assistance services for a fee. We generally don't recommend paying for such services, and anyway, you won't need them if you follow the procedures in this week's tasks. However, if you are destined to be a big spender with a PPC service (on the order of $10,000 or more per month), you may be able to get the free services of an account rep who can smooth over some of the bumps in the process.

Your PPC service may ask you to input your keywords and bids before you can complete the sign-up process. You can just enter in your company name as a keyword for now.

Tuesday: Prep Your PPC Keywords

Today you'll compile a list of keywords for your PPC starter campaign. Your top 10 or so target keywords are a starting point, but any terms on your long list from Chapter 6 are fair game.

Targeting the Long Tail

Perhaps you've heard of the "long tail" theory. It describes how our culture and commerce is moving away from a small number of very popular products (or movies, or dances, or even ideas) toward a very large number of niche products or activities. For example, not terribly long ago there were only three television networks that everybody watched (a *short head*). Now, there are hundreds of specialty networks, each with a much smaller audience (a *long tail*).

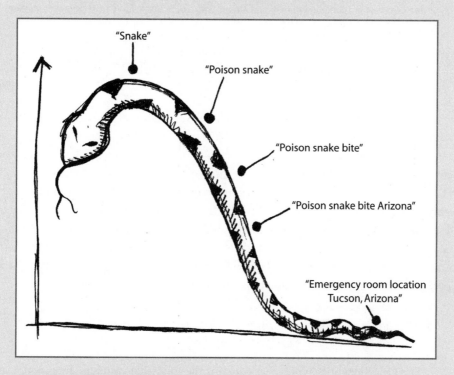

How does this apply to Your SEO Plan?

In SEO, a short head search is something like "motel," while a long tail search might be "baltimore pool motel airport." The short head search is very broad and is used commonly, while the long tail search is very specific and is used much less frequently.

Compared to organic optimization, PPC makes it much easier for you to target long tail searchers. Here's why: In organic SEO, each keyterm you target takes a certain minimum commitment of time and energy, so it wouldn't make sense to put hours of effort into rewriting your site for once-a-month, ultra-focused queries. In PPC, on the other hand, you can add your long tail keywords to your account for free—and pay only when they receive clicks.

Continues

> **Targeting the Long Tail** *(continued)*
>
> Why sponsor long tail searches? For one, they aren't likely to have much competition, which means lower costs per click. For another, by the time a searcher is using a long tail term, they are probably closer to the end of the buying process. This makes long tail searchers a very desirable group. Look again at the example: "motel" compared to "baltimore pool motel airport." Maybe you'd get 15,000 clicks for "motel" and only 100 clicks for "baltimore pool motel airport." But if you run a motel near the Baltimore/Washington International Airport with a pool, you're likely to get more reservations from those long tail visitors.
>
> Experiment with some long tail terms in your PPC campaign and you may discover some top performers that become candidates for future organic SEO efforts.

PPC engines have their own tools to help you figure out which terms you want to add to your campaign and how much you want to spend on each. However, we've found that it's often better to use our own simple spreadsheet, especially for small or new campaigns. Using a spreadsheet to record your keyword choices cuts down on the PPC interface learning curve, since everything you need is together in one document rather than partitioned in various PPC reporting or admin screens. And spreadsheets allow you a little more flexibility in manipulating parameters that matter to you, like maximum bid price or predicted click-through rate. We've created a worksheet that we think will be useful to you in the planning phase of your PPC campaign, called the PPC Keywords Worksheet. You can download it from www.yourseoplan.com.

 Now: Go to www.yourseoplan.com and download the PPC Keywords Worksheet.

The PPC Keywords Worksheet contains the following columns: Keyword, Category, Bid for Top Position, Estimated Click-Throughs, Estimated Cost, Conversion Value, and Landing Page URL. See Table 7.1 for an example of how Jason at Babyfuzzkin might fill out his worksheet.

Here's how you'll fill in your worksheet:

Keyword In the Keyword column, add your top-priority keywords and any additional keywords you're interested in testing. Review your long list of keywords from Chapter 6. Were there any terms that caused a lot of debate but didn't make the cut? Were there two terms that seemed equally promising? Results of this test PPC campaign will be a great tiebreaker.

How many keywords should you have in your PPC campaign? That depends on two things: your budget, and your desire to stay within the hour-a-day time frame. But we'll throw you a bone with this vague suggestion: somewhere between 10 and 50. For the purposes of this PPC trial period, it's best to keep your campaign smaller so that you can give proper attention to the details.

▶ **Table 7.1** Babyfuzzkin's PPC Keywords Worksheet

Keyword(s)	Category	Bid for Top Position	Estimated Click-Throughs	Estimated Cost	Conversion Value	Landing Page URL
baby clothes	baby clothes	$1.02	1,500	$1,530.00	high	http://www.babyfuzzkin.com/togs
baby gifts	gift menu	$2.11	360	$759.60	high	http://www.babyfuzzkin.com/gifts
baby shower gifts	baby clothes	$2.03	69	$140.07	high	http://www.babyfuzzkin.com/gifts
designer baby gifts	gift menu	$1.55	0.44	$0.68	medium	http://www.babyfuzzkin.com/gifts
designer infant clothing	baby clothes	$0.83	0.35	$0.29	high	http://www.babyfuzzkin.com/togs
designer toddler clothes	toddlers	$1.63	0.27	$0.44	medium	http://www.babyfuzzkin.com/togs
stylish baby clothes	baby clothes	$1.01	0.19	$0.19	high	http://www.babyfuzzkin.com/togs
unique baby shower gifts	gift menu	$1.72	5	$8.60	medium	http://www.babyfuzzkin.com/gifts

Landing Page URL For each keyword, note which landing page you want to send the visitor to.

Category Displaying the same ad for a group of related keywords helps reduce campaign management time. Since you've got an hour a day to work on campaign creation and maintenance, it would be reasonable to have from three to five categories of keywords. (Category names are not displayed to searchers. They are for administrative use only.) Even though more categories require more management and more ads, it's probably better to err on the side of too many categories than too few. Here are possible ways to group your keywords:

- **By landing page:** For example, an animal feed distributor may want to create categories for its Pet Care Tips page for terms like "overweight dogs" and its Horse Care Tips page for terms like "preventing colic in horses."

- **By target audience:** For example, a category called Pet Products for terms like "dog food" and "cat food" and another category called Livestock Products for terms like "bovine feed supplement" and "equine grain mix."

- **By concept:** You can categorize based on the needs your product or service fills or the concerns behind the searches. For example, a category called Low Cost for terms like "cheap dog food" or a category called Pampering for terms like "dog treats" or "dog rewards."

Bid for Position In the Bid for Position column, use the PPC engine to research the amount of money you would have to pay to get into the top spot for each of your keywords.

The PPC Keywords Worksheet doesn't make a provision for bidding lower than first place. This is for the sake of simplicity and not necessarily because we think you have to keep your ads in the top positions. You can always add a lower cost to the Bid column, but if you do, assume that the PPC engine's estimated click-through rate—and by extension, the estimated cost—is shooting high.

Estimated Click-Throughs In the Estimated Click-Throughs column, use the PPC engine to find the estimated click-throughs your ad will receive for each keyword in a given period of time (month or day).

Conversion Value In the Conversion Value column, enter your estimate of the value of the conversion in dollars. If a monetary estimate doesn't make sense for this conversion, give it a low/medium/high value based on how important a conversion for this term would be for your business. For example, a tree-trimming service might rank "large estate grounds maintenance" as high while ranking "cheap arborist" as low because a larger tree-trimming job means more green for them!

The Estimated Cost column has been programmed to calculate automatically. But if you'd prefer to use the number provided by your PPC engine, feel free to replace this column with that data.

Now: Fill in your PPC Keywords Worksheet for at least your top 10 keywords.

How Pandora Partners, Inc., Miscalculated Cost per Click for Six Months!

We once worked for a client (the name and some identifying details have been changed to prevent embarrassment) who was very enthusiastic about PPC because his campaign provided valuable conversions in a very competitive market. We came on board several months after his PPC campaign was in full swing, and we were pleased to see that this client had made his own spreadsheet to track important trends over time.

After a few days on the job, we made an astonishing discovery: Due to an unfortunate spreadsheet error (we're going to be charitable here and call it a typo), this company was working on the assumption that they were paying an average of $3.80 per click as opposed to the actual value of $0.26! Can you imagine how that affected their advertising budget, not to mention their opinion of the value of their PPC campaign? Can you imagine the smoke that rose up from our speedy phone-dialing fingers when we realized what they had been doing wrong?

Even if you're like one of us (hint: not the one of us with a degree in engineering) and gave up math class at an embarrassingly early age, you need to know this simple equation:

Cost per click = (cost) ÷ (# of clicks)

As we've mentioned, any PPC engine provides this kind of data for you. But if you ever decide to create your own reports, you can save yourself a big headache if you take some time at the start to double-check your own formulas against your PPC engine's prefab reports.

Wednesday: Write Your Ad Text

Depending on your talent with words, today may be a fun little excursion into copywriting, or it may be as frustrating as trying to bait a fishing hook with mittens on. If you have writers on your team, this is a great time to include them.

For each of your keyword categories, you're going to create a succinct, compelling ad that is substantially more interesting than your competitors'. You may want to write two or three ads for each category if your PPC service rotates ads for you. If your PPC service allows or requires a separate ad for each keyword, feel free to customize to your heart's content, but you can also do well with just one well-written ad for each keyword group.

Your HTML title and meta description tag for each landing page are a good starting point, but you'll probably need to edit them substantially for PPC use, in part due to editorial guidelines and character limits. You can read your PPC service's guidelines for lots of advice on writing ads (after all, they make money on your click-throughs, so they have every interest in your success!).

Here are some additional tips that we think will help you:

DO use keywords in the text. Studies show that people are more likely to click on your ad if the exact keyword they searched for is incorporated into your ad text.

DO be true to your landing page. Make sure that you write each ad with its intended landing page(s) in mind. Does the ad mention a specific product or solution? The landing page had better contain a clear path to it. Does the ad set up a need? The landing page should tell your visitor exactly how to fulfill it.

DO snoop on your competitors. If you're stumped, and even if you aren't, enter your keywords into the search engines and see what you're up against in the PPC venue. If everyone's ads are mentioning a certain topic, such as their low, low prices, you might not want to ignore it in your own ad. Then again, if you notice that you're competing against a clutch of nearly identical ads, you may want to describe yourself using language that will help you stand out.

DO use dynamic keyword insertion if it's available... You researched on Monday whether your PPC service of choice allows you to automatically insert searched-for keywords into your title. If a searcher enters the term "halogen bulbs" or "chandeliers," you may want to format your ad to say, "Halogen Bulbs and other lighting inventory" or "Chandeliers and other lighting inventory" to match the search. This can be a powerful way to attract the attention of your targeted audience.

...but DON'T insert the wrong keywords. If you've ever seen what appear to be inappropriate PPC ads, you can probably blame careless dynamic keyword insertion. It can create almost comical messages like "Tonsillitis: Buy Now at Shop-n-Ship.com." Likewise, if you're using broad matching, you might end up inserting nonsensical or misspelled words into your ads, so think through each keyword carefully in the context of your ad before using this feature.

DO include a compelling message. What makes your audience tick? Is it price? Is it the hope of succeeding at something or the fear of failing at something? Is it convenience? A desire for quality? A need to fit in, or to stand out? Use your ad text to speak to this need.

 Now: Following your PPC service's guidelines, write your ads. Store them in your PPC Keywords Worksheet or in your PPC service's admin screen, making sure your campaign is not turned on yet.

Thursday: Enter Your Data into the PPC System

Today's task is to transfer all of your keyword and cost preferences to your PPC account without making it "live" yet. For each keyword or group of keywords, you'll assign the attributes required by your PPC engine of choice, like cost per click, maximum bids, and daily/monthly budget cap. You already have these numbers in your PPC Keywords Worksheet. You'll categorize your keywords as you planned on Tuesday and insert the ads you wrote on Wednesday. You'll also assign appropriate landing pages for each keyword or ad. (And, to avoid wasting your money, make sure each landing page URL is working properly!)

Today may be a simple cut-and-paste job, or it might be a little more complex as you get used to navigating the campaign setup and management screens. But whatever you do, make sure your account isn't turned on yet. We're saving that for tomorrow.

Now: Enter all of your keywords, bids, categories, and ad content into the PPC system.

Friday: Turn On Your PPC Campaign

It's been two weeks since you sent out your site modification requests to your team or tasked yourself with making the changes. Is your site ready for its big debut? If you've finished optimizing your website, your landing pages will be clearly relevant to your PPC ads and targeted users will be able to find what they need. Don't flip the PPC switch until your site is ready. If your site content doesn't match your advertising campaign, it will confuse or annoy your visitors, and it may be removed by the PPC service for noncompliance of editorial guidelines.

Assuming your site is ready for the trick-or-treaters to come ringing the bell, let's get started. It's best to start this task early in the day so you can check that all is well before you go home for the night. Rather then spend a continuous hour on this task, we recommend you block out two half-hour segments of time. The first half hour you will use to turn on your account, which is probably as simple as changing the attribute "paused" or "offline" to "live" or "online." Later in the day, you'll spend another half hour checking in on your account to make sure all is well.

Here are things to watch out for:

- **No impressions.** Don't expect miracles, but do make sure you actually turned on the campaign.
- **Too many clicks.** If you're already close to blowing your budget after a few hours, something is out of whack. Either you underestimated the number of

clicks your ad would receive (you could have worse problems!) or you entered your bid price incorrectly.

- **The wrong ad showing up for the wrong keyword.** It would be a fairly easy mistake to, say, place an ad meant for your Industrial Products category into your Home Products category. Enter some of your keywords into the search engine and view your ads to make sure you haven't made this kind of error.

We do not recommend micromanaging your ads on a daily basis; the PPC engines' bid management tools should make this unnecessary. Regardless, today is a good day to monitor them closely to make sure you haven't made any boneheaded mistakes. Also, seeing your PPC ads online is a moment for celebration in your SEO campaign! After you turn on the account and check for mistakes, send out an e-mail to your team! Enlist them to help you catch any glitches that you may miss over the next few days. Throughout the rest of the plan, we've included days for you to keep an eye on, and generate reports from, your PPC campaign.

Today, before you forget, you will also want to record some of the basic setup information about your campaign in your PPC Keywords Worksheet. We know from experience that once you start running multiple PPC campaigns, or if you decide to share or hand off campaign management responsibility, it's great to have this information in an easy-to-find location:

- Date campaign was turned on
- Maximum monthly budget
- Total number of keywords
- Account login information

 Now: Turn on your PPC campaign and record your basic account data in your PPC Keywords Worksheet. Check your account later today for errors and unexpected results.

Week 4: Visibility Check and Monthly Reporting

You've had a productive month: getting your website up to snuff with a basic level of optimization, starting a link campaign, and turning on those PPC ads! Now, we're giving you a week to gather up all the information on what this work has accomplished.

This week is not just about producing a report, although certainly that's important. It's really about the thinking, planning, reviewing, and analysis that you do while you are gathering the information for your report.

A smaller SEO effort, like this hour-a-day approach, will have a high documentation-to-"work" ratio. In this case, it's a 1:4 ratio—one week out of every month devoted to gathering and reporting information. If you increased your SEO activities, this ratio would probably decrease: many of your reporting tasks would stay nearly the same. Regardless of the size of your campaign, a commitment to tracking and documentation will always separate the pack leaders from the also-rans.

Your daily assignments for this week are as follows:

Monday: Check Organic Status
Tuesday: Check Links
Wednesday: Check Conversions
Thursday: Monitor PPC Ads
Friday: Action Items

Monday: Check Organic Status

Last month, you established a baseline level for your site's visibility on the four major search engines. Today, you'll find out how your standings have changed. We'll ask you to check two values:

- Search engine rankings
- Indexed pages

Search Engine Rankings

For this task, you will perform the manual rankings check on the four major search engines for all of your top target keywords. You learned how to do this back in Chapter 6.

With your Rank Tracking Worksheet ready to go in your SEO Idea Bank, this task shouldn't take a whole lot of preparation.

Now: Now, open up your Rank Tracking Worksheet and fill in your website ranks for this month.

With your ranks for last month and this month side by side, it's easy to see any changes. We're going to guess that there hasn't been a whole lot of improvement to your ranks yet. Don't be alarmed—this is perfectly normal! After all, your basic site optimization has only been in place for a couple of weeks, and you may only have a few new inbound links. If you were starting from zero or you had some easy fixes in your optimization, you may have noticeable improvement in ranks this month. If you already had decent levels of visibility, you'll need to be patient.

Now it's time to go beyond the numbers, but first you'll need a document to do it in. Most of your Baseline Monthly Report, with the exception of the Quick Reference sheet, can be repurposed for your ongoing monthly reports.

 Now: Open your Baseline Monthly Report, and rename it (by choosing File > Save As) with the current date. This is now your current Monthly Report.

Start with the "Site Visibility" section, and in a sentence or two, summarize your standings this month as compared to last month. Here are some examples:

- We gained top-30 listings on MSN for three of our target keywords.
- We have a new #2 listing for the term "novelty napkin holders" on Ask.

Next, put on your thinking cap and flesh out these bare-bones facts with some juicy analysis. Why do you think that these changes occurred? What could be done to improve any less-than-pleasing situations? You're still getting your feet wet in SEO, so you might not feel as if you know how to do this, but we recommend you try. Possible analysis might look like this:

- We gained top-30 listings on MSN for three of our target keywords. Our text optimization probably had something to do with this.
- We have a new #2 listing for the term "novelty napkin holders" on Ask. However, since we already have top-10 listings on the other search engines for this term, I don't expect significant rank changes on those.

Over the next couple of months you will become more and more adept at this sort of SEO rumination.

 Now: Add your summary and analysis to the "Site Visibility" section of your current Monthly Report.

Indexed Pages

In addition to monitoring search engine ranks for your top keywords, we recommend checking in on the total number of pages indexed. You learned how to do this in Chapter 6 using a special search shortcut.

> **Now:** Check the total number of pages indexed on your site in each of the four major search engines. Record the value on your Rank Tracking Worksheet.

Why record the total number of pages indexed on a regular basis? For one, if you previously had obstacles to robot indexing on your site, you're likely to see a great deal of improvement here once those obstacles are removed. And, if you monitor this number, you may be able to catch and resolve any indexing problems before they result in a major drop in traffic.

If any of your landing pages were not indexed when you checked last month, be sure to look back again and see if your efforts have made a difference.

> **Now:** Check the indexing of any landing pages that were not indexed last month. Document status on your Rank Tracking Worksheet.

Looking to cut down on your workload? You can skip checking indexing if your landing pages were already indexed last month and you haven't made any changes to your website in the interim. Or skip checking the total number of pages indexed and focus only on your landing pages.

slacker

With a little sleuthing, you can see which search engine robots have visited your site. See Chapter 10, "Extra Credit and Guilt-Free Slacking," for more information.

xtra cred

Tuesday: Check Links

Today, you'll follow up on the link-building campaign that you started just a couple of weeks ago. We know you just started, but if you keep up with link building, each month you'll be faced with an increasingly long and gnarly tracking worksheet that will be nearly impossible to assess at a glance. That's why it's important to keep track of your link-building activities and accomplishments in a monthly summary report. You'll document the following in both words and numbers:

- Link campaign activities
- Google PageRank

Link Campaign Activities

Most likely, you've already had some correspondence, possibly even several back-and-forth e-mail communications, with possible linking sites. You may have also made directory submittals this month and explored many other linking opportunities. Today, review your e-mails and your Link Tracking Worksheet and briefly summarize these activities. Here are some examples of this kind of commentary:

- I contacted 14 website owners seeking new inbound links, and requested updated URLs from four others. Of these, our site received two link updates and one new link.
- On (date), I submitted our website to the Yahoo! Directory in the category:...
- Surfing the Web, I found a long list of sites that may wish to link to our website. Links will be requested after our new landing pages are complete.
- Three site owners stated that they would not link to us because...

If you received useful feedback from any site owners, such as a rejection letter that stated specifically why you were turned down, consider quoting it in your report so that the idea doesn't get lost in your e-mail inbox forever.

Google PageRank

Despite our misgivings about the usefulness of the Google PageRank value, we recommend that you track it for your landing pages on a monthly basis. Why? It's an easy way to gather "at-a-glance" numbers that can help you see changes in your status over time.

You can see Google PageRank just by browsing to your landing pages and reviewing the Google Toolbar that you downloaded in Chapter 6.

 Now: Browse to each of your landing pages and record the Google PageRank on your Rank Tracking Worksheet.

 slacker Google PageRank is good to know, but it's not essential. If you're short on time, you can skip this step.

Wednesday: Check Conversions

Conversions, especially if you've defined them properly so that they match the overall goals of your organization, are truly the bottom line of Your SEO Plan.

Last month, you established a baseline on conversions to the best of your ability. Maybe you've got plenty of cold, hard facts and were able to document "One percent of site visitors, and 7 percent of search engine-based visitors, completed an online purchase transaction." Or, perhaps you had to improvise a little: "According to the development department, very few of our donors have any awareness of the website's existence, and there is no evidence that any donations this month resulted from Web visits." If you don't have a conversion tracking method in place, you may not have much to write in this section. Make your best estimate—next month you'll devote an entire week to establishing conversion tracking.

Now: Open your conversion tracking document and record this month's data.

Take a look at this month's conversion data as compared to last month's. If there are differences, what caused them? Separating out all of the different factors that contribute to your bottom line—SEO efforts, seasonal effects, even regular month-to-month fluctuations—is almost impossible. Your mission over the coming months will be to separate out the effects of your SEO campaign as well as you can. If there are any results that you *can* attribute directly to your SEO efforts today, make a note of them in your report. Here are some examples:

- Listing our site in the Outdoor Lifestyle Directory has resulted in a branding boost and a 7 percent increase in page views.
- Since we succeeded in getting the Quilting Supplies page indexed in all four search engines, we have seen a 27 percent increase in cotton batting sales.
- Four hundred click-throughs on our PPC campaign resulted in 16 sales of wine gift baskets.

Now: Write your conversion data and commentary in your Monthly Report.

Thursday: Monitor PPC Ads

Each month, your report will include important information about your spending and accomplishments with your PPC ad campaigns. This month, be sure to touch on these points:

- Campaign setup info
- Monthly PPC performance data
- Top performing keywords
- Changes to campaigns

Here are some guidelines for making the most of the data you get from your PPC engine.

Campaign Setup Info

Since this is the first month that you have a PPC campaign, you will have a lot to say here. Which service did you choose and why? Are you focusing on a small number of popular keywords or going with a longer list of less-popular but more targeted terms? What is your goal for this campaign?

Monthly PPC Performance Data

You have a lot of flexibility to create comprehensive, customized reports using your PPC service. Later you'll use these to monitor, finesse, and drop the duds in your campaign. But for this Monthly Report, you just want to boil down the most important data for a 2-minute scan. At a minimum, this data includes the following:

- Total number of click-throughs
- Click-through percentage
- Total cost
- Average total cost per click
  And, if you're able to track conversions using your PPC service:
- Total number of conversions
- Conversion percentage
- Average total cost per conversion

We left the information brief, but you can go into a lot more depth here if you desire. Adjust your spreadsheet to suit your needs and preferences.

Now: Use your PPC service to generate a monthly campaign report, and enter the keyword performance data into your Monthly Report.

Keep your PPC service's campaign report open; you'll need it to complete the next section.

Top Performing Keywords

Looking through long lists of keyword data should be banned by OSHA! Whether it's a large PPC campaign with hundreds or thousands of keywords or a smaller one with a couple dozen, your keyword performance data can give you a major migraine. That's why we like to pull out some of the top-performing keywords for an eye-pleasing review.

First, you need to decide what you will consider good performance for your keywords. Some options are highest number of click-throughs, highest total number of conversions, best conversion percentage, best click-through percentage, highest total dollar amount spent, highest profit (dollar amount spent minus cost per click), and even a combination of multiple factors.

Once you have chosen your preferred performance measure, browse through your PPC service's campaign report and pull out the top 10 or so keywords based on performance. You will list them, along with their performance values, in the Monthly Report. See anything interesting or striking, like a new or unexpected performer? This information may lead to new strategies in your ongoing campaign.

Now: Record your top-performing keywords in the Monthly Report.

Campaign Analysis

Here is the place to record any changes that took place in your PPC campaigns this month: keywords bumped up or down the totem pole or changes to ad copy.

This is also the place to make your recommendations or plans for future changes: "Based on the success of our Purple Lampshade promotion, we will add a purple lampshade ad starting next month" or "Thirteen keywords with high click-throughs but low conversion rates will be dropped from the campaign."

With your PPC campaign monitoring complete, you're ready to finalize your Monthly Report with some forward-thinking analysis and action items.

Friday: Action Items

Here is the section that everybody on your team will turn to when they get this report. And even if you're working alone, this to-do list will be an indispensable reference as you move forward into the next month.

One of the challenges that we've faced time and time again in our SEO efforts is writing reports that are complete and meaningful, readable, and most important, *actionable*. Yes, actionable—it may be a made-up word, but it sure is an important idea in SEO.

Pearl of Wisdom: The best reports are not just repositories of information, they are also tools to guide your team through the next steps.

To assemble your action items, review each of the previous sections of the report. How is your organic search engine status? Do your pages still need basic optimization? Are there keywords you want to drop or add to your PPC campaign? And what are the next steps in your link-building campaign? Try to cover all activities, even the mundane ones like "Continue gathering inbound links." And be sure to include any budget or labor allotment approvals you will need for the upcoming month.

You're a professional, so we're betting you've seen an action item list or two in your lifetime. We bet you're used to seeing the following columns: Action, Person Responsible, Target Completion Date. Now, here's a curveball for you: We want you to add a column called *Reason* to your action items list.

The Reason column will be the hardest one to write. This is where you must provide a concise explanation of what good this action is going to do for your company. It hearkens back to what you learned in Chapter 5, "Get Your Team on Board": Educate your team for best results in SEO. Giving your team a quick explanation of the reasoning behind your requested change will eliminate the "Why in heaven's name am I being asked to do this extra work?" or "Why should I allot this extra budget?" reaction. And, being forced to write a reason for every action item will help you keep your own ducks in a row as well.

 Now: Write your action items, including the Reason column, in your Monthly Report.

You've been at this SEO thing for a couple of months now, and maybe you've even taken a liking to it. Next month, you'll get a little more technical about your site structure, conversions, and return on investment (ROI). Get ready to "establish the habit" of SEO!

Month Two: Establish the Habit

If it's true that it only takes 30 days to establish a daily habit, your SEO habit is now official!

This month, you'll tidy up your website's structure for improved SEO performance, and you'll get serious about tracking conversions. Then you'll spend a week honing your SEO research skills. And, as always, you'll document. It's all part of the clutter-clearing and routine-forming process that will keep your ongoing campaign cruising along.

Chapter Contents

Week 5: Site Structure Improvements

Last month, you took care of basic site optimization and knocked down obstacles to robot indexing of your landing pages. This week, you'll delve a little deeper into some techie decisions that can improve your site's optimization, indexing, and overall visibility success.

This week's tasks will involve a range of SEO skills, from PR-style communication to serious server geeking. It's a week when you will definitely want your team queued up and clued in to your needs and reasoning. Keep your meeting calendar handy as you review your daily assignments:

Monday: The Spider's-Eye View
Tuesday: Shape Up Your Site Map
Wednesday: Clean Up Ugly Listings
Thursday: Your Robots.txt File
Friday: PPC Quick Check

Monday: The Spider's-Eye View

Have you ever seen those photos that show what the world looks like to a dog? Or maybe you enjoyed the kaleidoscopic fly-cam scenes in the 1950s movie *The Fly*. Today you're going to learn how to take a search engine spider's-eye view of your website. Viewer discretion is advised: what you are about to see might be surprisingly scary.

As you learned in Chapter 3, "Eternal Truths of SEO," a search engine spider is simply software that goes through the Internet looking at web pages and sending information back to a central repository. It doesn't view content in the same way human site visitors do. Since spiders are an important—although by no means the most important—audience for your website, you want to know how your website appears to them. Today you will use a tool called a *spider emulator* to put on your spider's-eye view glasses and do exactly that.

For example, here is a typical web page, as viewed through the browser.

And here is the same web page, viewed through a spider emulator.

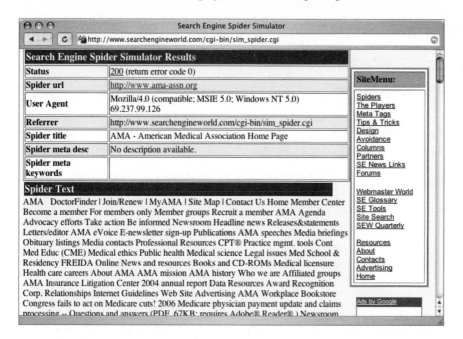

Are you scared yet? There are lots of spider emulators available on the web. We use http://searchengineworld.com/cgi-bin/sim_spider.cgi often because we like its simplicity and its built-in link checking feature. Another of our favorites is: http://tools.summitmedia.co.uk/spider/. You're going to view each of your landing pages through a spider emulator today.

Here's how to do it:

- Starting with your home page, go to http://searchengineworld.com/cgi-bin/sim_spider.cgi or the spider emulator of your choice and enter your page URL into the emulator.

- Once you see your page as it is seen by spiders, ask yourself some questions: Does this accurately represent the information I expected to see on my site? Is it readable and in the correct order? Are my target keywords present?

- For any noted problems, consider possible solutions. For example, if the well-crafted, keyword-rich content you added last month is not showing up, it may be that it's not rendering in standard HTML text. Print out this page and bring it with you to your web developer to track down the problem. Or, are you seeing the same nonsensical image ALT tag (for example, ImgFile01) repeating multiple times on the page? Make a note to have it removed or revised with appropriate keyword-rich descriptions.

- Perform this check for each of your landing pages.

Tuesday: Shape Up Your Site Map

Last month, we suggested creating a site map to help search engine robots navigate your site. If your website doesn't have a site map, today you'll consider creating one. If you already have one, you'll optimize it today.

Why Build a Site Map?

We think that just about every website can benefit from a site map, especially websites that contain more than 10 pages. Most people know that site maps are good for the user experience: they orient your site visitors and help lost visitors find their way to the right page. But there's even more benefit when you consider SEO. A site map can improve the search engine visibility of your website in several ways:

- By providing search engine robots with links to navigate through your site
- By pointing search engine robots to dynamic or hard-to-reach pages that might not be accessible otherwise
- By acting as a possible landing page, optimized for search traffic
- By providing ready-to-use content for the File Not Found page where visitors are automatically taken if they try to go to a nonexistent URL within your domain

If your site is small enough that links to every page are included in your *global navigation* (navigation provided on every page of your site) or absolutely every page on your site is available within two clicks from the home page, then you may not need a site map. But if your site is larger, and especially if it contains pages that may be hard for search engine robots to find, we highly recommend a site map.

Site Map Design 101

Simply put, a site map is a page that links to every page on your website. If you're like many web surfers, you visit a site map as a last resort when you can't find what you need or if there's no in-site search function. You're happy to forget it as soon as you leave it. But if a robot visits your site map, it's not going to forget what it saw, and it will be pleased as punch to come back on a regular basis. Here are a few pointers for treating both robots and human users well:

Include the most important pages. People will get lost if your site map contains too many links. That means, if your site has more than, say, 100 pages, you'll need to choose the most important pages and exclude the others. Here are our suggestions for pages to include:

- Product category pages
- Major product pages
- FAQ and Help pages
- Contact or Request Information pages
- All of the key pages on your *paths to conversion*, the pages that your visitors follow from landing page through conversion
- Your 10 most popular pages (you'll learn how to find these when you delve into your server stats next week).
- Top pages clicked from your internal search engine, if you have one (see Chapter 10, "Extra Credit and Guilt-Free Slacking," for more information on internal search engines).

xtra cred

Go easy on the autogeneration. Some content management systems will automatically generate a site map. As in so many other areas of SEO, we prefer the human touch. If you, or your tech teammates, are leaning in the automated direction, be sure you review the outcome carefully to be sure your site map has these characteristics:

- The layout is easy on the human eye.
- All links are standard HTML text that can be followed by spiders.
- The important pages (included in the preceding list items) are easy to find.

Look at other sites for design inspiration. Don't waste your time reinventing the wheel. There are hundreds, thousands, nay, bazillions of site maps out there on the Web. Use one you like as a starting point.

Optimize your site map. We don't mean you should think of your site map as one of your top-priority landing pages. But if done tastefully, your site map can actually contain a fair number of your target keywords, not to mention compelling text. For example, instead of a link simply labeled "Fungicides," your site map could contain more keywords: "Organic fungicides to eliminate lawn disease," with the most important keywords, "organic fungicides," as the anchor text. Similarly, why use a title like "Our Products" when you can say, "Our Earth-friendly herbicides, insecticides, and fungicides?"

Link to your site map from every page. Users have come to expect a link to your site map in the footer of every page on the site, so make use of this spot. If your site has a search box, you may also wish to add a link to the site map near the search box and even make a link to the site map a fixture within the site search results page.

Now: Design your new site map or shape up your existing site map using the preceding guidelines. Deliver your requested changes to your web developer or make the changes yourself.

For more site map design hints, see usability guru Jakob Nielson's website at www.useit.com/alertbox/20020106.html.

By the way, your site map isn't the same as your Google Sitemap. As you learned in Chapter 4, "How The Search Engines Work Right Now," Google Sitemaps is a service designed to allow webmasters to submit URLs and additional page information directly to the Google index. See Chapter 10 for ideas on how to get started with Google Sitemaps.

Wednesday: Clean Up Ugly Listings

During your site visibility assessments, you probably found at least one listing in the search results that made you cringe. A broken URL from your domain available to the searching public? An out-of-date press release announcing the hire of a long-gone CEO? Today you'll take steps to clean up some of these brand-busting uglies.

Here are some of the more common problems we've observed and how to deal with them. You probably won't face all of these problems, but we expect you'll see at least one:

Broken links The search engines don't want broken links in their results any more than you do. They will eventually figure out that a page doesn't exist and remove it from their indices. But why let a perfectly good search engine ranking go to waste? Try one of the following approaches:

- Since the URL is already indexed and may already have some good rankings, inbound links, or bookmarked traffic, consider creating a new page and saving it at the missing URL. However, do this only if it makes sense to create a new page with similar content—it would be awkward if your cabinet hardware products were listed at a page called "floral-arrangements.html."

- Talk to your IT people about setting up an automatic redirection, called a *301 redirect*, that carries traffic on this page to another page of your choosing. But don't make the common mistake of pointing the redirect to your home page! Choose the page on your site that best matches the one that has gone missing. And read up on techniques in Chapter 9, "Month Three: It's a Way of Life," for preventing this kind of *link rot* (insider lingo for the gradual increase in the number of broken links on the Web) in the future.

- Sometimes, broken links linger in the search results because your server fails to mention that the page is missing. That's right; it's possible for a server to return a "Page Found" message even if a page is missing! It's a riddle wrapped in a conundrum, but luckily it's an easy fix for your IT folks.

Out-of-date content You don't want your potential customers seeing outdated product descriptions, promotions that are no longer active, or last year's price list in the search results. The best and fastest approach to this problem is to update your site's content while keeping the file in the same location so that it doesn't lose its search engine status.

In some cases, a simple update may not be so simple. For example, suppose you have found a well-ranked search engine listing for your web page featuring the Snackmaster 2003 but your company no longer sells this older model. Your website now has a new page featuring the Snackmaster 2007. If you rewrite your 2003 page to describe your new product, your site will contain two pages with identical content, which is a search engine no-no as well as an administrative headache. Instead, it's best to edit the 2003 page content to include a notice that a new model is available and link to the 2007 model page. A 301 redirect would be another option, especially if there's no customer support or archival reasons to keep the old page live.

Private or inappropriate material There it is, staring out at you from between listing #5 and listing #7: Your company's holiday gift list, with addresses and phone numbers of all your best clients! You need to clean up your act, and fast. Here's how:

- Remove the page from your site. Or, leave the offending file live, but immediately remove the offending content.
- Then request removal from the search engines (see www.yourseoplan.com for links to removal URLs).

By leaving the file live but changing the content, you may benefit from a quicker update than if you took down the page altogether. However, you should be aware that a search engine's cached pages may retain a snapshot of the content for longer than you're comfortable with, and there are historical web archive sites that may display the content forever. If you have serious legal concerns—for example, if you posted a disclaimer that said, "All information on this site is medical advice" rather than "...*not* medical advice"—you can use the copyright search methods described next month to search for instances of your content throughout the Web and seek removal.

While these are all positive steps, in truth there's little you can do to prevent robots from indexing pages that are live and accessible. If you really do not want pages to be found, secure them behind a password!

www and non-www URLs in your listings In the eyes of the search engines, these two URLs are different pages:

- http://www.yourdomain.com/
- http://yourdomain.com

What's Popping Up at the Exploratorium?

Lowell Robinson of the Exploratorium, San Francisco's museum of science, art, and human perception, had a problem: how to display interactive video and Flash content on the museum's Science of Gardening website (www.exploratorium.edu/gardening). Most of this rich, interactive content was built within separate pop-up windows. Lowell and his team knew that this could wreak havoc on their search engine listings.

Their primary concern was not that the search engines would have trouble indexing the pages, but rather that the pages *would* be indexed and site visitors would click directly to the pop-up content—in a full browser window rather than a mini-pop-up window—without entering the Exploratorium website:

"After putting hundreds of hours into producing this rich content, we didn't want the search engines to index our pop-up windows as stand-alone web pages with no way to click to the parent website and none of our branding or credits displayed."

The Science of Gardening team came up with a clever solution: The web developer placed a *sniffer*, a piece of code that identifies the referring URL, on the pop-up windows. Now visitors who are already viewing the Science of Gardening website see the regular pop-up (see the left screen shot below), while surfers coming in from search engines or other links see the Flash or video content wrapped in a proper branding package, with easy access to the rest of the site (see the right screen capture below).

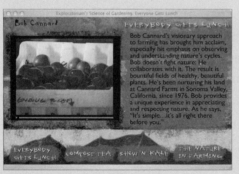 

While some less-than-ethical SEOs may use a sniffer to trick the search engines and confuse site visitors (a technique called cloaking), this is one example of using a sniffer to *help* the audience rather than deceive them.

Lowell's team learned an important lesson: You can't always control how people arrive at your website! If you have a website with significant content displayed in pop-up windows or within frames, be sure to check how they look as stand-alone pages and make sure that you are comfortable with them being potential entry points into your site. If you aren't, follow the Exploratorium's lead and take steps to make those windows shine! (Full disclosure: Lowell is the beloved husband of one of the authors, and yeah, he got a little free advice on this project.)

Now, *you* know and *we* know that these are actually pointing to the same page, and we figure that soon enough the search engines will get it right. But for now, most search engines have what industry insiders call a *canonical URL* problem (*canonical* is a programmer's term for "standard," so a canonical URL would be the standard or preferred URL for your website) and it can have a significant effect on your SEO success:

> **Pearl of Wisdom:** If your website is listed under more than one version of a URL, your ranks can suffer.

If your inbound links are distributed among different versions of your URL, the strength of these links can be diluted. You'll need to take these steps to deal with your canonical issues:

- Ensure that all internal links within your site point to the same URL. Choose a format and stick with it. You might even consider using absolute links (which include the full address of your website, starting with http://) rather than relative links. This will eliminate all canonical problems caused by internal links.
- Set up a 301 redirect that always points the "bad" URL(s) to your preferred URL. That will help search engines know which one is your preference. (By the way, this could be a tricky one for your webmaster, so don't suggest it without some sort of bribe in hand.)
- If there are inbound links from other websites pointing to the wrong URL format, write to them and ask for an update.

Other sites stealing your mojo Is there a listing on the search engines that looks like your website at first glance but is actually the website of one of your affiliates, vendors, or partners? Often, the best way to address this situation is with a direct phone call or e-mail requesting that the page be removed. Also see Chapter 9 for more information on searching for other sites that use your content without permission.

> **Now:** Work on cleaning up any problem listings that you previously identified in your Task Journal.

Thursday: Your Robots.txt File

A robots.txt file is the first file that a search engine robot visits on your website. Like a snooty nightclub bouncer with a velvet rope, the robots.txt file decides which robots are welcome and which need to move on to that less-exclusive joint down the street. Robots.txt can admit or reject robots on a sitewide, directory-by-directory, or page-by-page basis.

SEO folks often feel a special affection for the robots.txt file because it provides a rare opportunity to communicate with a search engine robot. However, its capabilities are really very limited. Robots.txt files exist only to *exclude* indexing. Just as a bouncer can keep people out but can't force anyone to come in, the robots.txt file can't do anything to entice a robot to spend *more* time or visit *more* pages on your site. Also, compliance with your robots.txt file is voluntary, not mandatory. The major search engines will generally try to follow your instructions, but other, less-reputable types might not. This is why you should not rely on your robots.txt file to prevent spidering of sensitive, private, or inappropriate materials.

Do You Need a *Robots.txt* File?

You may not need a robots.txt file. Without one, all robots will have free access to non-password-protected pages on your site. To decide if you need a robots.txt file for your website, ask yourself these questions:

- Are there any pages or directories on my site that I do not want listed on the search engines, such as an intranet or internal phone list?
- Are there any specific search engines that I do not want to display my site?
- Do I know of any dynamic pages or programming features that might cause problems for spiders, like getting caught in a loop (infinitely bouncing between two pages)?
- Does my website contain pages with duplicate content? (These should not be indexed or you may be penalized.)
- Are there directories on the site that contain programming scripts only, not viewable pages?

If the answers to these questions are no, then you do not need a robots.txt file. You've got the rest of the day off! If you have any yes answers, you'll prepare your robots.txt file today.

 Now: Determine whether you need a robots.txt file in your website.

Create Your *Robots.txt* File

Robots.txt files are very simple text files. To find a sample, go to www.yourseoplan.com/robots.txt and view ours, or go to just about any other site and look for the robots.txt file in the *root directory*.

The robots.txt file usually looks something like this:

```
User-agent: googlebot
Disallow: /private-files/
Disallow: /more-private-files/
User-agent: *
Disallow: /cgi-scripts/
```

In this example, Google's spider (called Googlebot) is excluded from indexing files within the two directories called private-files and more-private-files, and all robots (signified by a wild-card asterisk *) are excluded from indexing the directory called cgi-scripts.

There are numerous websites that will walk you through building and saving your robots.txt file. A very clear tutorial can be found here: www.searchengineworld.com/robots/robots_tutorial.htm. Answers to just about any question you could think of about robots are here: www.robotstxt.org. And we are particularly fond of the regularly updated listing of robot names, available here: www.jafsoft.com/searchengines/webbots.html.

Now: Create your robots.txt file and save it in the root directory of your website, or request that your webmaster do so.

If you are feeling any doubt about whether your robots.txt file is written properly, *don't* post it. The last thing you want to do is inadvertently shut out the search engines.

Here's a fun experiment—what do your Big Five competitors have on *their* robots.txt files?

xtra cred

Robots Meta Tags

A robots meta tag serves a similar purpose as the robots.txt file, but it is placed within individual pages on your site rather than in your root directory. A robots meta tag affects only the page it resides on. Chances are you don't need to use this type of tag, but here's a quick overview in case you do. You might choose to use a robots meta tag rather than a robots.txt file because you have only one or two pages you wish to exclude on the site, or maybe you only want to do a brief, temporary exclusion. Another possible reason is that you do not have access to the root directory on your site.

To exclude the robots from a page using the robots meta tag, simply include the following code in the HTML head of the page:

```
<meta name="robots" content="noindex, nofollow">
```

This will prevent search engine robots from indexing content or following links from the page.

 Now: Add robots meta tags to pages on an as-needed basis.

Friday: PPC Quick Check

Every Friday from now until the end of Your SEO Plan, we're going to ask you to check in on your PPC campaign. This weekly Quick Check will ensure that your campaign doesn't go dramatically out of whack over the course of a month. We estimate that your Quick Check will take about 15 minutes, but today you get a whole hour since it's a new process for you!

Here are the steps to include in your PPC Quick Check:

- Log in to your PPC account.

- Check your total campaign spending so far for this month. Is your campaign on track to spend your monthly budget on schedule? If you've set your daily budget appropriately, it's difficult to spend too much—but bugs on PPC engines are not unheard of. You should also keep in mind that spending too little can be just as bad as spending too much; you want to be right on target. If your campaign is low, you may wish to add more keywords or increase some of your bids. If your campaign is high, reduce bids or remove or disable keywords.

- For each keyword category, figure out how to sort the list of keywords by total amount spent. Some keywords are going to be naturally more popular and costly than others, so it's probably not realistic to expect that your spending will be distributed evenly among the keywords. If one or two keywords are using up too much of your budget and you don't think they're converting well enough, you may wish to temporarily disable them or lower their bids. Some keywords with extremely high click-through rates may need to be checked on a daily basis. If you've found a keyword that is gobbling up your entire budget, consider moving it into its own category so that you can watch and manage it more closely.

- If you are testing multiple ads for some keywords, review which are performing better. See Chapter 9 for more information on running a multiple-ad test.

- PPC engines are often so good at reporting that you won't need to do much documenting elsewhere. But until you get the hang of PPC, you may want to make a note of any changes to your account in your Task Journal.

Your PPC Quick Check will probably become second nature in time, but during Your SEO Plan we'll remind you each Friday.

Now, with your site structure improvements in place and your PPC campaign purring, you've never been more ready to get some serious conversion tracking underway!

Week 6: Conversion Tracking

Now that your SEO campaign is getting into its "humming along" phase, we think you're ready for the challenge of conversion tracking.

Conversion tracking is a simple concept to grasp: You count how many people are performing a desired action, you determine where those people came from, and you figure out what keywords they used if they came from a search engine. Here's the simplest scenario: Your goal is to get more *unique visitors*. You use data from your servers to tell you how many unique visitors came to your site and what search terms they used.

But tracking online activities like making a purchase, filling out a form, or downloading a file, not to mention offline conversions like phone sales and walk-in business, requires a more sophisticated tracking system.

This week you'll develop a plan for tracking the conversion goals you established in Chapter 1, "Clarify Your Goals." Think "baby steps": You probably won't finalize your tracking system, but you'll set the wheels in motion. This week you'll find the tools you need and some ideas for tracking even the most challenging types of conversions. Pop your head out of your cubicle and let your IT folks know you're going to be bugging them soon, because you'll need them to help you make this happen.

Here are your daily tasks:

Monday: PPC Conversion Tracking
Tuesday: Get to Know Your Basic Server Stats
Wednesday: Tracking Online Conversions
Thursday: Tracking Offline Conversions
Friday: PPC Quick Check and Link Requests

Monday: PPC Conversion Tracking

Your starter PPC campaign has been running for a few weeks now, and you have probably already have seen a nice influx of click-throughs. But do you know which, if any, of these click-throughs has turned into a conversion? For example, let's say you sell left-handed guitars. Your PPC reports can tell you the number of people who came to your site after searching for "left-handed guitars," and your server logs or sales figures can tell you how many people purchased a left-handed guitar, but to *tie together* those two actions requires some additional steps.

Both Google and YSM offer built-in conversion tracking that can connect the dots. Their systems keep it simple by answering only one question: which PPC click-throughs turned into conversions for your website?

How it works To implement the built-in conversion tracking on Google or YSM, you'll need to define a page or pages on your site that indicate a conversion has been completed. Very possibly, this will be your transaction completion page or confirmation page—it's wherever you say thank you to your customers for a purchase, download, registration, or form completion (you did remember to say thank you, didn't you?). You will put a tiny piece of code or image (also called a tag or tracking pixel) on that page to communicate with the PPC system. On Google, you can also assign certain variables like a dollar amount for conversion value. You will then be able to view information such as total conversions, conversion rate, and cost per conversion in your admin interface and reports.

Benefits Since you already have a PPC account, there is no easier way to monitor conversions from your SEO efforts and expenditures! The process requires very little technical intervention on your part and nothing in the way of server setup.

Google, always wanting a bigger piece of your organization's pie chart, also makes it possible for you to track campaigns you're running on other PPC services. Yahoo! offers a similar capability, called Marketing Console, for a fee.

Limitations As much as you may wish otherwise, your site visitors aren't going to march in lockstep through your site from entrance to conversion. Much more likely, they'll browse around your site, go to other sites, and then come back minutes, hours, or weeks later. When they return, they may perform another search or type in your site URL, or perhaps their web browser will remember your site address and fill in the URL for them. Whatever the case, you may have lost the link between the original keyword search and this conversion. Your PPC service may hold onto visitor information for some period of time, perhaps 30 days, using a cookie. This feature will save you from losing at least a portion of your wanderers.

Another obvious limitation of the PPC tracking systems is that they only track PPC visitors, not people who came in through organic search results.

Hey! Where'd Everybody Go?

We spoke with Anthony Severo, founder and managing partner of Vertical Spin, a business intelligence consulting company, to learn more about conversion tracking. One way that Anthony helps his clients is finding out where their site visitors are dropping out of the conversion process.

He explains: "Let's assume that I have a 1 percent overall conversion rate from the moment someone views the keyword on a search engine to the point at which the purchase is completed. That means that 99 percent of the visitors are not converting. This is great data, but you need to get to the next level of detail to take action and optimize the conversion rate. Where are the trouble spots:

- "Is the user not clicking through the ad [on a PPC sponsorship]?

- "Is the user getting to the site and immediately exiting?

- "Is the user engaged in the product description but not buying the product?

- "Are they dropping off in the checkout process?"

Through further analysis and experimentation, Anthony works to discover exactly why users are leaving the site.

For example, "…let's say that 80 percent of the users exit when checking out. This clearly identifies an issue with the checkout process. You can conclude that the visitor is engaged, they found the product they were interested in purchasing, and were ready to buy, but somehow had a problem with the checkout process. This issue could be

- "the checkout process is too tedious and time consuming;

- "the checkout process has a bug that prevents people from checking out (I experience this more often than you can believe);

- "the visitor continued shopping and somehow got distracted and never came back to check out."

The good news is, "If you can reduce this drop-off by even a few percent, it will greatly increase your conversion rate." Finally, a word of caution from someone in the know: "Tracking tools provide so much data and you can easily spend hours per day viewing it." For a streamlined approach, focus on the highest-priority metrics:

- "Am I driving visitors to the site?

- "Are they converting?

- "What are my ad costs?

- "What are my revenues?"

Take Anthony's words to heart with a focus on identifying drop-off and tracking actionable data and your SEO campaign will be sure to flourish.

Before you set up a PPC conversion tracking tool, be sure your organization is comfortable giving the PPC engine access to potentially sensitive information about your conversions. Some in the SEO industry have expressed concern that sharing this information will lead to security breaches or a rise in PPC prices.

 Now: Assuming you get clearance, set up conversion tracking on your PPC starter campaign.

With your conversion stats in hand, you'll have all the information you need to shape up your PPC campaign return on investment next month!

Tuesday: Get to Know Your Basic Server Stats

You have a website, which means you have a server, which means your server is probably making server logs. Like a good computer, it logs and logs and logs: who came to your site, where they came from, what browser they were using, and more. Each time any action is taken on your website, your diligent server log file makes a note of it.

We hope, for your health, that you never look at a server log file. Doing so can cause headaches, dizziness, and a desire to escape to the water cooler. What you want to see, instead, is output from a *web log analyzer*—software that takes the raw server log file ingredients and whips them up into an easy-to-digest serving of meaningful traffic data. (Don't confuse the web log we're talking about here with the other kind of weblog, the one called blog for short!)

The area of *web analytics*, the measurement and analysis of online activity, includes products ranging from simple to sophisticated. We've boiled it down into an at-a-glance table so you can get your bearings (see Table 8.1).

▶ **Table 8.1** Online Conversion Tracking at a Glance

Type of Tracking	Level of Complexity for You	Cost	Where Data Resides
Traffic only	Low	Usually low-cost add-on to your hosting package	Your hosting service's servers
Traffic + conversions (build-your-own)	High	Low	Your servers
Traffic + conversions (server-side)	Moderate	Moderate-to-high	Your servers
Traffic + conversions (client-side/hosted)	Low-to-moderate	Free (Google Analytics)-to-high	Third-party provider's servers
Conversions only (Band-Aid methods)	Low	Low	Your site visitors (until they choose to spill the beans, at which point it ends up on your servers)

Today, we're going to look at data that is available from the most simple, and often free, systems using information from your server logs. These include Webalizer and AWStats. Most commercial web hosting packages include at least this basic level of web log analysis. (See Figure 8.1 for an example.)

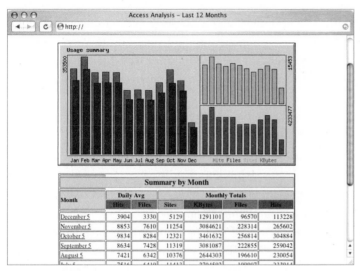

Figure 8.1 Basic website stats

Maybe you already have something like this available. If you're not sure, talk to your IT department and find out. Here is the information you'll want to regularly see from your server logs, at a minimum:

Unique visitors Knowing the total traffic to your website doesn't tell you much. It won't tell you whether your visitors are the ones you targeted, what path they took through your website, whether they made a purchase, or how happy they were during their visit. Nevertheless, it's one of those little numbers that you. just. need. to. know. Your log analyzer will do its best to determine a total number of unique visitors based on IP addresses and any other info it can gather. Admittedly, the number is not perfectly accurate. But it's a good tool for tracking trends. After all, what does it really matter if you had 1,015 or 1,045 unique visitors this week? What matters most is whether you're up or down from last week.

And while you're at it, banish the word *hits* from your vocabulary. *Hits* describes the number of times a request is made to your server, and *page views* describes the number of times an entire page is called by a browser. So if there are dozens of images on a given page, there will be dozens of hits recorded for each page view. Depending on your conversion goal, you may want to focus on the number of page views or unique visitors, but never hits.

Traffic to key pages Traffic to your landing pages, or other key locations on your website, can be a lot more meaningful than overall traffic to your website. Any web log analyzer worth its salt will be able to show you how many visitors are browsing the landing pages that you worked so hard to optimize.

Referrers After all your link-building efforts, wouldn't you love to know which sites are actually sending you traffic? After optimizing for the search engines, wouldn't you love to know which search terms your visitors used to find you? This is where your stats start to become truly useful to your SEO campaign. Your web log analyzer can tell you where your site visitors came from, and even more important, for those that came to your website from search engines, it can tell you the exact keywords they searched for. This can be a good source of ideas for finding new keywords to target. It may also help you identify inbound links you didn't know existed!

Keep in mind, referrer data is limited to folks that clicked to your site from another site on the Web. Users that typed your URL directly into their browsers, or clicked from a bookmark, or clicked from an e-mail, are harder to track.

Exit pages If it's good to know how visitors found your site, it's even more telling to know where visitors exited your site. Exit pages can be used to diagnose a whole host of problems, from poor navigation design to poorly targeted traffic. Don't be surprised if your home page is high on the list. It's common for people to arrive at your site and immediately realize it's not what they're looking for. Also, don't always assume that exit pages are the "bad guy." Some websites are set up so that when users click to make a purchase they are taken to a different site. If this describes your site, then exiting your site may be the best thing a user can do!

However, for most websites, exits represent your conversions walking out the door. If a large proportion of your visitors are leaving after viewing just one page, either you're inviting the wrong crowd to your party or there's something very unappetizing greeting them at the door.

Errors Among other things, your server will log a *404 error* ("File not Found") every time a user tries to access a nonexistent URL. This can help you find inbound—or internal—links that are using incorrect or out-of-date URLs. (By the way, your server logs will record a 404 error every time a search engine robot comes looking for a non-existent robots.txt file, which may be reason enough for you to add one to your website.)

The list of useful server stats could go on and on, but you have limited time, so we stuck with the basics.

If you already have access to your server stats through a web log analyzer, congratulations! Today, you'll look through it for the information just listed.

Now: Open up your server stats program (if it exists) and find the key information listed in this section. If you don't already have a way to view this information, read on.

If you do not already have a way to view server stats, this is the week you'll figure out how to make it happen. You have several options, including the basic server stats discussed today as well as more comprehensive tracking described in the next sections. You probably won't need to use a basic program if you are also implementing a more advanced system because the more advanced systems incorporate all of the info a basic program provides and more. Consider them all, and choose which is best for your organization.

Wednesday: Tracking Online Conversions

Today we're going to talk about options that allow you to take your basic server stats to the next level for your organic SEO campaign. Instead of recording separate chunks of data (like the number of unique visitors and the number of people entering your site for a specific term), you can set up tracking so that a visitor is "followed" from the time they enter your site until they perform your conversion goal. You already know this for your PPC clicks, but what about all the rest of your site visitors? With a comprehensive web analytics system in place, the seller of left-handed guitars can stop fretting about which of his optimized landing pages is encouraging more southpaw sales.

If you only have offline conversions to track, you can skip this day.

Setting up a comprehensive tracking system for your site is usually much more time intensive than the PPC conversion tracking you set up on Monday. So, think of today as a day to learn, compare, and get the ball rolling on one of these options:

- Advanced tracking systems
- Implementing your own solution
- Band-Aid methods

Here are some more details about each option.

Advanced Tracking Systems

Major providers of advanced tracking systems include Omniture, Web Side Story, Web-Trends, ClickTracks, and Coremetrics. Free or inexpensive options for smaller businesses are Google Analytics (see the sidebar "You've Gotta Love Google Analytics"), measuremap for bloggers, and GoDaddy, a website hosting provider that bundles a tracking service with its hosting options. Consult their websites for more information, or see our companion site at www.yourseoplan.com for links to reviews.

How it works Advanced tracking systems come in two flavors: *client-side tracking* (also called *hosted*, *tag-based*, or *on-demand* tracking) and *server-side tracking*. Client-side tracking generally works like this: You add a tiny piece of code or a tiny image to every page of your site. This little code communicates with a tracking system located on the vendor's server and the information is used to build detailed reports about activity on your site—for a monthly fee. Server-side systems provide similar capabilities but stay on your own servers, are purchased like software, and must be set up by your IT team. See Figure 8.2 for an example of an advanced tracking system.

You don't need to know the details of how these systems work. You just need to know how much they cost, what reporting options they provide, and whether your webmaster will let you add the little scripts to the page (you may meet some resistance based on security concerns).

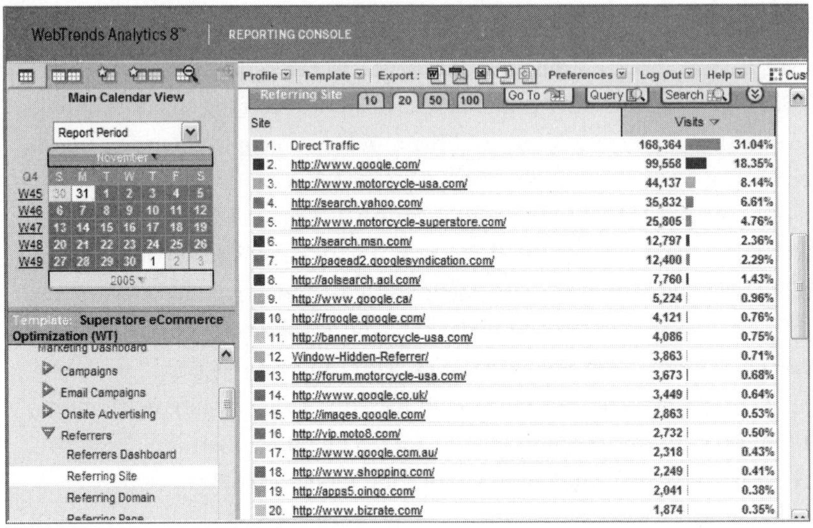

Figure 8.2 WebTrends data example

Benefits Both client-side and server-side tracking systems give you much more information about your site visitors than basic server log analysis or built-in PPC tracking will provide. What paths your users took, where they lingered, where they exited your site—the options are almost endless. Client-side systems provide the additional advantage that your part of the setup generally doesn't require heavy-duty IT involvement. If you know simple HTML, you may be able to do this part yourself.

Limitations Got time on your hands? It takes a serious time commitment to review and act upon the data you receive using this method. But consider implementing an advanced tracking system even if you don't see yourself cozying up with the data on a weekly basis. It's possible to review data on a monthly, even quarterly, basis and glean some fascinating and helpful information.

Client-side tracking also brings about the same security issues that PPC conversion tracking does. If data security is a major issue at your organization, server-side tracking will be the better option for you.

Another limitation is that both tracking methods are likely to undercount your visitors for various reasons, including the fact that users can disable the JavaScript or *cookies* (small pieces of text that are saved temporarily on the user's computer) that these techniques rely on.

You've Gotta Love Google Analytics

In 2005, Google pounced on the conversion tracking scene with Google Analytics. Previously a fee-based service called Urchin, Google Analytics can track *all* clicks, both PPC and nonpaid. The Web-based interface offers all the tools a small or medium business needs for SEO tracking and more. And, it's free!

Like many must-haves (Remember Cabbage Patch Kids? No? Well, then…remember the years-long beta phase of Gmail?), demand for Google Analytics significantly exceeded supply during its first few months of existence, causing Google to turn away many enthusiastic site owners. Growing pains notwithstanding, we predict that Google Analytics will change the face of conversion tracking for small businesses. Options that previously cost a bundle or required heavy hitting from in-house techies will be available to all small businesses for free. With enough businesses using it, Google Analytics could give organic SEO some of the accountability—and budget—that PPC already enjoys. We're looking forward to it!

Implementing Your Own Solution

If you've got the will and the IT firepower, creating your own tracking solution may be an option you find yourself considering.

How it works Your own tracking solution will be limited only by your time and programming capabilities. We recommend that you start simple: all you really need to do is count conversions and trace the conversions back to search engine traffic. For example, we once implemented a basic tracking system for our own employer's website. It worked like this:

- Every time a visitor came to the website, we set a cookie that recorded the referring URL, including searched keywords for those that came from search engines.

- Nothing else would happen while the user surfed around the site.

- And then, in the occasional event that the visitor submitted a request for information form (which was our conversion of choice), the cookie text was included along with all the other form information submitted directly to Sales.

Your own solution could include a wide variety of techniques to store important visitor data, including setting cookies, adding tags to pages on your site, and creating special tracking URLs. Your choice will depend on your specific needs and abilities.

Benefits There are a couple of advantages to building your own tracking system. One is that it can be customized to your needs and you won't get bogged down in data overload. Another is that it eliminates the security and privacy concerns that third-party systems cause.

Limitations If you have relatively few conversions, a basic do-it-yourself system might be feasible for you. However, the amount of programming you'd have to do to get close to the flexibility of a third-party solution is probably prohibitively high. As Anthony Severo told us, "I work with many small companies that start building their own solution because they can (typically you have a hot shot engineer who takes it on as a pet project) but then waste that critical engineering resource on something that they can buy for dollars a month."

Do you really want to get into the business of building and maintaining a tracking tool rather than focusing on your core business?

 Pearl of Wisdom: Building your own tracking tool is serious work, so you should seriously consider other options before traveling the do-it-yourself path.

Band-Aid Methods

Depending on your business, you may feel that the conversion tracking methods described previously are overkill. Or, you may not have the time, money, technical ability, or support to gather conversion data behind the scenes. The only thing left for you to do is to ask your visitors! Sure, it's not a perfect method, but it's *something*. Here are some suggestions:

Bust the "e-mail us" link. Replace any "e-mail us" links on your website with a "contact us" form. This will allow you to ask your visitors how they found you (but don't hold your breath for any details).

Don't miss an opportunity. Every form on your site has the potential to ask your visitors how they found you. If your site has a store component, you could provide a small incentive, like a discount on shipping, for customers who fill out a brief survey prior to checkout. Look through your site and make sure you're taking advantage of every opportunity to get your visitors to volunteer this important information.

Try an opt-in. If your website includes highly desirable content (for example, research papers, articles, or high-res imagery), you may be able to convince your site visitors to provide their contact information—and the all-important information about how they found you—in exchange for a download. However, proceed with caution on this option: web searchers as a rule cherish their anonymity. We are always dismayed to see businesses insist on a name and phone number before sharing product information. That's like expecting people to pay to see your advertising!

Conversion tracking: you know you want it! Now that you've digested the basics, you can use today to discuss it with your team. Then, it's decision time: which system will you start with? Remember, you can always start small—perhaps a free option—and upgrade later.

Now: Finalize your choice of conversion tracking system for online conversions.

Thursday: Tracking Offline Conversions

As we touched upon in Chapter 5, "Get your Team on Board," one of the more challenging areas to track is offline conversions like phone calls or walk-in customers. (If you have only online conversions to track, you can skip this day.) And if your website is out there trying to convince someone to, say, vote for a certain school board representative, how are you ever going to measure the contribution that your SEO work made to the campaign?

To track your offline conversions, you'll need to be creative. Here are a few ideas for some of the more common scenarios:

Set up a special phone number. If a large percentage of your sales take place over the phone, it may be difficult to show that the website, much less your SEO campaign, had anything to do with them. But there is one way: Set up a unique phone number and display it on your website—and nowhere else. Then, have your sales team monitor and track how many calls come in to that line and how many of those calls turn into conversions.

For a greater level of detail, you can sign up with services (such as ClickPath or Who's Calling) that will generate unique 800 numbers and dynamically display them on your web pages, linking each call to a keyword and ad source.

Run campaigns on things nobody else is promoting. You can get an inkling of the effects of your SEO work by promoting a specific event or product that nobody else in your organization has taken the time to promote. For example, if you put your SEO efforts into promoting Tuesday Night Half-Price Pickles and there is no other marketing for it, you can relish the thought that most of the people who show up found out about the event as a result of your SEO work.

Include coupons or promotion codes on your website. How will you know if walk-in customers used your website to research your products or services? One way is to create coupons or promotion codes on your website that these customers can print out and bring into your store for a discount. Sure, it won't tell you whether they used a search engine to find your site, but at least you'll have something to link your real-world traffic to your online traffic.

Cultivate communication. If your site goals fall into the persuasion category, give your users an opportunity to tell their stories with "Post your success story here" or "Share your smoking cessation tips" links. An increase in the number of postings can indicate your SEO success.

Simply ask. When all else fails, simply ask your offline customers or clients how they found you. It's not the most accurate information, but it's better than nothing. Be sure that your traditional marketing, sales, and PR team put out the question in print, on the phone, or in person whenever they have the opportunity.

 Now: Brainstorm with your team on options for tracking your offline conversions and finalize a plan.

Tracking the Intangible

Many organizations report that branding is a primary goal of their SEO campaigns. But how do you track these less-than-tangible factors? The Left Brain and Right Brain debate.

The Right Brain says, "Whether you call it Branding with a capital *B* or just 'keeping up appearances,' the image that your organization projects through the search engines is important. If the top-ranked website for your company name is a rant by a disgruntled former employee, or if half of your inbound links mention an outdated product name, you've got an image problem that SEO can help fix.

"Branding improvements may be a fringe benefit of your SEO campaign, or they may be a central goal. Either way, make sure you document outcomes like improved search engine listings; inbound link updates; cleanup of outdated, private, or inappropriate content; and mentions in other web media such as blogs or review sites. Keep a diary or log it in your Task Journal, and pull out these accomplishments when you need some good news in the analysis and interpretation sections of your Monthly Report! I think of these positive little pieces of information as 'exclamation point moments.'"

The Left Brain says, "I've spent so many hours pursuing and documenting branding advances in my SEO campaigns and, frankly, nobody seems to care unless it's presented just the right way. Things like eliminating references to nonexistent products and services and monitoring blog references, media mentions, and hate sites are so important that they need quantitative measurement. When the effectiveness of an SEO campaign comes into question, you need more than an exclamation point in your Monthly Report; you need hard data!

"Try to quantify your image-improvement accomplishments in some way. For example, 'Eight out of 14 of our misspelled listings have now been corrected,' 'Our company name has been mentioned on 63 blogs this month, up from 24 mentions in the previous month,' or 'Our specially designed landing page now outranks the 'hate site' listing for the keywords 'I Hate ZappyCo,' a phrase that approximately 250 people per month search for.' Companies like Buzzmetrics and Intelliseek work to measure activity in this arena, known as *consumer generated media (CGM)*. (I prefer to just call it 'buzz'!). Numbers will help provide a clear baseline and measurable change. You'll be glad to have facts and figures at the ready when you need to justify another round of SEO spending!"

Friday: PPC Quick Check/Link Building

Setting aside a day once a week for your PPC Quick Check and link building is the bare minimum you should do to build your traffic and conversions. Some people spend the majority of their SEO time on these two tasks. As advocates of the holistic approach to SEO, we don't recommend focusing most of your energy on just one or two activities. But, in general, you can always benefit from spending more time on links and PPC campaign tweaks.

PPC Quick Check

It's that time again...the PPC Quick Check is upon us!

 Now: Follow the same steps you followed in last week's PPC Quick Check. If you need to make any changes to your account, do so now.

Link Building

Think of your link-building campaign as a trickle of water etching pathways in rock. Every little moment you spend in pursuit of links can have a little impact on your incoming traffic and conversions, which will eventually add up to something substantial. Every Friday from here on out, you'll continue your link-building campaign. So, with whatever time you have left today, get working on those targeted links:

- Continue to move down your list of inbound links from your Link Tracking Worksheet, and request modifications as necessary.
- Continue to move down your list of potential linking sites and request new links. Remember to use your impeccable link-request etiquette and to write bulletproof correspondences!
- Surf for additional potential linking sites, and log any promising ones you find in your Link Tracking Worksheet.

 Now: Continue your link-building campaign.

With your conversion tracking plan in place, you'll get into an R&D groove as Your SEO Plan enters its next week!

Week 7: Research and Development

This week, we've chosen four open-ended hot topics for you to explore. We selected these topics because they're either a little too close to the cutting edge of today's SEO or require a little too much individualization from you for us to give you specific instructions. So you're going to do the research yourself, with guidance from us! The goal is for you to come away with an approach to use whenever you need to learn something new about search. If you're a naturally curious person, and if you find it easy to surf from site to site while staying focused on your goal, this week should be a snap. If you aren't yet confident in your advanced searching skills, or if you generally don't trust an answer unless you get it in writing from a paid expert, this week will help you stretch your abilities and save your money in the long run!

This week you'll start to get a feel for how to pursue your own SEO tactics and plans:

Monday: SEO News and Trends

Tuesday: Task Journal Investigation

Wednesday: International/Local Search

Thursday: Specialty Search

Friday: PPC Quick Check/Link Building

Monday: SEO News and Trends

SEO moves fast! In the weeks since you started doing SEO, there have probably been a few changes (significant or not so significant) introduced by the big engines, a brand-new search engine launched in beta, and, oh, about 40 rancorous discussions about what's "right" or "wrong" in any number of SEO forums. It might seem that every time you go out for a cup of coffee, you come back to a whole new set of important players, rumors, and must-haves that weren't there before.

You're busy, so nobody expects you to keep up with every little twist and turn along the SEO highway. In fact, staying a month or so behind the times can prevent you from crowding your brain with unnecessary SEO rumors and speculation.

Pearl of Wisdom: You can skip a heck of a lot of daily SEO minutia and still get enough of the overall story line to know what's important, as long as you keep the Eternal Truths of SEO in mind and stay focused on your audience and your desired conversions.

But we recommend keeping up at least a passing knowledge of SEO current events and stashing some solid SEO researching skills in your tool belt. When it comes time to do SEO on your own, you'll need them! Here's where to look:

*   SEO news sources
*   SEO forums
*   Blogs and e-mail newsletters

SEO News Sources

One day soon you're going to need to learn something about SEO, something specific to your own site that we didn't cover in this book. The Web is the only way to keep up with the latest SEO news and trends. Unfortunately, not every site is reputable, so you'll need to wear your heavy-duty BS filters. You can't go wrong if you stick with articles on the following sites:

Search Engine Watch, www.searchenginewatch.com Danny Sullivan, editor and world-renowned guru of search, offers reviews, updates, tips, and advice with mind-boggling attention to detail, helpful context, and insider information that nobody else comes close to. When we asked him what role his site plays in the SEO industry, he said, "I'd hope it's also seen as a good learning tool, especially for those who sometimes feel they may get lost among the many details of search and are seeking a resetting or a higher level view of what's going on." Bravo, Danny!

HighRankings.com, www.highrankings.com Jill Whalen offers cheerful, no-nonsense, often low-tech advice that's perfect for do-it-yourself SEOs of all stripes.

ClickZ News, www.clickz.com A little heavier on the marketingspeak, this site offers an impressive gamut of expert advice on all avenues of Internet marketing, not just SEO.

SEOmoz, www.seomoz.org Rand Fishkin's articles and tips speak to beginners and experts alike. An assortment of page analysis tools are available too.

Information Overload

A recent thread on a search forum asked SEO professionals how they spend an average day on the job. Looking at the responses, you would think that SEOs are paid based on the number of search engine blogs they read, how many SEO podcasts are filling their libraries, and how many thousands of forum postings they've racked up. We won't bash this lifestyle, but we realized long ago that there's no need to live it.

Reading SEO info online can make even a seasoned Internet researcher hyperventilate. There are so many acronyms, rumors, and arguments (not to mention posturing…do these people *really* read 826 search blogs every day?) and so much conflicting advice that even if you understand what's being said, you probably shouldn't believe it at first blush. Follow these words of warning as you get your bearings in the overstimulating world of SEO news and advice:

- Always check an article's date *before* you read the article. Some sites are better than others at letting you know whether you're reading something brand-new or a two-year-old history lesson from their archives.

- Beware articles posted on the websites of SEO firms. Many companies publish web articles and tips written by their in-house staff in an effort to improve their linkable noncommercial content and prove their worthiness in the SEO arena. These authors may be knowledgeable, or they may not be…it's very difficult to tell if you're new to the game. And these kinds of articles are often undated. Some of these authors may have moved on from the SEO company years ago! If you're inclined to follow the advice from an SEO firm, do a search for the author's name to help you determine if they are reputable in the SEO community.

Continues

SEO Forums

In our conversation with Danny Sullivan, he cautioned, "Forums probably aren't the best place for beginners. They should do a lot of reading from more focused sites before diving in. As for advice, be wary of everything and always remember that nothing should be taken as fact." To begin your own SEO forum research, start with these tried-and-true sites:

- forums.searchenginewatch.com
- www.highrankings.com/forum/
- www.webmasterworld.com
- www.searchengineforums.com

Jump in on the forums whenever you have a burning question that needs answering, but don't count on them for your regular SEO news fix.

Blogs and E-mail Newsletters

One of our favorite ways to keep up-to-date on SEO news is through blogs and e-mail newsletters. Here, seasoned and uncommonly generous SEO professionals distill the latest happenings into easy-to-read content. If you trust the source, you can trust the advice. Here are our favorite SEO blogs and newsletters:

- http://blog.searchenginewatch.com/blog/
- Aaron Wall's blog and newsletter at www.seobook.com
- www.mattcutts.com/blog (for Google-centric information)
- www.problogger.net (for those with blogs)
- www.jimboykin.com

As you continue surfing SEO sites, you'll probably see other premium content or regular e-mail updates; consider signing up for a subscription from sites you like. Then do what we do: let them pile up in your inbox, and set aside a time once a week (you can even get away with once a month) to pour yourself a cup of coffee and browse the SEO news.

 Now: Go read some SEO news!

Bonus points if you can slip something interesting and *au courant* about SEO into your next conversation with your boss.

Tuesday: Task Journal Investigation

Your Task Journal is only as good as your ability to tackle the issues you add to it. Today is a freestyle day, set aside for you to look into, or take care of, one of your Task Journal issues.

 If your Task Journal isn't yet filled with dozens of fascinating ruminations, look to Chapter 10 for some ideas to get you started.

 Now: Go learn more about an issue of your choice from your Task Journal.

Don't be surprised if, in the process of knocking something off your task list, you add several additional items. That's the sign of a truly productive research session!

Wednesday: Explore Local/International Search

Would your site benefit from a geographically targeted campaign? Whether it's Paris, France, or Paris, Texas, today you'll choose the area that interests you and determine whether you want to move forward in either of these:

- International search
- Local search

We'll give you an overview and point you in the right direction for further research.

International Search

The Internet knows no borders, but unfortunately, your SEO campaign does. If your target audience includes an overseas component, you need to learn strategies for international SEO and put a focused effort into your international visibility. Ask yourself, Which country are you targeting? Is your international audience composed of English speakers? Which languages do you want to target? Answer these questions for your organization, and then start your research on international SEO with these general guidelines in mind:

International PPC Google AdWords and YSM make it easy to add new campaigns and set them up for different countries and languages. If your international ads are in English, it's very simple to edit the targeting preferences on your current campaign to include additional countries.

You should custom-write your ads for non-U.S.-based site visitors, even if they are English speaking, to address their different terminology or needs. Separate sites or landing pages will also improve localization.

To target additional languages, you'll need to create new PPC campaigns with their own language and country settings. Google AdWords also allows you to target specific regions or cities within many countries. So, for example, if you want to sell to Ontario in English but to Quebec in French, you can specify which provinces will see which campaign's ads.

If you are marketing to a European audience, you'll also want to look into a PPC campaign with Miva, at www.miva.com, formerly espotting. This company has a large PPC presence in Europe.

International Organic Optimization Let's say you want your chic boutique website to rank well for searchers in France searching for the French words "parapluie jaune." One approach would be to choose this term as one of your top target keywords and optimize your landing page accordingly. Good start, but there's more you can do to optimize for the geographic audience you desire. Here are a few tips to help you sell more of those yellow umbrellas:

DO make sure your landing page is written in the language of the country you want to target. And your page titles and meta description tags should be in the target language too. Even though there's an HTML meta tag that allows you to specify which language your web page is written in, the search engine robots will probably ignore it and look at the web page text to make their own determination of language. Don't confuse the search engines by sticking substantial portions of several different languages on the same page.

DON'T use your home page for the sole purpose of selecting a language. If you are creating several subsites or site sections in different languages, don't waste precious home page real estate on choosing a language. Instead, include quality content in your most important language, with links to other language choices.

DO use a country-specific domain. Your site will get a lift if it has the appropriate country domain: This is a big clue to the search engines that the site should be shown to a searcher in your target country. And major search engines often allow their users to request only documents from their own country, so having the right domain will put you in the running.

DO consider building separate sites. Some sites redirect their international domains to their .com domain (for example, babyfuzzkin.co.uk and babyfuzzkin.de could both redirect to babyfuzzkin.com), and this is OK. Of course, it would be better—for your site and for your user—to create separate sites in separate languages (or in the various "flavors" of English), especially since key content like pricing and contact information may be different for each country.

DO seek inbound links from sites that are in your targeted countries. And be sure to request links in the appropriate language!

DO explore locally popular search sites. Google, Yahoo!, MSN, and Ask have a major presence worldwide, and if your site is in their indices, it will also show up on the international versions of their search sites (for example, google.co.uk). So you could focus on those four search engines and let it go at that. But there may be smaller search sites that play an important role in your country of interest. For example, Voila.fr is a major search engine in France. Your soggy Parisian seeking a "parapluie jaune" is just as likely to go there as fr.Yahoo.com, and perhaps more so. It's a little heavy on the exclamation points, but www.searchenginecolossus.com has a long country-by-country list of international search engines.

You've probably figured out by now that a fully fledged international SEO campaign is outside the scope of your hour-a-day commitment. It may even involve a major web development effort, creating unique sites for each of your targeted countries. But keep this in mind:

Pearl of Wisdom: Everything you're doing now for your SEO campaign will also help your international efforts in the future.

And once your SEO campaign has an established ROI, it will be easier to swing the additional resources for international SEO.

Now: Determine whether international search is right for your site, and determine who you need to speak with in your organization to get the ball rolling. Make a note of it in your Task Journal.

¡Hola SEO!

According to the Selig Center for Economic Growth, the buying power of the Hispanic market in the United States is expected to reach $992 billion by 2009—that's 9 percent of the entire market! The Spanish-speaking population within the United States is growing, and with it grows an important sector of the search world. Many of the major search engines have created portals specifically for this audience, for example, AOL Latino, Yahoo! Espanol, and MSN Latino. However, anecdotal evidence suggests that the U.S. Latino market searches extensively on the major English-based search engines using Spanish or English keyterms.

We won't claim to be experts in this domain. SEO for the Latino market is still relatively uncommon. But that also means it's a great opportunity to find untapped areas, maybe that top-10 Google spot you've been having such a hard time capturing! And, last we checked, PPC prices for terms in Spanish were much lower than their English counterparts.

Anyone ready to reach out to this audience may want to attend Search Engine Strategies Latino conferences—the first of its kind was scheduled in July 2006 (see www.jupiterevents.com for more info).

And remember, much of what you're doing in Your SEO Plan will aid your website in listings regardless of language. You're off to a great start already!

Local Search

In Chapter 2, "Customize Your Approach," we talked a little bit about the wonders of local search. Been waiting in line for coffee too long? Pull out your wireless PDA and search for another café in the vicinity. Sitting at home on a Saturday night? Order pizza and a video directly through the Web (and while you're there, join a social networking site!). What's good for the searcher is even better for the search-savvy local business owner. If your organization has a brick-and-mortar component and you'd like to use the search engines to gain walk-in customers, begin tackling local search today.

Local search, such as local.google.com and local.yahoo.com, to name two, is changing fast as additional searchers and businesses flock to it. So keep a sharp eye out for new products and procedures. As a general rule, you will want to approach local search optimization from two angles:

- Finding out which sites are feeding into the local search engine of your choice and submitting to them
- Creating your own local listing

Here's how to get started:

Who's feeding whom? Local search listings are usually compiled from a variety of sources, some of which you have control over and some of which you don't. Some local searches are fed by partner sites that focus on local listings, such as www.citysearch.com and www.insiderpages.com. There are a couple of ways you can check to see which sites are feeding into a search engine's local listings. First, you can check out the local search engine's frequently asked questions (FAQs) or review the Webmaster or Business Owner information that many of these services publish on their sites. You can also search for your competitors and see which sites are listed: Your competitor's actual site? A review from a content partner? See Figure 8.3 for an example.

Once you know which sources are included in the local search engine of your choice, you can go to them directly and attempt to get or improve a listing.

Make your own listing Last we looked, Yahoo! and Google provided easy-to-find links for business owners to submit their own company data to local search. It's free or cheap ("enhanced" fee-based options are available)...and worth it at almost any price, in our opinion. If local search is important to you, you should make it a priority to create your own listing because if the information doesn't come from you, it will probably come from someone else who doesn't have a personal stake in the listing's accuracy or success. They may not make it easy—yet—but it *is* possible for you to exert a little control over your local listing.

Check www.yourseoplan.com for submittal pages.

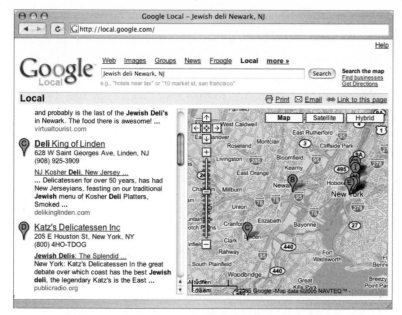

Figure 8.3 Different sites provide content for "Jewish Deli Newark, NJ" on Google's local search

Explore PPC localization. It's easy to test-drive a local PPC campaign. Just follow your PPC engine's instructions for selecting your targeted geographical areas, and assign a budget for testing. Keep in mind, though, that if your local competitors include national retail chains, at least one PPC expert, Kevin Lee of the search marketing firm Did-it.com, believes local PPC could be an uphill battle. When we asked Kevin what's coming up in local search, he shared these insights:

"My opinion is that for many sectors, the national players will be the dominant players in the local search marketplace. They have brand names and this gives them an advantage in the hybrid PPC auctions. Dominos and Pizza Hut can coordinate locally targeted campaigns and have significant resources. The local pizza place many also advertise, but there is only room for half a dozen pizzerias in the search result. So, the number of local players involved in an area doesn't increase revenue to an engine. Kinkos, Sir Speedy, and AlphaGraphics can also coordinate aggressive localized campaigns, making it difficult for the local business owner to break into the results profitably.

"For professional services, there are not many national companies, so local players will be active. However, once again, there will only be two or three Atlanta divorce attorneys who pay enough to be at the top and get most of the clicks."

Now: Determine whether local search is right for your site, and get the ball rolling. Make a note of unfinished business in your Task Journal.

Thursday Shopping and Media Search

These highly specialized segments of search are being built out as the major engines follow the trends of available media and website owner practices and preferences. Unlike
the niche directories you looked into last month, the specialty search you'll work on
today can be found predominantly as components of the major search engines. They
include the following:

Shopping search Sites such as Froogle, Yahoo! Shopping, MSN Shopping, not to mention large shopping engines such as Shopzilla and Shopping.com, allow merchandisers
to submit frequent updates of product details and prices.

Image search Sites such as http://images.google.com and
http://search.yahoo.com/images allow you to search strictly for images. If one of your
site's differentiating factors is its images, don't overlook image search as a way to snag
some targeted visitors. Depending on the search engine, optimizing for image search
may involve writing optimized image ALT tags and adding keyword-rich text immediately surrounding your images.

Video search Upload your video, set up your feed, or wait to be crawled! Any way
you slice it, video search is taking shape at sites like http://video.google.com and
http://video.yahoo.com, not to mention media search sites like singingfish.com. Since
video in general is difficult for search engines to crawl, some video search engines are
currently giving site owners an uncharacteristically high level of control over submitting, including metadata that you can include in video-specific *RSS* tags (we'll talk
more about RSS, sometimes called Really Simple Syndication, next month).

Like local search, these specialty search areas are still being developed and
refined. So rather than give you likely-to-be-obsolete steps for getting yourself optimized and listed, we're going to give you our methodology for finding out how.
Here are the steps:

Search as if your site depends on it. First, go to the specialty search engine and start
searching. You want to get the full picture of what the listings look like. Try searching
for your own organization, your competitors, product names, and commercial and
noncommercial sites. Get a feel for listings that seem compelling and listings that look
skippable, and try to put your finger on why they're coming across that way. Also,
keep an eye out for sites that are partnered with the search engine. For example, when
you search our favorite term—"Britney Spears"—on http://videos.yahoo.com, you'll
see a featured listing from Y! Music in a coveted top-of-the-screen position. You may
want to pursue a listing in a partner site, if it's at all possible.

One Cheeky Yahoo! Store

We spoke with Dexter Chow, co-owner with his wife, Anna, of Cheeky Monkey Toys in Menlo Park, California, about their experiences running a website companion to a traditional brick-and-mortar store.

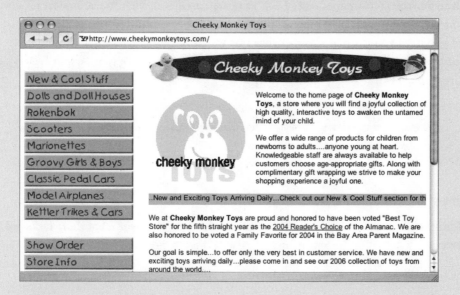

Their goals for the website, www.cheekymonkeytoys.com, are twofold: first, to direct visitors to their brick-and-mortar store with hours and location information, and second, to sell products directly online.

With the heavy demands of running the shop on a daily basis, Dexter simply doesn't have time to learn new web development technologies or search marketing strategies: "If there is a choice in where to spend time, the B&M side gets it." That's why he and Anna chose to use a Yahoo! Store for their website. The Yahoo! Store covers the HTML basics with a built-in editor that allows Dexter to easily maintain the store's product information online, includes e-commerce tools such as order processing, and—perhaps even more important—Cheeky Monkey listings are automatically integrated into Yahoo! Shopping results. Cheeky Monkey does well on Yahoo! Shopping searches "since we're hosted by Yahoo! and get indexed by them and pay money for Yahoo!'s searching indexing."

Many small businesses find the ease-of-use and search integration is worth the added cost of a Yahoo! Store. We think this can be a great choice if it suits your needs. But you don't have to stop there! Content on your Yahoo! Store site can also be integrated with Froogle listings, and Froogle does not charge a fee. (For more information on optimizing your Yahoo! Store, read *Starting a Yahoo! Business for Dummies* by Rob Snell [Wiley, 2006].)

Uncover the FAQs. A search engine's FAQ or Webmaster Information may contain a submittal form, or submittal guidance, and it may even give you some hints on how you can optimize your site and/or media components. You can visit www.yourseoplan.com for a list of links to FAQs and submittal forms for these services.

Use your research smarts. After you've got a handle on what the submittal process and the listings look like, read up on submittal or optimization tips in the SEO info sources you learned about earlier this week. It may be as simple as going to searchenginewatch.com and typing in "video search" or "shopping search." Don't forget to check the dates on these articles!

 Now: Explore the specialty search that matters most to you. Make a note of your hopes and plans as well as what you've learned about optimization and submittal for this venue in your Task Journal.

Friday: PPC Quick Check/Link Building

You started them in Chapter 7, "Month One: Kick It into Gear," but these tasks are never truly "done." It's time again to visit PPC monitoring and link building.

PPC Quick Check

Friday means...the PPC Quick Check is upon us!

 Now: Follow the same steps you followed in last week's PPC Quick Check. If you need to make any changes to your account, do so now.

Link Building

Get out your Link Tracking Worksheet and find more opportunities for targeted traffic!

 Now: Continue your link-building campaign.

Week 8: Visibility Check and Monthly Reporting

As you "Establish the Habit" of SEO, your workday should naturally begin to accommodate a small portion of SEO time. Likewise, you'll find it easier and easier to gear up and get through your monthly reporting. In fact, you might notice that you begin to feel disoriented if you go too long without grounding yourself with empirical data!

Your second Monthly Report will follow the same basic pattern as last month's. However, since last month, we've encouraged you to add several more options for collecting data, including server stats, online PPC and organic conversion tracking, and offline conversion tracking. You know your business, and you know what matters most. So, think of this week's tasks as a guideline, and don't be afraid to substitute your own revelations whenever appropriate. Refer back to Chapter 7 and your completed Monthly Report as you dive in. Your tasks for this week are as follows:

Monday: Check Organic Status

Tuesday: Check Links

Wednesday: Check Conversions and Image Improvement

Thursday: Monitor PPC Ads

Friday: Action Items

Monday: Check Organic Status

Two months have passed since you started optimizing your site, and that means that it's quite possible to start seeing some improvements in your rank and your traffic. It's time to pull up your Rank Tracking Worksheet and last month's Monthly Report from your SEO Idea Bank so that you can check and record values for the following:

- Search engine rankings
- Indexed pages

Search Engine Rankings

Once you have reliable conversion tracking implemented on your SEO campaign, it may be reasonable to drop your full four-search-engine monthly rank check. But, in order to keep up with "little things" like branding and competition, your monthly habits really should include checking your site's presence on at least one search engine for your top-priority keywords.

This month you paid special attention to problem pages and broken URLs on your site. As you perform your rank check, keep a close eye out for improvements or additional problem pages.

Now: Open up your Rank Tracking Worksheet and fill in your website ranks for this month.

Now it's time to interpret your results in this month's report. You've got three months of rankings to compare now—see any trends? Are you gaining confidence in your methods as you watch a certain keyphrase or page do well? Are you beginning to doubt a particular keyword choice?

Now: Open last month's Monthly Report and rename it (by choosing File > Save As) with the current date. This is now your current Monthly Report.

Jot down observations that matter in your report, and don't skimp on the analysis! Remember that trying to explain "why" is one of the most important, not to mention least-expensive, tools you have in your SEO repertoire. If you found anything from last month that requires a follow-up, don't let it fizzle away! Either update your report with your current take on things or make a note that this issue is still unresolved and put it on your Action Items list for next month.

Now: Add your summary and analysis to the "Site Visibility" section of your current Monthly Report.

Indexed Pages

Add another month's data to the total number of pages indexed. Again, you can start looking for trends.

Now: Check the total number of pages indexed on your site in each of the four major search engines. Record the value on your Rank Tracking Worksheet.

If any of your landing pages were not indexed when you checked last month, be sure to look again and see if your efforts have made a difference.

Now: Check the indexing of any landing pages that were not indexed last month. Document status on your Rank Tracking Worksheet.

As your Monthly Report begins to flesh out, be sure to review the action items from last month. You will want to report on completed items throughout the document in whichever sections are relevant.

Tuesday: Check Links

Reporting new inbound links is a very satisfying aspect of SEO. Today you'll document the following in both words and numbers:

- Link campaign activities
- Google PageRank

Link Campaign Activities

As you document your inbound link activities this month, don't just count on a correspondence from another site's webmaster to let you know that a link to your site has been added. Make sure to review your Link Tracking Worksheet and visit each page you've submitted to. Do a quick scan or search the page using Ctrl+F (or Apple+F for Mac) for your organization's name or URL, document a link if you find it, then move on to the next page.

You don't need to list all your new inbound links in your Monthly Report...that's what your Link Tracking Worksheet is for. But do mention any links that you find particularly exciting!

Now: Record new inbound links in your Link Tracking Worksheet and add commentary and analysis to your Monthly Report.

Google PageRank

Track Google PageRank for your landing pages. Now that you've got three months of numbers, you can start making informed guesses about whether Google views your pages as heavyweights or weaklings.

Now: Browse to each of your landing pages and record the Google PageRank on your Rank Tracking Worksheet.

Google PageRank is good to know, but it's not essential. If you're short on time, you can skip this step.

slacker

Wednesday: Check Conversions and Image Improvement

After spending a week climbing the web analytics learning curve, you know much more about tracking your conversions than in your previous Monthly Report. At the minimum, you've got some new ideas and plans in place—document them today!

Online and Offline Conversions

This month you spent a week focusing on improving your conversion tracking. You probably have some new information available, such as conversion rates from your PPC campaign, sourcing reports from your sales crew, or the number of coupons printed out and brought into your brick-and-mortar store. To avoid comparing apples and oranges, begin a new conversion tracking document for any new values you are now gathering.

Now: Open your conversion tracking document (or start a new one, if applicable) and record this month's data.

In the Monthly Report, describe any changes you have made to your information gathering methods:

- This month, we implemented conversion tracking on the PPC campaign.
- We will be tracking unique visitors to our home page and how many unique visitors reach the last page of the Save Our Schools article.
- We have created a Sales Diary document to record how many customers report that they used search engines to find us.
- A custom phone number was set up for use only on the website.

If you're still in the planning stages of your new conversion tracking system, document it! You may be surprised about the positive effect that writing down your plans has on your ability to carry them out.

Now: Explain your new tracking methods in your Monthly Report.

With your new methods clearly explained, summarize the data you have recorded. If any of your tracking methods are continued from previous months, discuss any observed changes and trends.

Now: Write your conversion data and commentary in your Monthly Report.

Image Improvement

As you were performing your rank assessment task on Monday, did you happen to observe any improvements to the image that your organization projects through the search engines? (Or, did you notice any new "uglies" or red flags?)

If branding is one of your goals for this SEO campaign, then these improvements deserve a rightful place at the table alongside other conversion goals. Make a note of them, and as we discussed in the sidebar "Tracking the Intangibles," put some thought into quantitative measures for ongoing tracking. Image improvements can be tracked in your conversion document or in the Monthly Report. (New red flags should be tucked away in your Task Journal for future fixing!)

Now: Now, record any image improvements in your Monthly Report.

Thursday: Monitor PPC Ads

This month you're going to build on your previous PPC reporting data by adding your conversion tracking data:

- Monthly PPC performance data
- Top-performing keywords
- Changes to campaigns

Monthly PPC Performance Data

Using the data you collect from your PPC engine and last month's report as a jumping-off point, boil down the important aspects of this month's PPC performance and add it to your report:

- Total number of click-throughs
- Click-through percentage
- Total cost
- Average total cost per click
  This month, you can add some new data (assuming you didn't have it already):
- Total number of conversions
- Conversion percentage
- Average total cost per conversion

Now: Now, use your PPC service to generate a monthly campaign report, and enter the performance data into your Monthly Report.

Keep your PPC service's campaign report open; you'll need it to complete the next section.

Top-Performing Keywords

With new conversion information on hand, you may wish to rethink your definition of keyword "performance." Last month, the keywords with the highest click-through rate may have been the ones you considered top of the heap. You may now want to look at conversion rates instead. Based on your new performance criteria, pull out the top-10 or so performing keywords from your PPC service's report and list them here.

Now: Record your top-performing keywords in the Monthly Report.

Campaign Analysis

Use this portion of the report to record any changes that took place in your PPC campaigns this month: new keywords, deleted ads, regrouped categories, and so on. Are you happy with your campaign performance so far? Any surprises? Discuss them here.

Now: Discuss PPC campaign changes or plans for the future in your Monthly Report.

Friday: Action Items

Since you're using last month's report as a template for this month's report, you have last month's action items available for easy reference. Don't clog up your monthly Action Items list by marking completed ones here; let your team focus on reading items that are still outstanding.

Now: Delete completed action items, and write new ones, in your Monthly Report.

By the way, we'll let you in on a little secret:

Pearl of Wisdom: The action items in your monthly report make great daily assignments once the tasks we've laid out in Your SEO Plan have run out.

With your second Monthly Report complete and making its way into the hands of everyone on your team, you're ready to move on to the third month of Your SEO Plan. Join us in the next chapter, where SEO becomes a way of life!

Month Three:
It's a Way of Life

With so many SEO elements—organic, paid, on site, off site—in the works for your website now, you've built up a holistic approach to SEO that you can be proud of. But don't rest on your laurels yet. SEO is never done!

This month you'll find SEO-friendly solutions for expanding your site's content, and you'll learn how to get more out of your starter pay-per-click (PPC) campaign. You'll smooth out any rough edges on your website's visibility, and you'll take reporting a step further.

9

Chapter Contents

Week 9: Build Content

Since Week 2 of Your SEO Plan, we've had you searching the Web for sites that may want to link to yours. Have you received the cold shoulder from most of these potential traffic sources? Or have you been slacking on link building because you think your site has no linkable content?

With more and better content, your search engine visibility will benefit in two ways: more people will want to link to it, and the search engines will find more unique pages to index. But building quality, linkable, preferably noncommercial content is easier said than done.

This week, you'll uncover opportunities that you may never have realized existed and scrub out obstacles, all with the goal of making your site more linkable. Your daily assignments for this week are as follows:

Monday: Discover Content You Already Have

Tuesday: Develop New Content

Wednesday: Optimize Non-HTML Documents

Thursday: Content Thieves

Friday: PPC Quick Check and Link Building

Monday: Discover Content You Already Have

You know how great it feels to find a twenty in the pocket of a jacket you haven't worn in a while? Today is the day you'll look for linkworthy and search-engine-friendly content that you didn't know you already had.

Here are some likely hiding places:

On Your Website What could you already have on your site that's linkable? Here are some possibilities:

- Product comparisons
- Research reports
- Industry news
- Free downloads
- Case studies
- Games
- Photo galleries
- Forums

You may have content on your website that just needs a little tweaking—perhaps a reorganization or a minor rewrite—to become linkworthy.

What Makes Content Linkworthy?

Everyone is talking about getting inbound links. Some SEOs are even focusing on strategies specifically geared toward building linkable pages, called *linkbait*. For the best chance of gaining inbound links, content should be

- original

- unique

- useful

- noncommercial (or subtle in its sales pitch)

- timely

- accessible without a password

- free of charge to view

And at the risk of stating the obvious, to be linkable, each page must *be linkable*—meaning it must have its own URL!

Perhaps you do have some of these elements on your site but they're intertwined with your less linkable, commercial content. If so, your site may benefit from a simple reorganization of materials. You can cluster this content, or links to it, within a new section of your site, aptly named "Resources," "Fun," or something similar. And remember, your goal is conversions, not just inbound links, so be sure to provide a clear path from this new section to your landing pages.

Sometimes, even a simple title rewrite can dramatically change the linkability of a page. For example, one type of content that often draws inbound links is a product comparison. Perhaps your site has a page that compares features of your product with your competition's. The only thing stopping it from being linkworthy is the title "Why Choose Us?" which strikes a commercial chord. Give this page a new, industry-specific but neutral title like "Compare Medical Imaging Products" and suddenly the exact same chart becomes potential linkbait.

By the way, consider this:

Pearl of Wisdom: Anything *not* free is just plain not linkable.

So you should separate out freebies such as freeware downloads or clipart onto their own page, for a linkability boost.

Your Sales and Promotions Everybody loves a bargain, and next to "free stuff," a sale or promotion is a strong contender for links. Trouble is, most websites move their promotions around, showing them temporarily at whatever URL seems to suit the moment. Take the smart approach: If your site runs promotions, make *one specific URL* for all promo materials! That way, linking sites will have an easy time sending you their bargain-hungry traffic—and you'll gain inbound links. If your organization runs promotions but somehow doesn't manage to get that content up on the website in a timely manner, put linkability on the list of reasons to turn over a new leaf.

Tools, Worksheets, and Sample Documents Are there any tools, worksheets, presentations, or documents that your organization is using in-house and might be willing to share? For example, countless SEO firms offer keyword assessment tools or other useful gadgets for free on their websites. Think they're doing it out of pure altruism? Nope. More likely, they're trying to attract links and repeat traffic.

Offline Marketing Materials You can add offline marketing materials, such as brochures and sales presentations, directly to your website in whatever format they were created in. However, from an SEO standpoint, HTML is still the best format for your web content. Here's why: Other websites might hesitate to link to non-HTML documents because viewing them may disable the "back" button. Also, many searchers will skip over links to non-HTML documents because they don't want to wait for a separate program to launch and they may not be in the mood for a long download. So, if your organization has a large amount of linkable content in non-HTML documents, see what it would take to re-create it in HTML. If that isn't possible, be sure to optimize your non-HTML materials. We'll show you how later this week.

E-mail Newsletters If you're already writing and sending out e-mail newsletters, why not add them to your site too? What appeals to your customers or opt-in readers may also appeal to linking sites.

Press Releases Press releases are excellent potential landing pages, naturally text based, keyword rich, and often linkworthy because they're news! In Chapter 5, "Get Your Team on Board," we discussed getting PR involved in optimizing press releases. If your organization hasn't been posting its press releases online, start now. But make sure the press release is linkable news before asking for links. New products fit the bill. New hires probably don't.

xtra cred Look to Chapter 10, "Extra Credit and Guilt-Free Slacking," for guidelines on optimizing press releases.

Now: Look for preexisting content within your organization that can be repurposed for your website, and make contact with the person who can help make the necessary changes to your site.

If you didn't have any luck finding usable content today, don't despair: tomorrow you will work on some easy strategies for creating *new* content.

Tuesday: Develop New Content

If yesterday's explorations didn't unearth any unique, linkworthy, and search-engine-friendly content for your website, you'll need to create some new content instead. Here are two approaches:

- Develop new content in-house.
- Use other people's content.

You'll look into these options today.

Develop New Content In-House

Of course, you could hire a staff of professional writers and set them to work full-time building fascinating, linkworthy content for your website. If you've got the budget for that, set down this book and call HR today! For everybody else, here are some ideas for building out your website content with limited resources:

Monthly Columns Is there anyone in your organization that might be interested in running a regular monthly (or weekly, but we won't hope for daily!) column on the website? Perhaps an "Ask the Expert" or "Helpful Hints" type of column, with no marketing agenda in mind. Once these columns build up steam, you might even begin sharing them with other websites through syndication or simply by contacting other site owners and requesting inclusion. Industry publications and e-mail newsletters are always looking for new content. But if you're going to be generous with your content, make sure you get as much SEO benefit as possible: articles posted elsewhere should always link back to your website.

Corporate Blog Many organizations are finding that the easiest way to keep a fresh presence on the Internet is through a corporate blog. This type of blog might allow contributions from many employees or just one. A blog can even be a great format for posting press releases.

The Need to Feed

As you learned in Chapter 2, "Customize Your Approach," blog-specific search works differently than standard search. If your content-building effort is taking you in the direction of blogs, podcast, vidcasts, vlogs, and so on, read on for tips to get your voice in front of the masses:

Ping me, baby First and foremost, make sure that your blog or 'cast is set up to send out a ping to an updating service (such as Weblogs.com, blo.gs, BlogRolling.com, or Ping-O-Matic, which will

Continues

ping a number of services for you). Most likely, your blog creation tool is already configured to contact an updating service (also called a *ping server*) automatically when your blog changes. Check your blog settings for this option.

Submit On www.yourseoplan.com, you'll find links to blog and podcast search engines to which you should submit your site. Luckily, these submittals are generally quick and easy. There are no titles and descriptions to carefully craft, just a URL to submit.

Pay special attention to specialty lists. Your weekly sermons should be listed at Godcast.com, and your deep-sea fishing advice will fit right in at codcast.net. Just kidding…better try sportsblogs.org.

Tag yourself Set up accounts with *social bookmarking* systems, searchable sites that allow members to save and classify, or "tag," URLs (del.icio.us, digg.com, and BlinkList.com are examples). Then make sure to tag each of your posts with keywords.

Get in the news If your website or blog contains regularly updated, unique, original content, it may qualify to be included on a news search engine such as Google News. Your site will be reviewed by an editor before inclusion, so don't waste your time or theirs with a submittal unless your content truly is news!

Blog your 'cast Some podcasting tools include creation of a blog that goes along with your podcast. This is a great opportunity for you to write accompanying text for your audio or video 'cast files (by the way, 'cast is just a trendy term for all sorts of podcasts. Every Web technology over 30 minutes old *must* have a nickname, you know). An example is shown here:

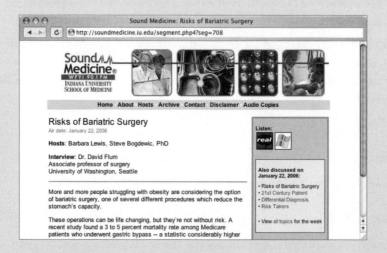

Potential subscribers will appreciate being able to read a description before downloading your podcast, and search engines—chronically allergic to audio and video content—will enjoy the tasty text treats you throw them in your synopses.

Compiled Resources You know your business, so you know the kinds of things your customers always seem to need help finding or figuring out. Resources such as useful links, FAQs, reviews, and a reference table or glossary can be good draws for inbound links (not to mention bookmarks and repeat visits!).

Interviews Interviews with bigwigs in your industry, or anyone else who your target audience finds compelling, can be a great way to fill out your website. For example, if your company sells home furnishings, an interview with an interior designer could provide content of interest to your target audience while giving the designer a publicity boost. Look for experts or service providers in fields similar to your own, and pick someone with a little flair.

Free Tools If your company has the technical chops for it, there's nothing like a free online tool for drawing inbound links. Translate dollars into yen; calculate shoe size in the European standard; figure out how many tablespoons of ground coffee it takes to brew a pot. As long as it's potentially useful to your target audience, it's a great idea. And you can gain even more linkage if you allow your tool to be used on others' websites. Just imagine: Suddenly your "teaspoons to quarts" conversion table is on every recipe website on the Internet—and each one includes a link to your site.

Use Other People's Content

Whoa, there! We're not saying you should go out on the Web, find some great content, and cut and paste it onto your website. There's this little thing called "copyright infringement" you'll want to watch out for. But there are some ways to use other people's content on your website without the Feds beating down your door. Here are a few ideas:

Articles Featuring Your Company Does your PR department keep a record of articles that mention your organization or include interviews or quotes from company representatives? See if you can get permission to add these articles to your website. (It goes without saying that you should stick to the complimentary ones.)

Syndicated Content It's quite easy to incorporate feeds onto your website—for example, industry news or blog posts. It's not unique content, but providing a group of topical links may add freshness and a sense that your site is up-to-date, thus increasing your linkability.

Forums or Classifieds One of our favorite ways to increase content is to let your users build it for you, with posts in message boards, classified ads, or product reviews. This is content that constantly updates itself and is eminently linkable. But it also sets you up for abuse, such as people submitting meaningless content (a practice called *comment spam*), so be sure you have a moderator or other system in place to protect your site if you're thinking of offering these features.

Guest Contributors Many talented writers and artists would love to have space on the Internet to display their work. Your contributors don't have to be professional writers. Many websites are nicely filled out with the free expressions of regular folks, from birth stories to bedtime stories.

Copyright-Free Content Copyright-free articles on subjects ranging from wedding etiquette to tax advice can be added onto your website, usually in exchange for a link or a courtesy notice. However, since this content is not unique, it's of little value for your search engine presence (and may even annoy your site visitors because they may have seen the same articles on other sites). So use it with caution, and only if you are certain it improves your site offerings.

An alternative to copyright-free content is Creative Commons (CC) content. The Creative Commons, at www.creativecommons.org, is a new type of copyright—you might call it a "some rights reserved" copyright. Explore CC content by searching for it using Yahoo!'s or Google's advanced search.

We've given you a pretty long list of possible ways to add content to your website; not every one will suit your needs or abilities. Today, choose which technique you'll try first. Set a goal for yourself, perhaps adding one new page of unique content each week, and get started today.

 Now: Set a content-building goal and get started.

Wednesday: Optimize Non-HTML Documents

There's no harm in posting documents on your website in non-HTML formats such as Word, Excel, PDF, or PowerPoint. All of these formats are indexed by the major search engines, and sometimes they rank well. However, good old HTML still has the upper hand in search. Non-HTML content can be a turnoff to searchers, as we mentioned earlier. Nevertheless, it can be optimized and serve you well, especially for the long tail of search. For example, while your home page might rank well for "model cars;" your product PDF could have a better chance of faring well for the term "die-cast model car assembly instructions."

Today, you'll learn a little bit about what makes non-HTML content work on search engines. Then you'll make any needed changes to your own docs:

- Metadata for compelling titles
- Content optimization
- When to remove

Metadata for Compelling Titles

Search results for non-HTML documents can be downright ugly, because the folks who wrote them never considered how these documents would be presented in the search engines. For example, take a look at this page of PDF search results for the term "umpire whistles."

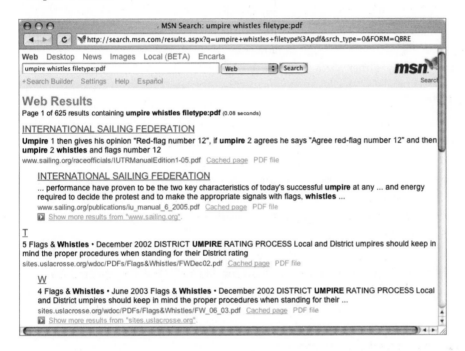

Look at listings number three and four: T? W? What kind of page titles are those? That just isn't going to cut it in the split-second decision world of search results.

Here are possible places that search engines will look for a page title for your document:

- The document title as specified in *metadata*, which is extra information you write to describe the document (and is stored in a file's properties but is not visible in the body of the document)

- The first 60 or so characters of the document's text

- The filename

- Any text in the document that you happened to format in a larger font.

Search engines will generally look for metadata first, so defining document metadata is the easiest way to improve your listings. In Adobe Acrobat and Microsoft Office applications, metadata such as Title, Author, and Keywords is very easy to define by selecting File > Properties or File > Document Properties. If you are using other programs to author your documents, look to their help pages for guidance.

Now: Open up one of your non-HTML documents and review the metadata. Insert an optimized page title if possible.

xtra cred
You can also define a description in the document metadata, but the search engines will generally gather a snippet from the document content anyway.

Content Optimization

Non-HTML documents are basically thrown in the mix with all the other documents and websites in a search engine's index. So, in addition to inserting metadata as described in the preceding section, you should follow the same SEO guidelines for non-HTML documents as you would for your regular web pages: include your target keywords in text, link to the document from other pages on your site, make sure URLs in the document are clickable so the search engine robots can follow them, and modify the content for improved snippets if desired.

slacker
We know it's not always realistic for non-HTML content to be edited based on SEO principles. And even if optimized, it's hard for non-HTML documents to rank well against HTML pages for competitive search terms. You may wish to skip optimizing the document content beyond basic metadata and hope for good results with the long tail of search.

Now: Make a determination about whether it's worth your time to attempt to optimize the visible content of your PDF files. If so, get started.

xtra cred
You can get a sense of how search engines see your non-HTML content by viewing the HTML alternate page created by Google. See Chapter 10 for more information.

When to Remove

You may be surprised to learn that keeping non-HTML documents—even if they rank well—can create disadvantages for your site. Consider the following:

- Files like PDFs and Microsoft Word documents are stand-alone entities, so they're not likely to be integrated into your site's navigation. If a visitor clicks on one of these files directly from a search engine, they may never even look at the rest of your site. You may want to weigh whether making your non-HTML content available to the search engines is worth the potential loss of traffic to the rest of your site.

- Since non-HTML documents will often be downloaded onto searchers' hard drives, it's possible that your content could be used in ways you don't condone. If you're concerned about this, don't put them on your site. At the very least, be sure that every document is clearly marked with authorship information, copyright notice, and your web address.

- Non-HTML documents may contain confidential information hidden in the metadata that you don't wish to make public, including things like tracked changes, comments, and speaker notes. It's always a good idea from a security standpoint to review metadata for your documents before posting them in public view. Workshare's free software, Trace, available at www.workshare.com/products/trace/, can help you weed out potential problems.

> **Now:** If you feel it's for the best, remove non-HTML files from your website or exclude them from indexing using your robots.txt file.

With metadata in your pages and content rich with keywords, your non-HTML documents may turn out to be healthy sources of targeted traffic for your site!

Thursday: Content Thieves

You're starting to develop a lovely collection of content on your website, but is somebody else nibbling at your piece of the pie? Unfortunately, the Internet remains something of a Wild West for copyright law. Other websites might steal your content simply by cutting and pasting, or they may use *scraping*, a more sophisticated technique of automatically grabbing content from your web pages, to steal material from your site and put it up on theirs.

You want to be aware of content thieves, not just because they are using your content to compete with you for search engine visibility, but also because they may be damaging your brand. An employer of ours once discovered that another company had repurposed large chunks of our website's marketing content—but *hadn't even taken the time to change all of the instances of our company name!* If your content is stolen by a similarly pathetic character, unwitting users might actually think that they are visiting *your* website, and that's something you certainly don't want.

There are several ways to check if your material is being repurposed elsewhere on the web. Here are a few:

Search for text. Using the search engine of your choice, search for a likely-to-be-unique text string (a sentence or two will do) from the body of your website, using quotes around the text. If the search engine finds sites other than your own, something fishy may be going on.

xtra cred Your competitors may be using your company name or proprietary product names in their PPC ads. Read Chapter 10 to learn more.

Use a page comparison site. Copyscape is a website specifically designed to help site owners find copies of their content online. A major limitation is that it searches only HTML content, not PDFs or other document formats.

Search for media. Stolen media such as images, audio, video, and Flash content is considerably harder to find than copies of your page text—for the very same reasons that search engines struggle with these formats in general. If media content is a significant portion of your site, you'll need to become an expert at using the media search options discussed in Chapter 8, "Month Two: Establish the Habit," to help protect your rights online.

xtra cred It's often easier to prevent media theft than react to it. If you're concerned about this, check in with your design team to make sure they're savvy to copy prevention options such as adding watermarks to images, building your Flash files in multiple pieces, or embedding your server information in media files.

Review your server logs. Other websites can display your media content such as images, audio, video, and Flash and make it look like it belongs to them. It's not uncommon for these nefarious nerds to point their links directly to your content on *your servers*. Not only does this infringe on your copyrights, it also puts an unfair burden on your servers, which are forced to serve up the content for someone else's site! Your server logs can help you find this sort of hijacking—yet another reason to make a habit of reviewing your stats.

Now you know how to look for misused materials on the Web. But what will you do if you find any? With any luck, a simple communication with the content thieves will clear things up. If not, you may need to contact the website host and request that the page be removed. Detailed advice and links to sample "cease-and-desist" letters can be found at www.plagiarismtoday.com.

 Now: Choose one of the methods listed in this section and search for copies of your web content. Begin pursuing any that you find.

Friday: PPC Quick Check/Link Building

It's time to continue your ongoing Friday tasks: PPC Quick Check and Link Building.

PPC Quick Check

Friday means…the PPC Quick Check is upon us!

Now: Follow the same steps as last week's PPC Quick Check. If you need to make any changes to your account, do so now.

Link Building

Today, you get your reward for a week of adding linkworthy content to your site. Your new content may give you some new possibilities for requesting links, and we *know* that having something noncommercial, useful, and unique to offer will make writing those link request letters a lot easier. This is where your whole week was leading you.

Now: Continue your link-building campaign with a focus on your newly-minted linkworthy content.

Now, with a website bodybuilding program in place for your organic SEO, it's time to spend a week toning your PPC campaign.

Week 10: PPC and ROI

Return on investment (ROI) is one of those fancy terms for a very simple concept: how much are you getting back compared to what you're putting in? Everyone wants a bigger, better ROI, and the best way to achieve one is to work within a framework that we like to call the *ROI loop*:

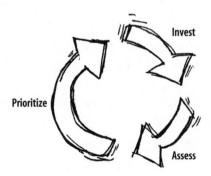

Over the past several weeks, you've invested both money and time in your PPC starter campaign. This week you'll move on to the next steps, assess and prioritize, and use what you learn to inform both your PPC and organic SEO efforts. We'll get you started on some new endeavors even as you take stock of older ones:

Monday: PPC Sanity Check

Tuesday: Organic Apples and Oranges

Wednesday: A/B Testing

Thursday: Close the PPC ROI Loop

Friday: PPC Quick Check/Link Building

Monday: PPC Sanity Check

Remember "algoholics," those people who obsessively follow the organic search engine algorithms? Well, we aren't trained in psychology, but we think we've identified two new SEO disorders: obsessively cutting out low-performing keyphrases because you can't stand the clutter (we call this PPC-OCD) and the inability to stop making little campaign changes (this is PPC-HD). The purpose of today's task is twofold: First, to give you some guidelines on how to "read" your PPC data like an expert, and second, to encourage those of you with itchy trigger fingers to make changes to your campaign without sabotaging its success.

Your PPC Sanity Check starts with lining up your PPC keywords from best performing to worst. So far, in the course of creating two monthly reports, you've identified your top performing PPC keyterms based on your own criteria. Probably you chose to order them by click-through rate, conversion rate, or some combination of the two. Today, using the same criteria, you're going to take a look at your entire PPC keyword list and decide whether it makes sense to delete any keywords.

 Now: Use your PPC service to create a keyword report for your campaign so far, and sort the keywords from highest to lowest performers.

As you look through your data, you may find that there is a fairly even spread of clicks or conversions throughout your list of keywords. Or more likely, you may find a nice group of performers at the top and a steep drop-off thereafter. Perhaps you even have a disturbingly long list of zero-performers. But is it really time to prune your PPC campaign? Probably not. Before you give in to your slashing instinct, take the time to apply some solid analysis. Here are the most common performance failures and possible ways to improve them:

- Keywords with low click-through rates
- Keywords with low conversion rates

Keywords with Low Click-Through Rates

As you learned in Chapter 4, "How the Search Engines Work Right Now," higher click-through rates will influence your rank on both Google AdWords and Yahoo! Search Marketing (YSM), so you may be tempted to start slicing and dicing keywords with low click-through rates. But while you may find these keywords bothersome, remember that you're paying for clicks, not ad views, so they aren't costing you extra money. Ask yourself a few questions that may help you turn these low performers around:

Is my ad text doing its job? Take an honest look at your ad copy to make sure it addresses your low-performing keyterm, and your audience, in a meaningful and compelling way. If the keyterm doesn't have its own custom-written ad, perhaps it should. Consider inviting another writer on your team to give your ads a tune-up. Or you may want to experiment with an *A/B split* (we'll tell you how later this week), which is an experiment that can help you get the most from your ad text.

Does the term have enough impressions for me to make a judgment call? Make sure you're getting enough ad views for your doubts about the keyterm to be valid. Sometimes, the number of impressions for an ad is so small that it's really not getting a fair shot at success. This is especially true if the keyterm is related to a seasonal or cyclical topic. Remember that terms on the "long tail" of search, which we described in Chapter 7, "Month One: Kick It into Gear," are naturally only going to get a very few impressions.

Did I start out with realistic expectations? This is a great time to reassess your trust in your PPC service's traffic prediction tool.

> **Now:** Review your keywords with low click-through rates and make changes for improvement if you determine it's necessary to do so.

Low Conversion Rate Keywords

Much more worrisome than the ad that isn't bringing in traffic is the one that actually *is* bringing in traffic but not resulting in conversions. You're going to hold these terms to a much higher standard than the low-click-through performers because every one of these clicks is costing you cash. But you may wish to give these underachievers a second chance before you dump them. Here are some questions you should ask:

Is the landing page a good match for the keyterm? You may be about to drop a keyterm when you should instead be planning to add a new page to your website to better accommodate it. At the very least, consider pointing a keyterm to a more appropriate landing page that already exists. Exploring different landing page options with an A/B split (described later this week) may also be in order.

Did I get caught in a word-matching snafu? If you are using a broad matching option, is it possible there's a broad match to your term that's drawing in the wrong audience? You can fix this with a *negative match*, a type of matching that excludes words you specify so that your ad doesn't show up for those terms. For example, you may want to sponsor the term "shredder" for your snowboarding site but you probably don't want to pay for clicks from people who are looking for those paper-eating office supplies. In this case, you'd want to exclude the words "paper" and "document" for this keyword.

Am I inadvertently using bait-and-switch tactics? If you owned a bike shop in Santa Cruz, California, you might think it's perfectly reasonable to sponsor the search terms "santa cruz bikes." Unfortunately, this is also the name of a popular brand of mountain bikes! Many of those click-throughs are going to be disappointed by your site. If you're in a situation like this, you'll need to review your ad text to eliminate ambiguity. Make sure your ads clearly represent your offering.

Now: Review your keywords with low conversion rates and make changes for improvement.

What's a Conversion Worth?

Determining the value of a conversion is anything but straightforward. The Left Brain and Right Brain share their perspectives.

The Left Brain says, "If you're paying for advertising, you need to have a way to determine if it's worth the cost. That means giving a numeric value to your conversions! For larger organizations, your marketing department probably already has a concept of the lifetime value of a new customer or client. For example, the PPC visitor who buys a digital camera online today may come back in a year for spare parts, and then recommend you to a business partner for a large purchase three years down the road."

The Right Brain says, "If your type of conversion is less tangible—for example, a visit to your Map and Directions page or downloading a white paper—you'll probably be hard-pressed to place a numerical value on it. This may be a case of 'I know it when I see it'—your gut will tell you that $10 per conversion feels like too much but $5 feels OK. If you can't place an exact value on your conversion, the best approach is to manage your campaign diligently so that you stay within your PPC budget and strive for the lowest cost per conversion possible."

Tuesday: Organic Apples and Oranges

Today, you're going to look for stand-out successes and unexpected disappointments among your PPC keywords so you can use that knowledge to adjust future organic SEO efforts. Why use PPC data to inform organic SEO? Because PPC provides data in a much more tangible form, quickly, and with less investment of labor than organic SEO.

With a quick scan of your PPC keywords reports, you can gain broad-brush insights like these:

- Your original keyword research led you to believe that a term is popular with searchers…but is it really? The number of PPC impressions it gets can help you confirm your suspicions.

- A keyphrase seemed targeted when you first assessed it…but is it? The number of click-throughs/conversions a term receives can give you a clearer understanding.

- A keyterm didn't make the cut for your organic top-priority list…but maybe it should have. If a term is a standout PPC success, you may have underestimated its organic potential.

Even with reams of PPC data in your hands, you may not arrive at any one finding or number that will make you say, "Eureka! I should change my organic approach in *this* way!" (But you can still just say, "Eureka!" for fun if you want. It's good for morale.) Factors such as low rank, less-than-stellar ad copy, or landing page problems can throw off any of the preceding "broad-brush" judgments.

Today, you'll use your PPC campaign data to judge the keyword choices you made at the outset of your Prep Month, looking for over- and underperformers that may need to be reprioritized. Here's what we look for:

- Keywords clusters
- Standouts and disappointments
- Next steps for your organic campaign

Keyword Clusters

Your PPC keyword assessment starts with reviewing the performance of clusters of related keywords. You can define a cluster as a group of stemmed keywords ("hangover cure," "natural hangover cures," "curing hangovers") or a group of conceptually related keywords (e.g., a "preventing hangovers" cluster vs. a "curing hangovers" cluster). This can give you an idea of the context in which your target audience is most interested in seeing those keywords.

Now: Download the PPC Cluster Worksheet from www.yourseoplan.com.

Next, follow these steps to assess the performance of keyword clusters:

- Sit down with a list of your top-priority keyphrases and your PPC report spanning the life of the campaign. (This can be the same report you used yesterday.)

- Go through your report and decide how you want to group your keywords into clusters. It might help to highlight different clusters in different colors as you go. You can define as few as two clusters or as many as you're interested in studying. It's OK to have leftover keyphrases that don't fit into any cluster.

- For each of the keyword clusters, copy total clicks and overall click-through percentage on a keyword-by-keyword basis into the PPC Cluster Worksheet. Or, if your conversion tracking has been in place long enough for some real data, enter total conversions and conversion percentage. See Tables 9.1 and 9.2 for examples.

- Use your PPC service to find the campaign-wide total number of clicks (or conversions, if that's what you're reviewing here) and the PPC Cluster Worksheet will calculate the percentage that each cluster is receiving.

Keep in mind, an accurate apples-to-apples judgment along these lines depends on the ranks for these terms being similar.

 Now: Gather clustered keyword performance data from your PPC campaign.

▶ **Table 9.1** Sample PPC Keyword Cluster Data for Cluster 1

Keyword(s)	Keyword Clicks/Conversions
mars rover	4
mars exploration rovers	55
athena rover	23
athena class rovers	99
Cluster 1 Clicks/Conversions	181
Cluster 1 Percentage of Total	**36%**

▶ **Table 9.2** Sample PPC Keyword Cluster Data for Cluster 2

Keyword(s)	Keyword Clicks/Conversions
space exploration	5
space science	2
space travel	7
space traveler	1
Cluster 2 Clicks/Conversions	15
Cluster 2 Percentage of Total	**3%**

Standouts and Disappointments

The truth is, there are lots of variables that get in the way of comparing PPC to organic performance. PPC and organic keywords are shown in different screen locations, in different contexts, and with different advertising messages and levels of keyword matching. Since the majority of searchers do not click on PPC results, you're not getting a full picture of the search population. But there are some things that PPC cluster data *can* tell you about your organic campaign:

Did you optimize for the right keyphrase variation? If you weren't sure whether you chose to use the right variation of a given keyword (e.g., "silk screen" vs. "silk screen printing"), this might give you enough data to convince you to make some edits to your landing pages.

Did you focus on the right user scenario? As you learned in Chapter 4, personas and scenarios are just ways to structure your thinking about your targeted audience and what you want them to do on your site. Looking at the data from the PPC keyword clusters, you might be surprised to see that one cluster is much more effective than the others (for example, the "monogram" cluster is getting more clicks or conversions than the "embroidery" cluster).

Did you miss any goodies? When you created your PPC keyword list, we asked you to toss in more than just your top-priority organic terms. Take a look now…are any of those added terms upstaging your top-priority list?

Next Steps for Your Organic Campaign

Now that you've gained some fresh insight on how your PPC keyphrases are performing, you'll use it to "close the loop" and adjust your organic campaign accordingly.

Did you find any keyterms outside of your original organic top-priority list that have any of these characteristics:

- Have a high conversion rate, even though they may have only a moderate number of impressions so far
- Are slightly more focused (or stemmed) versions of your top-priority keywords, and are coming through with noteworthy clicks and/or conversions
- Just appear to be logging a promising number of impressions

Conversely, were there any terms from within your original organic top-priority list with these characteristics:

- Logged few or no impressions
- Had plenty of impressions but no click-throughs
- Brought in lots of clicks but had a low conversion rate

Now: Make a list of promising new keyterms from your PPC campaign or existing organic ones whose PPC performance was below your expectations.

Consider the promising new keyterms for your next round of organic SEO. Does a place exist for these new terms on your site right now? Maybe they're already well matched with a landing page and it's just a matter of inserting them into the text and meta tags. As you incorporate new keywords into your organic efforts, you may want to drop underperformers from optimization and tracking.

Whether you start modifying your organic efforts today or put it off until your entire team reaches consensus will depend on your personal and organizational preferences.

Analysis Paralysis

Closing the ROI loop on your PPC campaign can range from an art form to a purely automated process. The Left Brain and Right Brain describe differing approaches.

The Right Brain says, "A little knowledge is a wonderful thing. But a limitless supply of raw data—which PPC services are very good at delivering—is difficult to wrap your mind around. An average do-it-yourself SEO may have a very hard time tackling this data, much less arriving at a meaningful take-away.

"So don't expect perfection, either in your campaign or your ability to assess it! It's all about evolving toward a better ROI. Start simple, with the broad-brush, trust-your-gut-instinct ways that help determine if your SEO campaign is on the right track. If you're not comfortable with your method of assessment, keep your budget small until you find the method that's manageable for you and that offers data you feel you can trust. Remember, the ROI loop is a circle, not a straight line."

The Left Brain says, "I agree that some degree of instinct-based approach is needed for difficult-to-track conversions. But for more straightforward e-commerce sites, or anyone with a clear method of measuring profit per conversion, PPC offers the opportunity to be more empirical in your approach. For one, you know what your conversions are worth, so you can set your bids as high as possible while still delivering a comfortable profit margin.

"Of course, bids are not the only factor in PPC ranking, and they may not even be the most important one. After all, even a top-ranked ad is worthless to you if your ad copy is no good. Ongoing scientifically run A/B testing can help you improve both your ads and your ROI. And there are even comprehensive, automated PPC campaign management solutions, such as the proprietary one used by Did-it.com, that will help track and analyze your PPC campaign for you. If you're ready to invest in closing the loop in a more sophisticated way, these solutions might be a good match for you."

Wednesday: A/B Testing

Civil engineers know that the best kind of earthquake testing for a building is this: *a real earthquake*. A/B testing is a way to get that type of real-world information for your SEO campaign.

Commonly used in the direct mail industry, A/B testing (also called an A/B split) is a practice of sending out two different advertisement designs and comparing their sales. On the Web, A/B testing can be used to compare the conversion rates for PPC ads, for landing page designs, or even for two different "Buy Now!" buttons.

There are several ways to approach an A/B split. Read through the following options and determine which one best fits your campaign.

- A/B Testing: Proper
- A/B Testing: Practical
- A/B Testing: Page-Based

A/B Testing: Proper

A scientifically robust A/B test would follow these steps:

- Create two identical PPC ads.
- Point both ads to the same landing page.
- Let both ads run for a while. The period of time (be it a day, a few days, a week, or even longer) before they are both showing approximately the same click-through or conversion rates is your testing period.
- Keep one ad the same throughout the test (this is called the A ad).
- Make *one* edit to the other ad (for example, change "Purchase low-cost dental insurance" to "Purchase discount dental insurance").
- After each edit, wait one testing period. Did the change increase or decrease the ad's performance (either click-throughs or conversions)? Don't forget to keep records!
- Try again with another edit.
- Lather, rinse, and repeat. With each testing period you learn whether the edit will help!

The scientific approach is great, but we know the real world rarely presents the opportunity for ivory tower–style research. And that's why we're hoping you'll look into the approach described next.

A/B Testing: Practical

If you're using Google AdWords, A/B testing for PPC ads is easy! Just write one or two additional ads for each of your Ad Groups. As clicks come in, Google automatically judges which ad is more effective and will increase its prominence for you automatically. If you have Google Analytics in place, you can use a ready-made A/B testing function for comparing the effectiveness of two different ads.

A/B testing on YSM takes a little more determination because you can't run two different ads for the same keyword at the same time. Instead, try testing your A/B split over consecutive testing periods rather than simultaneous ones.

A/B Testing: Page-Based

If you have a conversion tracking system in place, you can pursue a landing page A/B test. Here's how to compare the effectiveness of two landing pages for the same PPC ad:

- Find a PPC ad that's been running long enough to gather meaningful performance data. Select a period of time (like a month) of its history and record performance data. This period of time is your testing period.
- Build a new landing page for use with the ad. This should be an "orphaned" page, one that doesn't have any links to it other than from your PPC ad. For meaningful testing, you don't want this page to be indexed by the search engines, so exclude it using your robots.txt file. (You learned how to do this in Chapter 8.) Let your designer have fun with graphic text; this page doesn't need to be robot friendly. Since you know that the audience for this page is a little more "qualified"—that is, they clicked a specific PPC ad—make sure the copy is tightly focused to that audience.
- Now, sit back for a testing period and assess: Is the new PPC landing page delivering more conversions than your original landing page did for the same ad?

Some campaigns find that the extra level of targeting that is possible with a PPC-only landing page translates into more conversions.

 Now: Choose your favorite method of A/B testing, and set up your first testing period.

Does A/B testing have its limitations? Of course it does. You may figure out that one ad is doing better than another, but unless you interview your target audience, you'll never know exactly *why*. And if you're only measuring click-throughs, and not the outcome of the visit, A/B testing sure won't tell you what those clicks are worth. Plus, your tests are limited to your ideas for edits, so unless you're a master at thinking outside the box, there may be big improvements that you miss. Nevertheless, A/B testing is one of the few ways of getting real data on the persuasiveness of your SEO message.

Thursday: Close the PPC ROI Loop

Today you're going to start a new "invest" cycle in your PPC ROI loop. You'll drop the duds—unsalvageable low-performing keywords—from your PPC campaign. And you'll line up some promising new PPC keyterms and adjust bids based on performance data so far.

Add New PPC Keyterms

Adding a few new keyphrases to your PPC account is a fairly flexible process. You can do this in any number of ways:

- Use your PPC service's keyword tool to suggest additional terms.
- Grab some more terms from your preliminary organic keyword list that didn't make the cut for top-priority optimization.
- Go for the "long tail" and add some longer, highly focused versions of existing terms.

Now: Brainstorm more ideas for keywords in your PPC campaign. If your budget allows, add them to your account.

Adjust Bids Based on Performance

Each Friday during your PPC Quick Check, you've been adjusting your PPC bids to keep your spending balanced and on schedule. Now, if you have PPC conversion tracking in place, you can also adjust bids based on conversion performance. If you found any unexpectedly high or low conversion rates among your PPC keywords, you may wish to increase or decrease your bids for them today.

Now: Adjust bids for keywords with unexpectedly high or low conversion rates.

Drop the Duds

At this point, you have a good sense of which keywords are pulling their weight in your PPC campaign. You also know which ones may deserve a second chance. Now you'll drop any that are working against you. Here are the keyterms we call "duds":

- Low or zero click-through-rate terms that are costing you more in administrative work than you think they're worth (tasks that eat up time include appealing an editorial decision, closely monitoring a very expensive term, or just performing routine management on a campaign that has grown too large over time)
- Terms for which you're paying more per conversion than your estimated conversion value
- Terms that don't accurately represent your offerings

If any of these factors are true, then go ahead and slash. You can always add them back later if you regret your choice.

Now: Comb through your low-performing keywords and delete those that are actually having a negative impact on your campaign.

Friday: PPC Quick Check/Link Building

It's Friday! Time to wind down your SEO workweek with the PPC Quick Check and another day of link building.

PPC Quick Check

Perhaps you were so busy assessing your campaign's lifetime performance this week that you didn't get a chance to give your account a proper once-over to keep costs in check and keyword performance humming.

Now: Follow the same steps you performed in last week's PPC Quick Check. If you need to make any changes to your account, do so now.

Link Building

Get out your Link Tracking Worksheet and find more opportunities for targeted traffic!

Now: Continue your link-building campaign.

Now that you've spent a week pruning and feeding your PPC campaign and planting the seeds for a healthier ROI, it's time to dig your site out of some common SEO challenges.

Week 11: What's Your Problem?

You're nearing the end of Your SEO Plan, so this week we'll give you a chance to tie up loose ends and chase down any remaining trouble spots in your search engine presence:

Monday: New Site, New Problems

Tuesday: Copywriting to Improve Your Search Results Snippets

Wednesday: Catch Up with Your Team

Thursday: Fun Tools for Site Assessment

Friday: PPC Quick Check and Link Building

Monday: New Site, New Problems

It happens all the time, for big reasons or little ones, and it's one of the greatest challenges to an SEO campaign: a website redesign in which all or most of the URLs on the site change. Suddenly, every inbound link to your site is outdated. Bookmarks lead to broken links. Traffic plummets. Your search engine ranks drop off the map! And these problems can linger long after the revamp.

If your site was recently redesigned, or you're still working through repercussions from a long-ago revamp, or even if you're planning your site's next incarnation, here are some ideas for handling the sticky situations that crop up:

Page Redirects Do all your outdated pages redirect to appropriate new ones? Don't just redirect them to the home page. Ideally, each old page would redirect to a new page with similar subject matter. If this is not the case with your site, your task for today is to create a list of old URLs that are still getting traffic and the new URLs that they should be redirecting to. Then send it to your IT team member, who can help set things right using a server setting called a *301 redirect*.

File Not Found Page Do you have a kinder, gentler File Not Found (*404 error*) page? The page should, first and foremost, apologize to your patient readers for not being the page they're looking for. Next, it should *help them find the page they're looking for!* This could be by providing a site map, search box, or suggested links. If your File Not Found page is not helpful, your task is to propose new traffic-friendly content for the page and either implement it or deliver it to the person who can do so.

Inbound Links Do you still have a multitude of links pointing to your old pages? If so, your task is to sweep the Web for links to your old URLs and request updates. We showed you how to find links that point to a specific page in Chapter 6, "Your One-Month Prep: Baseline and Keywords."

Internal Links Did you clean up your old navigation? You'll never know until you check. Run a *link validator*, a program that checks your website for broken links internally. Tomorrow, you'll learn where to find these and other fun tools.

Massive site revamps have been known to cause more harm than good. So we would be remiss if we didn't tell you this:

Pearl of Wisdom: Sometimes it's best to follow the old maxim If it ain't broke, don't fix it.

Before you think about a site redo just to "keep things fresh," take stock of whether you're satisfied with your rankings, whether you have a good number of inbound links, and most important, whether your site satisfies the overall goals of your organization. Maybe, just maybe, you don't want to tempt fate with a redesign.

Prevent Link Rot

Next time you redesign your site, use URLs that you won't need to change—*ever*. Put some serious thought into file-naming conventions that will grow and expand with your website. Here are some rules of thumb:

- Don't name files with words like *new*, *old*, *draft*, *current*, *latest*, or any other status markers in the filename. This status will surely change as "new" files become "old" and "draft" files become "final." (It's a common problem! Last we checked, there were 581 listings in Google containing the preposterous filename final2.html—*for shame!*—and 456 listings for final3.html.)

- Name nested folders by year, and possibly month, for press releases or other dated materials (for example, http://www.yoururl.com/press/2005/august/newproduct.html). Try to put files in their final location as soon as they are launched rather than starting them out in the "current" folder and moving them later.

- Leave out any information that may change in the future. For example, you don't want to include the name of a current copywriter in the filename. This URL will feel outdated and awkward three years from now when that individual no longer works at the company. Names of servers, the city where you're headquartered, or any other contemporary information should also be left off of filenames.

Follow these guidelines, and your search engine presence may survive the next site redesign without a hitch!

 Now: Choose from the "new site, new problems" tasks listed in this section, and get started on the one that most applies to you.

Tuesday: Copywriting to Improve Your Search Results Snippets

In Chapter 7 you learned that searchers choose which result to click in a matter of seconds. Of course you want your site to have the best possible representation in the search results—and that means you need a snippet that's on your side!

For example, which of the following search results would you be more likely to click? This one?

Mizuho Securities Co., **Ltd.** - TOPPAGE
shadow, shadow. shadow, shadow. **Mizuho** logo Image. shadow, shadow. shadow, shadow.
Mizuho Securities Co., **Ltd.** shadow. shadow shadow. News TOPICS ...
www.**mizuho**-sc.com/english/ - 42k - Feb 8, 2006 - Cached - Similar pages

Or this one?

> **Mizuho Bank, Ltd.**
> **Mizuho** Bank aims to become Japan's most powerful commercial bank by providing comprehensive, high value-added financial services as the customers' bank of ...
> www.**mizuho**bank.co.jp/english/ - 17k - Feb 8, 2006 - Cached - Similar pages

Both of these examples show snippets from websites that are divisions of the same corporation. Why does one snippet look deliciously clickable while the other looks more like a Dadaist poem? Stay tuned:

- How snippets work
- Check your snippets
- Your snippet makeover

How Snippets Work

A snippet is text taken from a web page and shown when that page is listed in the search results. All four of the major search engines currently use snippets for many (but not all) search results. The most important thing to understand about search result snippets is that they are different depending on what keyword has been searched. For example, a Google search for the term "animal cloning" returns this snippet.

> **animal cloning**
> The study of **animal clones** and **cloned** cells could lead to greater ... As far as **animal cloning** is concerned, all **cloning** for research or medical purposes in ...
> www.rds-online.org.uk/pages/ page.asp?i_ToolbarID=5&i_PageID=162 - 48k -
> Cached - Similar pages

While a search for the term "animal cloning dolly" returns a different snippet for the same web page.

> **animal cloning**
> **animal cloning**. **Dolly** the sheep may have been the world's most famous **clone**, ... How was **Dolly** produced? Producing an **animal clone** from an adult cell is ...
> www.rds-online.org.uk/pages/ page.asp?i_ToolbarID=5&i_PageID=162 - 48k -
> Cached - Similar pages

Notice how each snippet includes the keywords that were searched? That means a search for your company name will return a much different snippet than a search for another of your target keywords will, even if both results point to your home page!

The specifics of how snippets are chosen vary for each search engine, but here are the basic rules:

- In general, the search engine finds the first instance of the searched keyphrase in the visible text on the page and displays it along with roughly 50 to 150 characters of surrounding text.

- The snippet often excludes titles and navigational elements.

- If the landing page doesn't include the exact phrase searched, the snippet will show sentences that include the various words in the phrase.

- Searched terms will be bolded in the snippet, while stemmed and plural versions of the words (clon**ed**, clon**ing**, clon**es**) may or may not be bolded as well.

Check Your Snippets

The first step toward optimizing your snippets is reviewing them! To check your snippets, simply open the search engine of your choice and search for your target keywords. Scroll to your search result and see what you find.

 Now: Review your snippets for each of your target keywords on the four major search engines. Make a note of any that you wish to improve in your Task Journal.

 slacker   If your website is not ranking in the top 30 for a target keyword, you can skip the snippet improvement for now.

 xtra cred   There may be other keywords you want to check as well. If you know phrases outside of your top-priority terms that are bringing traffic to your website, take a look and see if those snippets could use a makeover too.

Your Snippet Makeover

If you came across some snippets that you would like to improve, here are some possible approaches:

Add text. Sometimes, improving a snippet is as simple as adding one keyword-rich introductory sentence to the beginning of your page copy. Be sure that it is formatted the same as the rest of the page copy—titles and headers may not show up in snippets. And use your good copywriting skills so it doesn't seem jarring or "tacked on."

Remove ALT tags. One of the less-appealing items in many snippets is repetitive image ALT tags. A graphic button displaying the words Free Delivery in February! should have an ALT tag containing matching text. But a tiny graphic that is used to create a corner on a button does not need an ALT tag stating "white button corner." The page will be just fine without it. (Yep, that's what caused the poetic, but completely ineffective, "shadow, shadow, shadow" listing for Mizuho Securities Company that we showed you earlier.)

Change your error messages. As you learned in Chapter 7, search engine robots come calling at your website without any of the plug-ins, cookies, or JavaScript enabling that your site may require. If you're not careful, your search engine snippet might end up looking like this.

USGS (US Geological Survey) **EROS**, Sioux Falls, SD
Your browser does not support script. Your browser does not support script. Your browser does not support script. About **EROS** ...
eros.usgs.gov/archive/nslrsda/ - 8k - Cached - Similar pages

We've already shown you the best ways to avoid this kind of listing: be a stickler for good robot-readable content. But if you still have the odd error message making its way into the search results, remember that these messages are usually written by programmers without a marketing once-over. You might want to get in the loop!

Restructure the page. If your page is built using Cascading Style Sheets (CSS), it may be a simple endeavor to move scripts around in the source code so that navigation or other less-optimized content is situated below the page copy. This won't make any difference to your users viewing the page in the browser, but to search engines it will make your page copy come first. This may be a good strategy if your snippets are getting bogged down in navigation text.

Now: Assemble your suggested edits for snippet improvement. Deliver them to whomever needs to make the changes, or complete the edits yourself.

This is one of those rare opportunities for you to see rather sudden and dramatic changes in your listing quality. You may even notice the difference in just a few days, the next time your pages are spidered.

Wednesday: Catch Up with Your Team

You're well into the third month of Your SEO Plan now—how is your team holding up? Are you all working together like a well-oiled machine? Or is your "team" more like a collection of squeaky wheels, revolving doors, and bottlenecks?

In Chapter 5, we covered some strategies for encouraging members of your organization to join your SEO effort. Here are some good questions that may help you keep everyone on the same path:

Are my edits getting implemented? This is a biggie for many in-house SEOs: just getting simple (or not-so-simple) edits made to the website may require jumping through design, IT, and even legal hoops. If your recommended edits aren't being taken care of, take time today and figure out why. Are you sending your requests to people who don't have authority or access to make the changes? Are your requests playing second fiddle to another department with more "pull"? Or, did enthusiasm wane after the first round of edits didn't turn out the hoped-for quick results? Get the inside scoop on the holdup so you can take steps to flush it out!

Is anybody reading my reports? Are your monthly reports collecting virtual dust in your colleagues' e-mail inboxes? Are your action items chronically not checked-off? You may want to consider making some changes to your reports to gain a better audience. Next week you'll read about ways to structure your reports to encourage buy-in from your team.

Is SEO integrated into our processes? For Your SEO Plan to succeed, it needs to be part of the web development process. That means an SEO review before, during, or (worst case) after changes are made to the website. It also means integration of SEO considerations into the website style guide, if your organization has one. If you're feeling like an outsider, or if you think SEO is being given short shrift, you need to work on ways to integrate SEO into company processes. This means you may have to take on the role of SEO evangelist: Write up the first draft of an SEO style guide and deliver it to your developers. Ask to be included in copywriting or design meetings. If you don't overdo it, you can even send articles or SEO tips to a team member who might benefit from this information.

How's that conversion tracking going? Last month, you started setting up conversion tracking for your organization. If your system requires participation by members of your team (for example, you need Sales to track calls from a special 800 number), revisit it today and see if it's working. Are you getting the information you need? If not, what needs to change?

Will the Real Home Page Please Stand Up?

You met search engine expert P.J. Fusco in Chapter 5, where she shared advice for getting your team on board. Here, P.J. tells a cautionary tale:

"We needed to optimize a handful of pages in a 4,000-page e-commerce site. One of the elements required was meta tags—unique title, description, and keyword attributes for eight different pages....

"The project manager informed me this portion of the organic project was complete, so I audited the work. Everything looked good, except for one thing. *Every single page of the site contained the meta tags for the home page.* Can you imagine what a search engine spider thinks when it's trying to index 4,000 pages all proclaiming to be the official home page of the company?"

You've heard of Murphy's Law: If anything possibly can go wrong, it will. Add to that our sad little truth: If any project is going to get rushed through, glossed over, or ignored, it will be SEO. Nobody is going to look after SEO details the way you, the SEO team leader, will. So keep P.J.'s experience in mind, and be sure that you have a process in place to check your team's SEO-related edits, even when you're *sure* nothing can go wrong.

Who's in it for the long term? Which members of your team have the energy, talent, and mindset for a sustained effort? By now, you have enough SEO experience that you can spot the personalities with a natural affinity for this work. Now it's your turn to be the squeaky wheel: do what you can with your higher-ups to keep those people on your team for the long term.

> **Now:** Ask yourself the preceding questions and start sending e-mails or setting up the needed meetings for improvement.

Since your SEO team is made up of people who, like you, are busy doing other things, it's natural that your team's interest and ability to focus will wax and wane. So don't be surprised if you need to do check-ups as you did today on a regular basis.

Thursday: Fun Tools for Site Assessment

From time to time throughout Your SEO Plan, we've pointed you to helpful tools available on the Web. Today, we'll share a few more of our favorites! Every one of these can help your search engine visibility; read through the descriptions and spend your hour exploring the ones that interest you the most:

Link Validator There are many free tools online to check your website for broken links on a page-by-page basis. (For example, LinkScan/QuickCheck at www.elsop.com/quick/ and several spider emulators do this.) However, it's much more useful to run link validators sitewide. One site that offers a deeper crawl is www.dead-links.com.

Slow Page Load Checker Your site visitors and prospective customers aren't the only ones who grow weary of slow-loading pages; spiders may also give up and walk away. A good online tool for checking page load time can be found at www.websiteoptimization.com/services/analyze. Another tool that checks load time along with spelling and several other HTML code factors can be found at www.netmechanic.com/toolbox/html-code.htm.

Link Popularity Comparison Use the tool at www.marketleap.com/publinkpop/ to compare your website's link popularity with that of your competitors.

Keyword Density Tools www.live-keyword-analysis.com offers a quick and easy way to check keyword density in any text you choose.

Your Own Browser Here's a tool we know you already have: a browser. In Chapter 6, you learned how to view page source using your browser. You can also use your browser as a makeshift spider emulator. Here's how: Select Preferences from your browser menu. Then, figure out how to turn off image display and disable JavaScript. You can choose to reject all cookies while you're at it. Voila! Your browser is now a speed machine and a crude approximation of a search engine robot.

Accessibility Check One of the fringe benefits of Your SEO Plan is that it will improve your website's accessibility for the disabled. By the same token, a more accessible website will tend to be more robot friendly as well. Jan Schmidt of Collaborint Web Management Services, a web design and development firm specializing in web accessibility, explains that many SEO practices "not only make it more efficient for search engines to crawl a website and index the content but can also improve the disabled user's experience by providing easy-to-navigate links and machine-readable page text."

Tools are available to check your page with everything from voice browsers to color-blindness simulators. We recommend you start with Cynthia Says, a free Web-based tool located at www.cynthiasays.com. Links and descriptions of many more accessibility tools can be found here: www.w3.org/WAI/ER/existingtools.html.

Sandbox Detection Tool In Chapter 4 you learned about the Google sandbox. The Sandbox Detection Tool, www.seomoz.org/tools/sandbox-tool.php, will help you analyze whether your site is trapped in Google's temporary holding pen.

xtra cred

If you're the type to spend hours testing out gadgets and techno-goodies, there are a couple of SEO tool smorgasbords that you may enjoy: www.webuildpages.com/tools/default.htm and www.faganfinder.com/urlinfo/.

Now: Explore your favorites from the list of tools in this section.

Warning: Heavy use of SEO tools may result in an increase in the size of your Task Journal. Embrace it! Good SEO means never running out of things to do!

Friday: PPC Quick Check/Link Building

It's time once again to make sure your PPC campaign is on track, and to keep those links coming!

PPC Quick Check

It's Friday...time for the PPC Quick Check.

Now: Follow the same steps you performed in last week's PPC Quick Check. If you need to make any changes to your account, do so now.

Link Building

Think of link building as an opportunity to compensate for some of the lost traffic that might result from any problems you found this week.

You've done a lot of good for your site over the last few weeks. Now you'll have the opportunity to track your accomplishments in your Quarterly Report.

Week 12: Visibility Check and Quarterly Reporting

Just like the talk you may be planning (or planning to avoid) with your significant other, the Quarterly Report is the time to turn your attention to the long-term view. SEO and your website have been in a relationship for three months now, four if you count the Prep Month. What's it all about? Where are you going? Are you committed to your keyword choices? Do you think it's time to start playing the field and looking for additional landing pages? Do you have an itch to check out new competitors?

As with last month, think about this week's reporting tasks as a guideline, and don't be afraid to substitute your own observations or methods whenever appropriate. Refer back to last month's completed Monthly Report as you go. Here are your tasks for this week:

Monday: Check Organic Status

Tuesday: Check Links

Wednesday: Check Conversions and Image Improvement

Thursday: Monitor PPC Ads

Friday: Action Items

Monday: Check Organic Status

Just like last month, it's time to pull up your Rank Tracking Worksheet and last month's Monthly Report from your SEO Idea Bank so that you can check and record values for the following:

- Search engine rankings
- Indexed pages

Search Engine Rankings

Whether you're checking your ranks on multiple search engines (as you have been doing since your Prep Month) or you've evolved your reporting process to include more conversion tracking and less rank tracking (as we discussed in Week 8), look through at least one search engine and record your ranks today.

Just Another Monthly Report?

We've cautioned you not to forget about reporting…but maybe you forgot anyway. And we've also cautioned you not to generate reports more frequently than once a month…but maybe you got a little excited. Whatever your past reporting problems, the Quarterly Report has a lot of cleansing power.

Here's why: Performing special in-depth tasks, like checking ranks for a greater number of key-words, and revisiting your most visible competitors, can give you a snapshot of your campaign's big picture performance that might yield some very telling results. If you have extra time to spend on campaign analysis, the Quarterly Report is the time to do so. That's why this week is full of extra credit ideas.

Conversely, if you've been a slacker about reporting—we mean a real slacker, not the kind we condone—now is your chance to make good on collecting that all-important data.

What's more, planning for a slightly more robust report on a quarterly basis can help you get other people off your back as you go about your regular SEO activities. If you have a group of extremely enthusiastic colleagues who have been hounding you for more and more data and analysis, the Quarterly Report is a great time to placate them. Practice saying this: "That's a fascinating ques-tion. I'll pay special attention to it in the Quarterly Report."

Don't worry, though, if you don't have any more time than usual to devote to reporting. There's still great value in your regular routine and much to be gleaned from four consecutive monthly visibil-ity checks.

This month you paid special attention to your site's snippets. As you perform your rank check, keep an eye out for improvements.

 Now: Open up your Rank Tracking Worksheet and fill in your website ranks for this month.

 xtra cred There may be reasons for checking additional keywords outside of your top-priority terms on a quarterly basis. See Chapter 10 for details.

 Now: Open last month's Monthly Report and rename it (by choosing File > Save As) with the current date. This is now your Quarterly Report.

It's been three months now. You can probably start to formulate the kind of confident cause-and-effect analysis that looks like this:

- After our optimization efforts caused a boost in rankings, our rankings have stayed relatively stable.

- Even though our optimization efforts took place in June, our ranks continue to fluctuate. This is due to the high level of competitiveness of the keywords we are tracking.

- Still no top-30 ranks in Google, even for our company name. It's probable that we are still sandboxed!

Feel free to add a liberal sprinkling of qualifying words like *probably* instead of *certainly* and *unlikely* instead of *definitely not*. These words are staples in the SEO expert's repertoire of reporting verbiage. Sure, one day the algorithms may come out of hiding and your competitors may send you a bulleted list of their most recent SEO activities, but until then, it's perfectly fine to make educated guesses.

Now: Add your summary and analysis to the "Site Visibility" section of your Quarterly Report.

Indexed Pages

If you were a diligent slacker and haven't been checking your site's indexed pages, slack no more! It's worth at least a quarterly check.

Now: Check the total number of pages indexed on your site in each of the four major search engines. Record the value on your Rank Tracking Worksheet.

If any of your landing pages were not indexed when you checked last month, or if you didn't see one or more of your landing pages in the search results during your manual rank checks, verify that each one is indexed in all four search engines now. If a page should get knocked out of a search engine's index, it could mean a significant loss in potential traffic for you, so it's important to catch it now.

Now: Check the indexing of your landing pages. Document status on your Rank Tracking Worksheet.

Tuesday: Check Links

Who added new links to your site? Today you'll document the following in both words and numbers:

- Link campaign activities
- Google PageRank

Link Campaign Activities

As you document your inbound link activities this month, remember to review any pages providing new links. You want to be sure that they are linking to your site using the best possible linking text and descriptions.

 Now: Record new inbound links in your Link Tracking Worksheet and add commentary and analysis to your Quarterly Report.

 slacker   You can stop looking into link requests that are more than two or three months old. It's better to focus on future links than waste time checking for previously requested ones that you're unlikely to receive.

 xtra cred   If you have server log analysis in place, you can check to see if any of the inbound links you received are bringing in visitors. Peek into your server stats and find the most effective inbound links that are a direct result of your link-building activities. So what if it's a drop in the bucket compared to what Yahoo! brings in? It's still a traffic source you can take direct credit for. Write about it now in the analysis. (Sorry, we don't have a worksheet for tracking brownie points.)

Google PageRank

If you've chosen the slacking path and haven't collected Google PageRank for your landing pages so far, do it now. Looking at PageRank on a quarterly basis can help you catch big problems, like zero PageRank on any of your landing pages.

 Now: Browse to each of your landing pages and record the Google PageRank on your Rank Tracking Worksheet.

Wednesday: Check Conversions and Image Improvement

Last month you began the process of implementing more sophisticated conversion tracking. If you've got a shiny new tracking system in place, good for you! If you're still working on it, continue to track conversions any way you can, as we've encouraged you to do since your Prep Month.

Online and Offline Conversions

As we mentioned last month, if you're just starting out with a new conversion tracking method, start a new tracking document to avoid comparing two different types of data.

Now: Open your conversion tracking document (or start a new one) and record this month's data.

Analyzing conversions may be tricky this month if you don't have three or four months of similar data. Do what you can. If you started with rock star conversion tracking methods and you've got a nice, continuous stream of data to analyze, this is the time to look for trends that influence the future of your SEO campaign. Should you focus on a particular subset of your target customers? Should you make a bigger effort on ironing out sitewide technical difficulties that are blocking conversions? Could usability or copywriting be a factor?

Depending on your organization—and your place on the totem pole—these kinds of judgments may be best presented as "thoughts" or "suggestions," not directives. Big changes may best be left to a committee decision.

Now: Write your conversion data and commentary in your Quarterly Report.

Image Improvement

Your image and branding improvement work this month, and your findings from your website analysis using the fun tools last week, shouldn't go unrecorded. Maybe this month you'll be able to make some statements like these:

- PDF files were optimized for better indexing.
- A new CEO blog was started to increase linkable noncommercial content and develop relationships with online readers.
- I was unable to find any instances of stolen content on the Internet in our competitors' sites.
- Our keyword density for the term "comforter covers" on our home page is on par with those of our competitors.

Now: Record any image and branding improvements in your Quarterly Report.

Thursday: Monitor PPC Ads

Today you'll continue to gather PPC performance and conversion data.

- Monthly PPC performance data
- Top performing keywords
- Changes to campaigns

Monthly PPC Performance Data

Using the data you collect from your PPC service, and last month's report as a jumping-off point, boil down the important aspects of this month's PPC performance and add it to your report:

- Total number of click-throughs
- Click-through percentage
- Total cost
- Average total cost per click
- Total number of conversions
- Conversion percentage
- Average total cost per conversion

 Now: Use your PPC service to generate a monthly campaign report, and enter the performance data into your Quarterly Report.

Keep your PPC service's campaign report open; you'll need it to complete the next section.

Top Performing Keywords

You've done a lot this month to determine which of your PPC keyphrases are earning their keep. Use what you've learned to list your top performers.

 Now: Record your top-performing keywords in the Quarterly Report.

Campaign Analysis

This month, we walked you through several tasks that may have resulted in big changes in your PPC account. Did you do some housecleaning? Did you take a new tack? Or were you reassured that your PPC campaign is heading in the right direction? Summarize it briefly.

Now: Discuss PPC campaign changes—and your reasons for making them—in your Quarterly Report.

xtra
cred

You've identified your Big Five organic search competitors. Have you considered who your Big Five competitors are in the PPC realm? Although shifting bids and position-jockeying may make this hard to pin down, you've been working on PPC long enough now that you may be able to list your PPC Big Five in your Quarterly Report.

Friday: Action Items

Action items are your way of communicating with your team that your SEO effort is continuing and that you have your priorities in place. Action items can also be a way to formally request your teammates' help in your organization's SEO efforts.

Do You Need a Report Card…for Your Reports?

You've lived with your reports for several weeks now. Do you forget them as soon as you finish them? Are you secretly glad that nobody has popped over to your desk to discuss them? If so, you need to improve your reporting style.

For Yourself: Think of your monthly reports as a distillation of the most important elements of your Task Journal. Your reports should be peppered with items that were resolved or completed every month, and your action items should contain the Task Journal's "most wanted" list.

Use your reports to motivate yourself. Sometimes the only way to muster the energy to complete a less-than-enjoyable task is the satisfaction you get from knocking it off your Action Items list. The "I can't stand to see that again" factor is very helpful in your Task Journal. Don't underestimate the power of the "I can't stand for the *team* to see that again!" factor in your report.

If you are finding it very difficult to complete your reports every month due to other monthly obligations, consider taking advantage of SEO's forgiving timeline and shifting your SEO reporting to another time of month.

For Those Reading Your Report Ask what they want to see! Would the people reading your report like briefer explanations? More detail? Less negative phrasing? Would selective bolding increase their ability to scan the document?

Continues

Do You Need a Report Card…for Your Reports? *(Continued)*

Are your reports being studiously ignored by your busy colleagues? Consider setting up a monthly or quarterly meeting to discuss them with the people who have the biggest stake in your SEO success. This may encourage them to be more diligent about reading your reports.

Or, maybe you need to improve your delivery style: Perhaps you could deliver your reports in hard copy rather than electronic form. Or, put the action items in the body of the accompanying e-mails.

You may also wish to add or remove individuals from your mailing list: Stop delivering the report to folks who aren't holding up their end of the deal, or start delivering the report to their bosses so they can justify the time spent on SEO tasks.

Making just a few minor improvements to your monthly reports could result in a better reception, and more cooperation, from your team.

 Now: Delete completed action items, and write new ones, in your Quarterly Report.

 xtra cred   The Quarterly Report is an excellent place to reassess your campaign and realign your organization-wide SEO priorities. As a starting point, why not dig out your Quick Reference sheet from the Baseline Report you compiled in your Prep Month? It might be time to update it!

Moving On: Forging Your Own SEO Path

Congratulations! Since you've opened this book, you've absorbed a tremendous amount of SEO knowledge, been promoted to SEO team leader, and become even more valuable to your organization. The "scripted" portion of Your SEO Plan is over, with the exception of some helpful ideas for extra credit and slacking in the next chapter.

You may have noticed that the further Your SEO Plan progressed, the less we held your hand and the more you had to create your own directions. That's because, as SEO expert Jill Whalen said, there really is no cookie-cutter solution. You have to go where your organization needs to go, where your competition forces you to go, and where your market allows you to go. As you move forward on your own, you have endless options, but here are some possible ways to proceed:

- Make every day a Task Journal day, with the exception of a day a week set aside for link building and PPC checks and a week a month set aside for visibility checks and reporting.

- Start Your SEO Plan over again with a new audience or conversion goal in mind.

- Start Your SEO Plan over again with a new set of landing pages in mind.

- Start combing through your site, page-by-page or section-by-section, and optimize based on your current best practices.

- Ask your marketing team about what short-term promotions are coming up. A contest? A seminar? A sale? Make sure you have a say in any promotional text that's going up on your site, and consider setting up your PPC campaign to promote it for the short term.

- Depending on what you've learned, you may want to drop PPC and go full-bore on organic SEO. Or vice versa!

Intelligent Outsourcing

Maybe you've developed into a full-fledged SEO expert over the course of reading this book. But it's also possible that you've discovered that it's not your favorite pastime and you're ready to outsource. In the years that we've been in the SEO industry, we've seen growth in the number of quality SEO service providers. At the same time, we've seen at least 57 varieties of snake oil on the market! If you do choose to go the outsourcing route, keep the following caveats in mind:

- Watch out for any guarantee of a specific search engine rank. A legit search marketing service will not guarantee a rank that they don't have control over.

- Some companies direct your traffic through intermediate pages on their own hosted domains and then "turn off" your traffic when the contract is terminated. You need to have control over your own content and traffic, so don't agree to this type of business arrangement.

Snake oil

Continues

- There are only a small number of important search engines to rank well on, so anyone who is talking about rankings on "thousands of search engines" is probably best avoided.

- Good search marketing is time consuming, and there are no shortcuts. If a company is charging $79.99, you are not getting a legitimate full-service solution.

The best news is, now that you know so much about sensible, effective, and holistic SEO practices, you'll be able to make informed judgments about any SEO help for hire that crosses your path.

The world of search is ever changing, and Your SEO Plan will need to change with it. Technological advances in personalization, local search, demographic targeting, synonym recognition, keyword categorization, and so on will require constant adjustment on your part. Will social bookmarking systems and "human intelligence" replace search engine algorithms? Will organic SEO become obsolete as PPC dominates? Will search become integrated with television and search marketing replace TV ads? Whatever the future holds, we hope this book will help you enter it with great SEO habits in place and a strategy for continued learning. Continue to give SEO an hour a day, every day, and you'll be able to ride the waves of change with confidence.

Extra Credit and Guilt-Free Slacking

Since you're not a full-time SEO professional, sometimes other work obligations will get in the way and you'll need to give your campaign a little less attention. Other times, your website's unique problems or your own curiosity will inspire you to dig deeper. In this chapter we'll help you sort it all out by defining a range of reasonable slacking and extra credit behavior.

10

Chapter contents:

The Slacking Spectrum

Be honest: Did you flip to this chapter before you even started your SEO campaign? Have you been planning to do the bare minimum from the get-go? If you expected us to disapprove, you're wrong. Let us reassure you:

 Pearl of Wisdom: Any amount of properly executed SEO that you can muster will bring about *some* positive effect.

And this is especially true if your competitors are doing absolutely nothing in the way of SEO.

Slacking, as we're using the word here, simply means taking an honest look at your time and abilities and determining whether you can put off, or even blow off, a task or a group of similar tasks. Slacking can be the result of a simple judgment call; for example, if a task we assigned in Your SEO Plan didn't apply to your site, don't do it. Or slacking can be a path you're forced to take due to a lack of time, budget, or manpower.

Take heart: There's really nothing wrong with having a slacker mentality as long as you follow these important Dos and Don'ts about slacking and SEO:

DON'T beat yourself up. Periodic dips in SEO activity are to be expected for busy people in dynamic organizations. An occasional bout of inattentiveness to your campaign is common. Dropping the ball every once in a while is no reason to abandon your SEO efforts altogether.

DON'T slack if your competitors aren't. If you are in an extremely competitive market, there's probably no easy way to shirk. You will have to work harder on your SEO campaign to see changes for the better. Likewise, if one of your sleepy competitors wakes up to SEO, you'll need to step up your efforts accordingly or suffer the consequences.

DON'T blame it on the budget. Just as you don't need a big SEO budget to be an overachiever, you don't need to slow down on SEO just because you're low on funds. Site edits, link building, landing page A/B testing, and competitive analysis—to name just a few—are tasks that most organizations can do at no extra cost.

DO be realistic. If you anticipate that you *never* will be able to devote an hour a day to your SEO campaign, it's time to think about sharing the load with a coworker or hiring a consultant. (We gave some guidance on hiring SEO help in Chapter 9, "Month Three: It's a Way of Life.")

Ideas for Reducing Your SEO Workload

For many sites, an hour a day pretty much *is* the bare minimum you can get away with for an effective SEO campaign. If you're starting a new SEO campaign, following the plan as written from your Prep Month on through to the end of Week 12 will give your site the best shot at success.

Throughout the Plan, we've pointed out tasks that we feel can be dropped without a major impact on your SEO outcome. But if you think you need to trim down your SEO campaign even further, you may be looking for a little guidance on how to do it.

Some Slacking Is Not Guilt Free

Priorities will vary from organization to organization, but there are a few tasks you should never slack on because they form the foundation of your entire SEO campaign:

- Defining your conversion goals
- Identifying your audience
- Researching your keywords

And there are also certain red flags that you should not ignore because they can cause all of your other efforts to be wasted:

- Problems, such as coding errors, that block the search engines from indexing your landing pages
- Problems, such as broken links, that dump your audience into dead ends instead of delivering them to your site

Here are some ideas for bringing Your SEO Plan in line with your own less-than-perfect reality, whether it's related to your time, your budget, or your team's willingness to help:

Cut out early. Consider going through the Prep Month and stopping after Month One of the Plan. Choosing your keywords and getting them onto your site using sound SEO methods is a substantial step forward and may help you realize a positive change.

Cut out PPC activities. This is a no-brainer if you have no money to spend on it. Unlike PPC, organic SEO will continue to deliver improvements long after you've quit devoting time to it.

Cut out organic activities. Cutting organic SEO and focusing only on PPC may be a smart strategy if you are short on labor and have a healthy budget to work with. With

PPC, you can expect quicker success than with organic SEO alone. But proceed with extreme caution: If your site isn't optimized for your target audience, it may not be an effective destination for PPC visitors.

Cut reporting loose. If you seriously don't have the time, consider delegating your site visibility check to someone else in your organization. Yes, this will seriously handicap your ability to analyze and improve your campaign. But asking an administrative assistant to gather numbers for you is better than not tracking at all. After all, if nobody's collecting information about your site's performance, how do you know whether you're wasting what little time you *do* have to spend on SEO?

Do it all, but with a smaller scope. If you're low on time, do your slicing the way the SEO consultants do: by limiting your campaign to fewer conversion goals, audiences, or landing pages. For example, focus on only one product line or one landing page, whittle down your top-priority keywords to just a couple, or focus on only one segment of your potential audience. In this way, you're still working toward increasing your targeted traffic using a holistic approach to SEO.

Be a dedicated dud-dropper. We'd love to be able to list SEO tasks in order from the best to worst effort-to-results ratios. But these factors vary widely from organization to organization—one website's success story is another's sob story. So, you will need to track your own results and figure out for yourself which SEO tactics are working for you and which are wasting your time. Once you have some data under your belt, feel free to slash and burn.

You may have the big idea to strip down Your SEO Plan to just focus on Google ranks and nothing else. While this is a common sentiment expressed by clients we've come across, it really isn't a reasonable slacking mindset. There are couple of reasons why you shouldn't act on this kind of Google-centric instinct. For one, achieving good ranks in Google for any meaningful keyphrase requires the opposite of slacking; it's hard work! And second,

 Pearl of Wisdom: Google does not exist in a vacuum.

In fact, a well-rounded approach to SEO is the *only* kind that will improve your website's ranks in Google. You can't really strip out all but the Google-related tasks and have less work to do.

Slacker Stories

Just like the rest of your campaign, your slacking plan will be customized. Here are a few fictional examples of well-constructed "slacker" efforts:

Focusing on PPC Jeanna works at a five-person B2B software development firm. As the only admin staffer, she is responsible for everything from payroll taxes to coffee filters. She had hoped to spend an hour a day on SEO, but other crises are always interfering with her plans. Still, her boss is looking for results. As she learned in Chapter 2, "Customize Your Approach," one of the advantages of a B2B business is a high conversion value. That means that even a small number of conversions can pay off big for her organization. Jeanna convinced her boss to invest in six months of highly targeted PPC. She devoted about one hour per week to managing the campaign and a full day each month to documentation. Who knows? Maybe the new accounts that can be attributed to the PPC campaign can be used to hire Jeanna an assistant!

Focusing on a single goal or audience Alonzo is in Development at a mid-size nonprofit. The organization is optimistic about using search to improve volunteer awareness as well as to increase online donations. However, with limited time and almost no knowledge about the volunteer side of the organization, Alonzo chooses to focus his SEO efforts on online donations first and move on to volunteer awareness later.

Lengthening the process Laura works in Marketing at a medium-size B2C selling school supplies. She took advantage of the traditionally slow spring season to get started on her SEO campaign—the Prep Month and Month One only. She'll be able to see some advances from the basic optimization and continue with the remainder of the plan when time allows.

The Extra Credit Continuum

Extra credit in SEO doesn't require as much soul-searching and premeditation as slacking. Usually extra credit is just a natural extension of what you're already doing with your site. SEO encompasses a wide variety of disciplines and activities, from creative writing to coding. You may just discover one aspect of it that grips you and run with it.

But, if you're extremely gung ho on SEO extra credit, we will wave this yellow flag:

Pearl of Wisdom: Don't go so deep in any one area of SEO that you ignore everything else.

If you're going full bore on the technology side of SEO, make sure it's balanced out with a fully developed organic approach too. We've said it before: A holistic approach is best.

And, one more thing: Keep your perspective. There is a difference between extra credit and wasting your time. Checking ranks every day, logging daily unique visits (unless you have a short-lived or time-sensitive campaign), and spending all your time trying to decipher Google's algorithm are not worth the effort. Turn your attention instead to more reasonable tasks like researching new keywords and gleaning new ideas from competitors or legitimate never-ending tasks like link building.

Day-by-Day Extra Credit Tasks

As you went through your Prep Month and Your SEO Plan, we listed several options for extra credit for you to pursue if you've got the time and inclination. Remember, each of these tasks is a spin-off of a specific task in Your SEO Plan. So be sure to read the original task that matches the month, week, and day listed here before you get started.

Prep Month, Week 1, Tuesday: Internal Search Function

In Chapter 6, "Your One-Month Prep: Baseline and Keywords," we mentioned that the internal search on your website can teach you about your site visitors, giving insights into who they are and what they need. If you already have an internal search engine on your website, don't let its data go to waste! Data from your internal search engine can help you determine the following:

What are your site visitors searching for? If you sell shrimp deveiners and your internal search function is logging a lot of searches for "shrimp deveiners," that might be a good thing...or it may not. It's certainly nice that your visitors seem to want your product. But why do they need to search for it in the first place? Why can't they find it by navigating your site? Finding a large number of searches for your top-priority keywords in your internal search means that you need to make this content easier to find.

What's the (key)word on the street? When you were choosing keywords in the Prep Month, we advised you to try to get into the minds of your potential customers. The in-site search engine is a great tool for doing just that. Are they searching for "shrimp de-veiners," "shrimp deveiners," or something unexpected, like "shrimp cleaners"? Keep in mind, though, that this audience, having already decided to visit your site, may not behave the same as your general search engine audience.

Who's coming to your site? If most of your site's internal searches are related to finding a job in your organization or some other activity that doesn't relate to your intended conversion, it may be an indication that a substantial portion of your site visitors are not your target audience.

Are they getting where they need to go? Find the top 10 phrases entered by users of your internal search engine. Then, take each of them for a spin. What results came up? Were they your preferred landing pages or some crusty press releases? Depending on the technology behind your search function, you may be able to improve the results by adding your own metadata (usually in the form of keyword tags) to your website's pages. (Before you try to go extra-extra credit, take note: These tags are not recognized by the search engines.)

For example, for your Sale Products page, you can assign keywords like "discount" or "clearance"—even if these words don't appear on the page—and your internal search will then be able to show your Sale Products page to anyone searching for those terms. Of course, you should never manipulate your internal search results to be irrelevant; you don't want to display your Sale page when someone is searching for "returns," for example. But it's your site, and assigning reasonable synonyms and related concepts to your search function's metadata may be helpful to both your visitors and your conversion goals.

If you do this kind of extra-credit analysis, your internal search will be much more than a helpful feature for your visitors…it will also be a marketing tool for *you*!

Prep Month, Week 3, Friday: Checking Competitors' Directory Presence

In Chapter 6, you researched whether your competitors were sponsoring PPC campaigns. It may also be helpful to know whether your competitors have taken the time to create directory listings. Finding a directory listing, whether paid or unpaid, is an indication of how well your competitors are covering all their SEO bases.

Start by searching Yahoo!'s directory:

*   Open your web browser and go to http://dir.yahoo.com. This page allows you to exclude search results other than Yahoo! Directory listings.

*   Moving one by one through your Big Five competitors list, search for each competitor's name.

*   Since this is such a specific search, there will probably be very few listings. Look for one belonging to your competitor.

*   If you don't find your competitor's listing, search for a product or service that they offer. If this search turns up no listings, broaden your search to a general term related to what they offer. If you still don't find your competitor, you can feel comfortable that they probably don't have a directory listing.

You can do the same with the Open Directory or niche directories that you think are appropriate for your own site. Whether the directory listing is fee based or free is actually not important here. What's important is knowing whether a competitor is aggressive and savvy enough to find a directory and get their site listed.

Your SEO Plan, Week 4, Monday: Robots Visiting Your Site

In Chapter 7, "Month One: Kick It into Gear," we discussed search engine indexing of your landing pages. With a little sleuthing, you can determine which search engine robots have visited your site and when.

To scope out robot visits to your site, do the following:

- First, find the name of the robot that you are interested in monitoring. Table 10.1 lists the robot identifiers for the four search engines we've featured in this book, but be prepared for some variations.

▶ **Table 10.1** Robot Identifiers for the Four Major Search Engines

Search Engine	Robot Name
Ask	Teoma
Google	Googlebot
MSN	msnbot
Yahoo!	Slurp

- Then, review your website stats program. Look for a section called "User Agents," "Robots," or "Browsers" (servers interpret a search engine robot as a type of browser).
- Depending on the sophistication of your stats program, you may be able to specify a date range and view robot visits. You might even be able to see exactly which pages within your site were visited.

If this all feels a bit too tedious, you may wish to look into software that provides simple yet detailed reports on robot visits. One such program is Robot Manager, available here: www.websitemanagementtools.com.

Your SEO Plan, Week 5, Tuesday: Google Sitemaps

In Chapter 8, "Month Two: Establish the Habit," we talked about building a site map page for your website. The Google Sitemap is a specially formatted "map" made just for Google's search engine spider to use as its very own key to navigating your site.

Google Sitemaps (in beta as of this writing) is especially helpful if Google has a hard time indexing your site; for example, if your site has a very large number of pages or dynamically generated pages. Here are the basics:

- You'll first need to create a specially formatted file—a Sitemap—using Google's Sitemap generator tool. Google's help page at www.google.com/webmasters/ sitemaps/docs/en/faq.html has the scoop on how to generate a Sitemap and where you need to put it on your site. However you create it, the resulting Sitemap document contains the list of URLs that you want Google to crawl and, if you wish, additional data such as how often the page is updated and how important each page is to you.

- To get Google to notice the Sitemap, you must sign up for a Google Sitemaps account and perform a few steps so that Google can identify and validate your file. With all this squared away, you're in business.

- Using your Google Sitemaps account, you can review basic data about your URLs, including whether they were indexed, which (if any) errors they returned, and what search terms your visitors used to find them. You can even view PageRank summaries of your site's pages and get your hands on some other cool tools: page analysis, robots.txt info, and more. This data is not the same as Google Analytics (which is much more detailed and customizable), but it's great for finding red flags.

Google Sitemaps, essentially, allows two-way communication between you and Google, which, as you learned in Chapter 4, "How the Search Engines Work Right Now," is a relatively new and wonderful thing. Using Google Sitemaps *won't* help you rank higher or increase your PageRank, and it doesn't guarantee that your pages will be indexed. But it can certainly give your deep or dynamic pages a fighting chance!

You can sign up for your Google Sitemaps account here: www.google.com/webmasters/sitemaps/siteoverview.

Your SEO Plan, Week 7, Tuesday: Task Journal Investigation

In Chapter 8, we advised you to spend a day working on items in your Task Journal. If your Task Journal isn't yet filled with dozens of fascinating ruminations, here are some ideas to get you out there and investigating:

- Is there a site that offers an award for your organization's product or service? Can you get your site in the running? Try a search for "[your product] web award" or "[your industry] web award".

- Can you search for your site in a way that causes your meta description tag to show up on the search engine listings? Try searching with your URL only or with text that appears only in links to you but isn't on your site. Is your meta description tag showing up the way you expected? Do you see any funny characters? Did it get cut off earlier than you expected?

- Similarly, try to find searches that make your Open Directory or Yahoo! Directory listing show up in the results.

- Are you unintentionally spamming the search engines? Search for old pages on your site that are still live and displaying the same content as your new pages. Check to make sure your pages aren't doing something silly and spammy, like displaying text that's the same color as the background.

- One of our favorite mysteries to investigate: Exactly which page on your site does Google think is your "official" page? (You learned about a related topic—canonical URL problems—in the section "Week 5: Site Structure Improvements" in Chapter 8.) Search for your organization's name and check the URL that Google returns for this search. It may be your home page, or it may be an alternate domain, or it may something else deep within your site. Are you surprised? Dismayed? What's the reason that this URL is displaying? Is it the number of pages linking to this page? Is it that the "official" URL is the only listing your site has in the Open Directory?

- Do you know how to search like an expert? Try using advanced search operators on your favorite search engine. For example, Yahoo! allows you to build your own search shortcuts. You can define a shortcut so you can type just "!pix" into the search box and Yahoo! will automatically search for "pictures of ethanol vehicles" or whatever you prefer. Or, try one of the numerous built-in shortcuts, listed here: http://tools.search.yahoo.com/shortcuts/. Are there any that your target audience might be using?

- Are your competitors tracking their conversions using Google Analytics? Peek into their source code and look for the Google Analytics tracking tag. (Just search for the text string "google-analytics" in their code, and you'll see the script.)

- Are there any additional domains that your organization should own? For example, do you own a .org domain name but not the .com? If a searcher had to guess at your site's URL, what do you think it would be? And, when is your current domain set to expire? Make sure you don't inadvertently let it run out.

- Howz yore spelleng? Search for misspellings of your product or service and see what comes up.

- Do a little volunteer work for the search engines by helping them clean spam out of their listings. Every major search engine allows you to report spammers; Google's spam reporting tool can be found at www.google.com/contact/spamreport.html.

- What are people saying about your organization on discussion boards? Look to Lycos Discussion Search at http://discussion.lycos.com to find out. Or, see where you stand on the blogs at www.blogpulse.com.

Your SEO Plan, Week 9, Monday: Optimizing Press Releases

In Chapter 9, "Month Three: It's a Way of Life," we encouraged you to get your organization's press releases online. Follow these guidelines to maximize your press release visibility:

- Include keywords in press release titles and page copy, but don't go so overboard that you sacrifice good writing. There is no magic formula for the perfect keyword density. Find the same balance that you found for your landing page text.

- Be sure to include links to relevant locations on your website. However, since press releases generally will not be edited after the fact, pay close attention to choosing URLs that you do not expect to change in time (see the sidebar "Prevent Link Rot" in Chapter 9 for more information on URL file-naming conventions).

- Submit your press releases to free online wire services and consider a fee-based distribution service if your release is particularly newsworthy. PRWeb at www.prweb.com is one of the best-known online distribution services.

- Don't count on newswires alone to distribute your press release. Find on-topic publications, blogs, or journalists and send them a brief, personalized e-mail including a link to your press release.

- Feed, feed, feed—make an RSS or Atom feed for your press releases. This will help them get listed in news services and blog search engines. To simplify this process, you can even use a blog creation tool to post your press releases.

  Many in the media use search engines to find information on the Web. If you spend the time to optimize and distribute your press releases, you're making great strides in improving your search engine visibility and media presence.

Your SEO Plan, Week 9, Wednesday: How the Search Engines View Non-HTML Documents

In Chapter 9, you worked on optimizing non-HTML documents for your site. You can get a sense of how search engines see your non-HTML content by viewing the HTML alternate page created by Google.

Next to every search result for a non-HTML document, Google presents a "View as HTML" link. For example, here is the listing for a PowerPoint presentation.

> [PPT] Friday, August 27, 2004
> File Format: Microsoft Powerpoint 97 - View as HTML
> The news story listed "Pick-Your-Own" vegetables, hayrides, a "Pizza Patch" garden
> displaying ingredients in pizza, a **farmer's market**, a festival, tours, ...
> www.agednet.com/quiz.ppt - Similar pages

Click on the listing title and your browser will either display or download the PowerPoint file. But click on "View as HTML" and you will see this page.

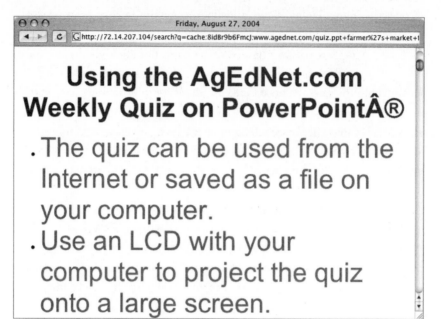

Viewing Yahoo!'s "cached" version of PDF files is a very similar experience.

Even if you choose not to spend time optimizing your non-HTML documents, we suggest you review this alternate version. Many of your potential site visitors will look here first before investing in a download. Nobody expects these pages to look perfect, but you don't want them to be an embarrassment to your organization.

Your SEO Plan, Week 9, Thursday: Content Thieves

In Chapter 9, we gave you pointers for sussing out sites that may be using your copyrighted content. But have you checked for PPC advertisers who are targeting your company name or your proprietary product names?

What you find may come as a surprise to you, especially if you haven't been performing regular checks on these terms in the search engines. Other advertisers may be using your targeted searches as an opportunity to display their own ads. For example, if your business happens to make a well-known snack food, you might see an ad for a diet supplement among search results for your product. You can read your PPC service's terms of service to determine whether these advertisers are breaking any rules. If you think they are, consider politely contacting the PPC service or the advertiser to let them know your interpretation of the situation. If this type of advertising is permitted, file this knowledge under "good things to know about your search competitors."

And beware the affiliates you never knew you had—and probably never wanted! Is your product name showing up in the ad for a shopping site? If so, does that shopping site actually sell your product? We've seen it time and time again: Due to haphazard use of dynamic keyword insertion, shopping sites create ads for a specific product but deliver only a landing page saying that the product isn't found on their website. It doesn't benefit you or the shopping site to let this practice continue, so if you find that you're in the middle of a bait-and-switch PPC ad, contact the shopping site and politely request that they remove it.

Your SEO Plan, Week 12, Monday: Checking Additional Keywords

Starting with your baseline report, and for every monthly report thereafter, you checked your website's search engine presence for your top-priority keywords. There may be legitimate reasons for checking additional keywords outside of your 10 or so top-priority terms on a quarterly basis. Here are some examples:

- Your site contains a laundry list of keywords for which you can reasonably expect good ranks without a formal optimization plan. An example of this situation might be a movie fan site with a good representation of several celebrity names or a product review site with multiple instances of several product names or brand names.

- In past SEO efforts, additional landing pages on your site were optimized for keywords outside of your current top-priority terms.

- You have been using an automated rank checker because you scaled up Your SEO Plan for several additional keywords. Consider checking rank manually once a quarter, at least for a portion of your keywords (see the section "Week 2: Baseline Assessment" in Chapter 6 to review the benefits of a manual rank check).

Whether you've followed Your SEO Plan to a T, had to make some tough choices to cut out some tasks, or have earned yourself an A for extra-credit effort, be proud of yourself! You're an SEO pro!

Appendix

In this appendix, you'll see screen shots of the worksheets that are referenced throughout the book. These documents can be downloaded from the Search Engine Optimization: An Hour a Day *companion website,* www.yourseoplan.com.

From Chapter 1, "Clarify Your Goals," you'll recall the Goals Worksheet, named GoalsWorksheet.doc, a Word document where you can record the specific goals of your organization. This worksheet will help you lay the foundation for your entire SEO campaign.

SEO: An Hour a Day
Goals Worksheet

Business Goals
(Fill in the blanks. Use as many or as few spaces as you need.)

Primary Goal	
Additional Goal	
Additional Goal	
Additional Goal	
Additional Goal	

Website Features
(Check all items below that exist on your website, or are future goals for the site.)

This is included on my web site now	This is a goal for the site in the future	Rating (Excellent/ Good/Fair/ Poor)	
☐	☐		Corporate history, news, and press releases.
☐	☐		Executive biographies.
☐	☐		Product and service information
☐	☐		Online purchasing/donation
☐	☐		Support for existing customers/clients/students
☐	☐		News and current events
☐	☐		Articles, white papers
☐	☐		Religious, philosophical, or political content
☐	☐		Online request for

In Chapter 6, "Your One-Month Prep: Baseline and Keywords," we introduced several worksheets to help you organize Your SEO Plan. First off, there's the Keywords Worksheet (KeywordsWorksheet.xls), an Excel spreadsheet where you can list possible target keywords for your website along with important measures that will help you finalize your top picks.

SEO: An Hour a Day

Keywords Worksheet

Keyword(s)	Search Popularity: Wordtracker	Search Popularity: YSM	Relevance	Competition Level	Landing Page URL
Top Keywords					
All Keywords					

Next, the Site Assessment Worksheet (SiteAssessmentWorksheet.doc) provides a checklist of factors to quickly assess the current optimization level of your website's landing pages.

SEO: An Hour a Day
Site Assessment Worksheet

Home Page URL:	
Yes/No	
	This page has a unique HTML page title.
	The HTML page title contains my target keywords.
	This page contains 200 or more words of HTML text.
	HTML text on this page contains my exact target keywords.
	This page can be reached from the home page of the site by following HTML text links (not pull-downs, login screens, or pop-up windows).
	The HTML text links from other pages on my site to this page contain my target keywords.
Landing Page URL:	
Yes/No	
	This page has a unique HTML page title.
	The HTML page title contains my target keywords.
	This page contains 200 or more words of HTML text.
	HTML text on this page contains my exact target keywords.
	This page can be reached from the home page of the site by following HTML text links (not pull-downs, login screens, or pop-up windows).
	The HTML text links from other pages on my site to this page contain my target keywords.
Landing Page URL:	
Yes/No	
	This page has a unique HTML page title.
	The HTML page title contains my target keywords.
	This page contains 200 or more words of HTML text.
	HTML text on this page contains my exact target keywords.

The Rank Tracking Worksheet (RankTrackingWorksheet.xls) is an Excel spreadsheet that you'll use every month to document your website rank and indexing status, both key indicators of your site's search engine visibility.

SEO: An Hour a Day

Rank Tracking Worksheet

| | Search Engine Rank | | | | | Notes |
	Baseline - (date)	Month 1 - (date)	Month 2 - (date)	Month 3 - (date)	Month 4 - (date)	
Search Engine: Google						
Keyword						
Keyword						
Keyword						
Keyword						
Keyword						
Keyword						
Keyword						
Keyword						
Keyword						
Keyword						
Search Engine: MSN						
Keyword						
Keyword						
Keyword						
Keyword						
Keyword						
Keyword						
Keyword						
Keyword						
Keyword						
Search Engine: Ask						
Keyword						
Keyword						
Keyword						
Keyword						
Keyword						
Keyword						
Keyword						
Keyword						
Keyword						
Search Engine: Yahoo						
Keyword						
Keyword						

The Task Journal Worksheet (TaskJournal.doc) is a simple template that allows you to stay focused on Your SEO Plan by giving you a place to record outstanding questions, thoughts, and issues that come up as you work. Rather than constantly going off on tangents, you will revisit your Task Journal items when time allows.

SEO: An Hour a Day
Task Journal

Date	Task or Question	Resolved?

Finally, you can use the Competition Worksheet (CompetitionWorksheet.xls) to document the basic site optimization and search engine presence of your major competitors.

SEO: An Hour a Day

Competition Worksheet

Competitor 1: (Name)

	URL	Keywords of Note	Basic Optimization (yes/no)	Number of inbound links	Google PageRank
Home Page					
Interior Page 1					
Interior Page 2					
Interior Page 3					

General Characteristics of site:

Overall Site Ranks:

PPC Sponsorship Assessment:

Additional Notes about this competitor:

Competitor 2: (Name)

	URL	Keywords of Note	Basic Optimization (yes/no)	Number of inbound links	Google PageRank
Home Page					
Interior Page 1					
Interior Page 2					
Interior Page 3					

General Characteristics of site:

In Chapter 7, "Month One: Kick It into Gear," you started Your SEO Plan in earnest with basic site optimization, link building, and setting up a pay-per-click campaign. Three worksheets help with these efforts: First, the Site Optimization Worksheet (SiteOptimizationWorksheet.doc) provides a template for detailing the edits you will need on your website.

SEO: An Hour a Day
Site Optimization Worksheet

Landing Page 1 (Home page)

Page URL:

HTML Title:

Meta Description:

Meta Keywords:

Text/Content Edits:

Landing Page 2 (Page name)

Page URL:

HTML Title:

Meta Description:

Meta Keywords:

Text/Content edits:

Landing Page 3 (Page name)

Page URL:

HTML Title:

Meta Description:

Meta Keywords:

Text/Content edits:

The Link Tracking Worksheet (LinkTrackingWorksheet.xls) is an Excel spreadsheet where you can document your ongoing link-building communications. Keeping this information organized will help you keep track of gains made and avoid embarrassing faux pas such as resending a link request after it's already been accepted.

SEO: An Hour a Day
Link Tracking Worksheet

URL of linking page	Requested Landing Page	Contact Email or URL	Date Requested	Link Received?	Notes
Link Update Requests					
New Link Requests					

And the PPC Keywords Worksheet (PPCKeywordsWorksheet.xls) is a convenient place to assemble all of the information you will be entering into your first PPC campaign.

SEO: An Hour a Day

PPC Keywords Worksheet

Keyword(s)	Category	Bid for Top Position	Estimated Click-throughs	Estimated Cost	Conversion Value	Landing Page URL
				$0.00		
				$0.00		
				$0.00		
				$0.00		
				$0.00		
				$0.00		
				$0.00		
				$0.00		
				$0.00		
				$0.00		
				$0.00		
				$0.00		
				$0.00		
				$0.00		
				$0.00		
				$0.00		
				$0.00		
				$0.00		
				$0.00		
				$0.00		
				$0.00		
				$0.00		
				$0.00		
				$0.00		
				$0.00		
				$0.00		

Total Click-throughs:	0					
Total Cost:	$0.00					

In Chapter 9, "Month Three: It's a Way of Life," we introduced the concept of clustering your keywords into groups in order to better analyze your PPC click-throughs. This Excel worksheet, called PPCClusterWorksheet.xls, allows you to compare the performance of these keyword clusters.

SEO: An Hour a Day
PPC Cluster Worksheet

Enter Campaign Total Clicks/Conversions here:

Keyword(s)	Keyword Clicks/Conversions	Click-through or Conversion Rate	Cluster Clicks/Conversions	Cluster Percentage of Total
Cluster 1				
			0	0%
Cluster 2				
			0	0%
Cluster 3				
			0	0%
Cluster 4				
			0	0%

Glossary

301 redirect A server setting that redirects traffic from one URL to another while sending a 301, or "permanent," status code to the requesting client. Also called permanent redirect. See also *client*.

404 error The error returned by a web server when a requested file cannot be found.

A/B split A method of comparing the performance of two sponsored listings, landing pages, or other promotional content. Also called A/B testing.

algoholic A person who obsessively follows search engine algorithm changes.

algorithm Any step-by-step procedure for solving a problem. In SEO, a search engine algorithm is the formula that search engines use to determine the ranking of websites on their results pages.

ALT tag A tag included in the source code of an image to define alternative text for site visitors who cannot or do not wish to view graphics. The ALT tag may also be displayed while an image is loading or when a user's mouse is placed over the image. Also called ALT text or IMG ALT tag.

anchor text HTML text that links to another location on the Web. Also called linked text or linking text.

Atom A web feed format.

authority page A web page that search engines recognize as having an outstanding level of trust, as represented by inbound links, among other websites in a topical community.

backlinks See *inbound links*.

banned Removed from a search engine's index.

black hat An SEO methodology that includes techniques not in compliance with the search engines' guidelines for webmasters. Also used to describe a person who engages in black hat techniques.

blog Shorthand for *weblog*, a regularly updated, journal-style web page that is generally presented in reverse chronological order (most recent entries at the top) and allows readers to post comments. Also used as a verb: *to blog*, meaning to write in a blog. See also *vblog*, *splog*.

blogger A person who blogs.

Blogosphere The entire community of blogs and bloggers.

bookmark search sites See *social bookmarking*.

broad matching A pay-per-click keyword matching option in which an advertisement is displayed for all search queries that include a given keyword or phrase—in any order, with or without additional words. Variants, synonyms, and plural forms are generally also included in broad matching.

canonical URL The preferred, or primary, form of a URL. Many websites are displayed using more than one URL format, for example, http://www.yoursite.com and http://yoursite.com, and it can be difficult for search engines to determine which is the canonical form.

Cascading Style Sheets (CSS) A website coding method that allows developers to control the style (font, color, background, and more) and placement of content, often in files that remain separate from the content itself.

client A program or computer that requests information from another computer over a network. For example, when a Web browser such as Internet Explorer requests a web page from a Web server, that browser is the client in the client-server relationship.

client-side tracking A web analytics technique that includes adding small scripts or images to web pages and monitoring user activity via a third-party server. Also called on-demand, tag-based, or hosted tracking.

cloaking A deceptive technique of showing different content to search engine robots than would be seen by visitors accessing a web page via a standard browser.

collaborative tagging A process that allows many people to label shared content with their own keyword labels, called tags. See also *social bookmarking*.

consumer-generated media (CGM) Information created and shared among consumers online using venues such as blog entries, email, personal websites, social bookmarking sites and message boards.

contextual advertising Pay-per-click listings that appear on websites other than search engines. Such listings are generally matched to the content of individual web pages through an automated matching algorithm. Also called contextual placement.

contextual placement See *contextual advertising*.

conversion funnel A desired conversion path defined by a marketer or website owner. The conversion funnel is generally a linear, step-by-step process leading directly from site entry to conversion. It is conceptualized as a funnel shape because some users will depart from the path, leaving fewer users at the end than were at the beginning, while others will be "funneled" into completing a transaction. See also *conversion path* and *scenario*.

conversion (offline) An offline action taken by a website visitor that accomplishes the site owner's intended goal. Examples include telephone-based purchases and visits to brick-and-mortar locations.

conversion (online) An online action taken by a website visitor that accomplishes the site owner's intended goal. Examples include online purchases, downloads, and specific page views within a website.

conversion path The web pages that a site visitor passes through between entering a website and completing a conversion. See also *conversion funnel*.

conversion tracking The process of monitoring and measuring conversions.

cookie A piece of text placed on a user's hard drive by a website. The information it contains can be accessed by the site that originally placed the cookie but generally not by other sites.

crawl See *index*.

directory A categorized, descriptive list of links to web pages, usually created and maintained by human editors.

doorway page A web page, usually outside the parent website's navigational structure, designed to serve primarily as a destination for search engine traffic and immediately redirect that traffic to pages within the parent website. This term is generally applied to spammy pages that are used strictly for search engine traffic. See also *landing page*.

dynamic keyword insertion Automatic placement of keywords into pay-per-click ads to match the keywords entered by a search engine user. For example, the same ad may display the title "Save 30% on dog food" or the title "Save 30% on cat food," depending on whether the searcher used the query "dog food" or "cat food."

elevator speech Marketing slang for a brief but informative overview that one gives about oneself or one's business. So called because all of the important points should be delivered in approximately the duration of a 30-second elevator ride.

entry page See *landing page*.

eyeballs Slang for visitors to a web page. Can be used as a synonym for *market share*.

geotargeting A service that is offered by pay-per-click services and allows advertisers to specify the geographic region(s) for their ads to run.

global navigation Links that are displayed on every page of a website.

Googlebombing See *link bombing*.

graphical text Text that is contained in image files such as JPEGs or GIFs. This text generally cannot be read by search engines.

GYM Abbreviation for "Google, Yahoo!, and MSN."

hit A communication made from a web browser to a website server requesting an element of a web page. When a web page is viewed, each separate item (such as a graphics or media file) on the page will log one hit to the server.

hosted tracking See *client-side tracking*.

HTML page title Code contained in an HTML document that that briefly describes its contents. This text is usually displayed in a web browser's title window. In search engine results, the HTML page title is displayed as the first line of a listing. Also called HTML title tag.

impression In online advertising, a single act of viewing a web page or advertisement.

inbound links Links pointing to a website from other sites. Also called backlinks.

index A search engine's database of web page content. Also, the act by a search engine robot of following website links and gathering content. When a web page is included in a search engine's database, it is said to be indexed. Used as a synonym for *spider* and *crawl*.

invisible text Text on a website that is not visible to a site visitor using a standard browser.

keyword A word or phrase describing an organization's product or service or other key content on its website. A word or phrase entered as a query in a search engine. Also called keyterm, keyphrase, and keyword phrase.

keyword density The number of times a keyword or phrase appears on a web page divided by the total number of words on the page. Usually expressed as a percentage.

keyword grouping The practice of categorizing sponsored keywords into groups to simplify pay-per-click campaign administration.

keyword exclusion See *negative match*.

landing page A web page that is focused on a key audience or topic and that serves as a destination for search engine traffic. In this book, landing pages are the focus of optimization efforts. Also called entry page.

link bombing A coordinated effort to manipulate search engine results for a certain search query by linking to a website using the keywords in the linking text. Also called Googlebombing.

link rot The gradual increase over time in the number of broken links on the Web or on an individual website. Also called linkrot.

link validator Software that checks the working status of links within a website.

linkability A web page's perceived potential for receiving inbound links.

linkbait Web content that has high linkability or that is specifically created to draw inbound links.

long tail Search queries that are significantly longer, more focused, and less frequently used by searchers than average search terms. Short, more generalized, and more popular search queries are sometimes referred to as "short head" in comparison. See also *short head*.

metadata Hidden comments that describe characteristics of a document, such as its author, file structure, or keywords. Metadata can be used by search engines to help determine relevance and rank.

meta description tag Metadata contained in an HTML document that describes the content of a web page. Search engines may display this tag in their search results.

meta keywords tag Metadata contained in an HTML document that lists keywords related to the content of a web page. Search engines may use this tag to determine relevance.

meta search engines Search sites that display combined results from several search engines.

meta tag Code contained in an HTML document that holds metadata. See also *meta description tag* and *meta keywords tag*.

metrics Measurements or methods of evaluation.

mobile search Web search sites or tools designed to be accessed with mobile devices such as cell phones and PDAs.

negative match A pay-per-click keyword matching option that prevents a sponsored ad from displaying if a particular keyword is used by a searcher. For example, a percussion website may want its ad to display for the term "drum" but not "ear drum." In this case, "ear" could be designated as a negative match. Also called keyword exclusion.

niche directories Directories that provide links to sites that focus on a similar theme or that relate to the same industry. Inclusion in niche directories can be paid or unpaid.

offline marketing Methods of marketing that do not involve the Internet. Examples include direct mail, billboards, and print advertising. Also called traditional advertising.

off-page factors Optimization factors that are not contained in an organization's own web pages. Off-page factors, such as the number and quality of inbound links, cannot be directly edited by website owners and must be influenced indirectly.

on-demand tracking See *client-side tracking*.

on-page factors Optimization factors that are contained on an organization's own web pages. On-page factors, such as HTML page title and text content, can be directly edited by website owners.

online marketing Methods of marketing that utilize the Internet. Examples include search engine optimization, direct emails, and banner advertising.

organic SEO Optimization efforts for areas of search other than pay-per-click.

PageRank Google's proprietary measurement of the importance of a web page. PageRank values vary from 0 to 10, with 10 being the highest level of importance. Also called PR.

page view The group of hits that together make up a single viewing of a web page.

paid inclusion A service offered by some search engines that allows site owners to submit a list of URLs for the search engine to index and recrawl on a frequent basis. See also *trusted feed*.

paid listing An advertisement displayed on a search engine or directory in response to a search query entered by a user. Fees for advertisers are typically charged on a pay-per-click basis. Also called sponsored listing, PPC listing, and PPC ad.

paid placement See *pay-per-click*.

path to conversion See *conversion path*.

pay-per-click (PPC) A form of advertisement in which an advertiser designates the specific keywords for which its listings will appear in the search results. The advertiser pays a fee to the search engine each time the listing is clicked. The subset of SEO tasks that encompasses setup and management of such listings. Also called paid placement and pay for performance.

persona In SEO, a fictitious personality created by marketers or website owners to represent a potential user of a website. Generally, several personality traits are defined, and these are used to help determine and analyze likely behaviors on the website. See also *scenario*.

personalized search Search results that vary based on the searcher's profile and past behavior.

ping In programmer's lingo, a way to check the validity of a link or connection between two computers by sending a small packet of data and waiting for a reply. In the Blogosphere, a communication between a blog and a ping server indicating that the blog has been updated. In more general parlance, any type of contact between two parties that checks on the status of the communication, as in, "She hasn't RSVP'd yet. I'll ping her tomorrow."

ping server A service that receives notification (a ping) from a blog every time the blog is updated. Usually the blog owner sets up this communication with a ping server as a means of gaining additional distribution.

ping spam The practice of using pings to misrepresent content that is not genuine blog content or has not actually been recently updated.

robot Software used by search engines to travel the Web and send content from web pages back to the search engine for indexing. Also called spider and crawler.

robots.txt A text file containing code that can exclude certain pages or folders from being indexed in the search engines. Can also be used to block access for a particular robot. The robots.txt file must be located in the root directory of the website.

root directory The top directory within the file structure of a website; it contains all other directories. Generally represented by a / after the domain name.

RSS Abbreviated form of Really Simple Syndication, a web feed format. It can stand for other terms as well, such as Rich Site Summary and RDF Site Summary.

scenario In SEO, a definition of a persona and a particular need of that persona (for example "college student seeking laptop covers"). The scenario may also define the actions that the persona may take on a website to reach satisfaction.

scraping An automated technique of copying content from one website to another. Often used as a method of stealing content.

Search Engine Marketing (SEM) See *Search Marketing*.

Search Engine Optimization (SEO) See *Search Marketing*. The term *SEO* may also refer only to organic SEO.

search engine optimizer (SEO) A person who performs search engine optimization.

Search Marketing A wide variety of tasks intended to improve a website's ranking and listing quality among both paid and unpaid results on search engines, with the ultimate goal of increasing targeted traffic to the website and achieving more conversions. Also called Search Engine Marketing and Search Engine Optimization.

search popularity The frequency with which a keyword is used as a query on search engines.

search query The keywords entered into a search engine.

SERP Abbreviation for Search Engine Results Page.

server-side tracking A web analytics technique that includes setting up software directly on the server that hosts the website being tracked.

shallow-wide An SEO technique of distributing keywords across a large number of unique landing pages.

short head Search queries that are short, generalized, and frequently used by searchers. Longer, more focused, and less frequently used terms are sometimes referred to as "long tail" in comparison. See also *long tail*.

sniffer Software that intercepts and monitors activities over a network. In SEO, a sniffer can be used for cloaking or for practices such as determining the speed of a user's web connection or filtering out suspicious traffic.

snippet Strings of text taken from a web page and combined for use as a summary or description of the page's content.

social bookmarking The use of shared lists of Internet bookmarks. Social bookmarking sites allow registered users to save and share bookmarks and classify them with user-defined keywords, called tags. See also *collaborative tagging*.

social networking In Internet terminology, creating person-to-person connections through participation in a website that facilitates social connections. Examples include dating sites, blog hosts, and social bookmarking sites.

social search Any system that uses community-sourced information to determine search results.

source code In SEO, the HTML text and tags that define a web page.

spam Any of a wide variety of deceptive or abusive online practices, including sending unsolicited advertisements, misrepresenting a website to search engines, and posting non-sensical comments to blogs in an attempt to increase the visibility of a website. Can be a noun or verb (*to spam*).

spam comment A blog or forum comment that contains gibberish or irrelevant content and is intended only to promote the website of the person posting the comment.

spider See *robot*. May also be used as a verb, "to spider," in which case it is synonymous with "to index."

spider emulator Software that attempts to reproduce the way a search engine spider would see a web page. Also called spider simulator.

splog Shorthand for *spam blog*. A blog containing stolen or nonsense content, which exists only to promote affiliate sites or get page views for advertising.

sponsored listing See *paid listing*.

stemming Combining variant forms of a word for one stem, or root, word. For example, *listen*, *listens*, and *listening* all share the same stem word.

tag-based tracking See *client-side tracking*.

topical community A group of websites that share a common subject matter. Also called topical neighborhood.

trusted feed A service offered by some search engines that allows website owners to specify a list of pages to be indexed. This is particularly helpful for websites that include content that would otherwise be hidden from search engines. Usually a paid service, trusted feed does not guarantee an improvement in ranks. Also called XML feed. See also *paid inclusion*.

unique visitors The number of different individuals who visited a website one or more times during a given period. This measure is based on available—but often incomplete—information. For example, two visits by the same person using two different computers would generally be logged as two unique visitors, while two different people using the same computer would generally be logged as a single unique visitor.

usability The elements of a website's design and copywriting that affect a site visitor's ease of use and navigation.

visible text Text on a website that is visible to a site visitor using a standard browser.

vblog Shorthand for *video blog*.

web feed A file that is created by a website owner and is intended to be retrieved and displayed by other websites. Generally includes summary information and a link to the primary content page. Web feeds are often used for blog and news content. See also *web syndication*.

web analytics The measurement and analysis of online activity, especially page visits, conversions, and search queries used to find individual pages. See also *metrics*.

weblog See *blog*.

web log analyzer A software program that parses raw server log data and presents it in a more easy-to-read format. Also called log file analysis software.

web syndication The practice of making content available to other sites through web feeds. Generally, a title and summary are displayed on the syndicating site with a link to the primary content page.

white hat An SEO methodology that includes only techniques that stay within the search engines' guidelines. Also used to describe a person who engages in white hat techniques.

XML feed See *trusted feed*. May also be used as a synonym for *web feed*.

Index

Note to the Reader: Throughout this index **boldfaced** page numbers indicate primary discussions of a topic. *Italicized* page numbers indicate illustrations.